Step-by-Step Service Guide to the VW BEETLE
by Lindsay Porter & Dave Pollard

FOREWORD

The average car today has a water-cooled, in-line, four-cylinder engine, mounted at the front of the car requiring little or no servicing for anything up to 20,000 miles. Its owners can (and do) treat it as simply a convenient method of getting from A to B and look forward to the 'sealed-for-life' engine bay.

The Beetle is not an average car and it's important that Beetle owners are suitably different. The Beetle demands of its owner that he or she becomes part of its life, that motoring becomes a shared experience with equal input from both parties. There's no doubt that VW's Wunderwagen responds like no other car to copious amounts of TLC - Tender Loving Care!

It's not that it will actually cease to function immediately without it; indeed, the high quality of build in all areas is one of the main factors which has helped it record sales of more than 21,000,000 (count the noughts - that's twenty one million...) world wide - and it's still selling!

Unfortunately, this inherent strength also makes it easy prey for lazy owners who can't be bothered to do the basic service tasks necessary to ensure a really long life. Consequently, it's essential to take great precautions when you're buying your Bug. If you don't know the car inside out, take along someone who does. A looked-after Beetle can be manna from heaven; a neglected one can lead to the overdraft from hell!

The Beetle was designed to be 'The People's Car' and, as such, it is incredibly hardy and relatively easy to work on - as long as you understand what you are doing. That's what this book is about. It won't turn you into a fully-fledged mechanic, able to dismantle your engine by the roadside. But equally, it will show you how to service your Beetle on a regular basis, to keep it in top condition so that dismantling the engine won't be necessary for a long time to come.

Major jobs may need specialists or specialist equipment, but by regular and efficient servicing, you'll cut down on the need for those. The 'stitch in time' principle is the one we preach and practice.

THAT FEEL-GOOD FEELING

When owners of modern 'Euroboxes' scoff at the mere notion of 3,000 mile service intervals (and they will), the Beetle owner can take heart from the fact that at least his car can be serviced and repaired by the competent DIY owner. And when those micro-chipped, turbocharged wonders splutter to a halt at the side of the road and require AA relay because of a blown fuse, the Beetle driver can bask in the warm knowledge that most of his on-road problems can be solved with a Swiss Army Knife and a piece of string!

Dave Pollard

CONTENTS

Keep a record of every Service you carry out on your car.

Lindsay Porter
Porter Publishing Ltd

Introduction

Over the years, I have run any number of cars, from superb classic cars, modern cars, to those with one foot in the breakers yard. And I know only too well that any car is only enjoyable to own if it's reliable, safe and basically sound - and the only way of ensuring that it stays that way is to service it regularly. That's why we have set about creating a series of books which aim to provide you, the owner, with all the information you might need in order to keep your car in tip-top condition. And if your car is not as reliable as it might be, you will be able to give your car a 'super service', using the information contained in the Servicing section of this book, and bring it back to good, reliable order.

Porter Publishing Service Guides are the first books to give you all the service information you might need, with step-by-step instructions, along with a complete Service History section for you to complete and fill in as you carry out regular maintenance on your car over the months ahead. Using the information contained in this book, you will be able to:

◆ see for yourself how to carry out every Service Interval, from weekly and monthly checks, right up to longer-term maintenance items.
◆ carry out regular body maintenance and rustproofing, saving a fortune in body repairs over the years to come.
◆ enhance the value of your car by completing a full Service History of every maintenance job you carry out on your car.

I hope you enjoy keeping your car in trim whilst saving lots of money by servicing your car yourself, with the help of this book. Happy motoring!

Acknowledgements

This book has been a real team effort, with lots of people contributing time, expertise and no little brain-ache to ensure that it is full of good stuff whilst being easy and straightforward to follow. That the project has worked is due in no small measure to a number of people, such as Zoe Palmer who helped with the research for several sections of this book, as well as having spent countless hours on the original concept behind this series of books. John Rose and John Mead (Technical Editor) have also been enormously beneficial in terms of their expertise and experience and Lyndsay Berryman of Pineapple Publishing has laid out and typeset this book. It's a pleasure to work with such people, professionals all and thoroughly nice folk, to boot!

In fact, one of the great things about this exciting new project is the positive, enjoyable spirit in which the whole thing has taken place. We were fortunate to be able to tap into the expertise of Iain MacLeod, proprietor of Macvolks. Apart from being technically well qualified, Iain actually lives and breathes Beetles and this enthusiasm shines through in all his work. Many of the 'Inside Information' notes here are gems he has passed on to us - and to you!

Others who have provided invaluable assistance include Peter Stevens of Autobarn, VW parts suppliers of Pershore and VW rebuild specialist Simon Woodall of Beetle Specialist Services; Bill and Sandy Beavis, who let us run riot over their car for the rustproofing section and Sony (UK) Ltd., who supplied a CCD-FX700E video camera which was used to great effect for researching some of the more complex dismantling sections. Also thanks to 'Trish Giles, who helped to make sure that the servicing information flowed logically, Peter Stant, who demonstrated the bodywork repair techniques seen in this book and my wife Shan who put her great experience in book-matters to excellent effect. Father and son Robin and Paul Wager supplied the beautiful Beetle featured on the cover and Kevin Brock produced the superb Beetle line drawing that appears now and again on these pages while Simon Woodall supplied the car for the back cover photos.

Specialist expertise also came from Dunlop/SP Tyres, Roger McNickle of Dinol GB Ltd, Mike Lomas at the Motorworld Bodyshop in Abingdon, Gunson's, who supplied the very useful DIY test equipment, Kamasa tools, who supplied almost all of the great range of tools used here and from David's Isopon who supplied expertise on bodywork repair and body filler that is second to none, and from Partco and AP Lockheed. And of course, there are our old friends Richard Price and Dawn Adams at Castrol whose advice we are always pleased to receive and whose products we can always unhesitatingly recommend.

VAG (UK) allowed us to use some of their superb illustrations, which make understanding some of the more complex pieces much easier. Most non-original illustrations were prepared by Davan Designs.

Many thanks to everyone listed here as well as to anyone else whom we might inadvertently have missed.

Using This Book

Everything about this book is designed to help you make your car more reliable and long-lasting through regular servicing. But one requirement that you will see emphasised again and again is the need for safe working. There is a lot of safety information within the practical instructions, but you are strongly urged to *read and take note of Chapter 1, Safety First!*

To get the most from this book, you will rapidly realise that it revolves around two main chapters. *Chapter 3, Service Intervals, Step-by-Step* shows you how to carry out every service job that your car is likely to need throughout its life. Then, the final Section, *Service History*, at the back of this book, lists all of the jobs described in *Chapter 3*, and arranges them together in tick-lists, a separate list for each Service interval, so that you can create your own *Service History* as you go along. When you have completed the three years of *Service History* included in this book, continuation sheets can be purchased from Porter Publishing.

Keeping your car in top condition is one thing; getting it there in the first place may be quite another. At the start of *Chapter 3*, we advise on carrying out a 'catch-up' service for cars that may not have received the de-luxe treatment suggested here. And then there are four other chapters to help you bring your car up to scratch. *Chapter 4, Repairing Bodywork Blemishes* and *Chapter 5, Rustproofing* show how to make the body beautiful and how to keep it that way - not something that is usually included in servicing information but bodywork servicing can save you even more money than mechanical servicing, since a corroded body often leads to a scrapped car, whereas worn out mechanical components can usually be replaced. *Chapter 6* shows you how to carry out *Fault Finding* when your car won't start, and *Chapter 7* describes *Getting Through the MoT*, an annual worry - unless you follow the approach shown here. With *Chapter 2, Buying Spares* describing how you can save on spares and *Chapter 8, Facts and Figures* giving you all the key vital statics, we hope that this book will become the first tool you'll pick up when you want to service your car!

CHAPTER 1 – SAFETY FIRST!

It is vitally important that you always take time to ensure that safety is the first consideration in any job you do. A slight lack of concentration, or a rush to finish the job quickly can often result in an accident, as can failure to follow a few simple precautions. Whereas skilled motor mechanics are trained in safe working practices you, the home mechanic, must find them out for yourself and act upon them.

Remember, accidents don't just happen, they are caused, and some of those causes are contained in the following list. Above all, ensure that whenever you work on your car you adopt a safety-minded approach at all times, and remain aware of the dangers that might be encountered.

Be sure to consult the suppliers of any materials and equipment you may use, and to obtain and read carefully any operating and health and safety instructions that may be available on packaging or from manufacturers and suppliers.

IMPORTANT POINTS

ALWAYS ensure that the vehicle is properly supported when raised off the ground. Don't work on, around, or underneath a raised vehicle unless axle stands are positioned under secure, load bearing underbody areas, or the vehicle is driven onto ramps.

DON'T suddenly remove the radiator or expansion tank filler cap when the cooling system is hot, or you may get scalded by escaping coolant. Let the system cool down first and even then, if the engine is not completely cold, cover the cap with a cloth and gradually release the pressure.

NEVER start the engine unless the gearbox is in neutral (or 'Park' in the case of automatic transmission) and the hand brake is fully applied.

NEVER drain oil, coolant or automatic transmission fluid when the engine is hot. Allow time for it to cool sufficiently to avoid scalding you.

TAKE CARE when parking vehicles fitted with catalytic converters. The `cat' reaches extremely high temperatures and any combustible materials under the car, such as long dry grass, could ignite.

NEVER run catalytic converter equipped vehicles without the exhaust system heat shields in place.

NEVER attempt to loosen or tighten nuts that require a lot of force to turn (e.g. a tight oil drain plug) with the vehicle raised, unless it is properly supported and in a safe condition. Wherever possible, initially slacken tight fastenings before raising the car off the ground.

TAKE CARE to avoid touching any engine or exhaust system component unless it is cool enough so as not to burn you.

ALWAYS keep antifreeze, brake and clutch fluid away from vehicle paintwork. Wash off any spills immediately.

NEVER syphon fuel, antifreeze, brake fluid or other such toxic liquids by mouth, or allow prolonged contact with your skin. There is an increasing awareness that they can damage your health. Best of all, use a suitable hand pump and wear gloves.

ALWAYS work in a well ventilated area and don't inhale dust - it may contain asbestos or other poisonous substances.

WIPE UP any spilt oil, grease or water off the floor immediately, before there is an accident.

MAKE SURE that spanners and all other tools are the right size for the job and are not likely to slip. Never try to 'double-up' spanners to gain more leverage.

SEEK HELP if you need to lift something heavy which may be beyond your capability.

ALWAYS ensure that the safe working load rating of any jacks, hoists or lifting gear used is sufficient for the job, and is used only as recommended by the manufacturer.

NEVER take risky short-cuts or rush to finish a job. Plan ahead and allow plenty of time.

BE meticulous and keep the work area tidy - you'll avoid frustration, work better and loose less.

KEEP children and animals right away from the work area and from unattended vehicles.

ALWAYS wear eye protection when working under the vehicle or using any power tools.

BEFORE undertaking dirty jobs, use a barrier cream on your hands as a protection against infection. Preferably, wear thin gloves, available from DIY outlets.

DON'T lean over, or work on, a running engine unless strictly necessary, and keep long hair and loose clothing well out of the way of moving mechanical parts. Note that it is theoretically

possible for florescent striplighting to make an engine fan appear to be stationary - check! This is the sort of error that happens when you're dog tired and not thinking straight. So don't work on your car when you're overtired!

REMOVE your wrist watch, rings and all other jewellery before doing any work on the vehicle - especially the electrical system.

ALWAYS tell someone what you're doing and have them regularly check that all is well, especially when working alone on, or under, the vehicle.

ALWAYS seek specialist advice if you're in doubt about any job. The safety of your vehicle affects you, your passengers and other road users.

FIRE

Petrol (gasoline) is a dangerous and highly flammable liquid requiring special precautions. When working on the fuel system, disconnect the vehicle battery earth (ground) terminal whenever possible and always work outside, or in a very well ventilated area. Any form of spark, such as that caused by an electrical fault, by two metal surfaces striking against each other, by a central heating boiler in the garage 'firing up', or even by static electricity built up in your clothing can, in a confined space, ignite petrol vapour causing an explosion. Take great care not to spill petrol on to the engine or exhaust system, never alow any naked flame anywhere near the work area and, above all, don't smoke.

Invest in a workshop-sized fire extinguisher. Choose the carbon dioxide type or preferably, dry powder but never a water type extinguisher for workshop use. Water conducts electricity and can make worse an oil or petrol-based fire, in certain circumstances.

FUMES

In addition to the fire dangers described previously, petrol (gasoline) vapour and the vapour from many solvents, thinners, and adhesives is highly toxic and under certain conditions can lead to unconsciousness or even death, if inhaled. The risks are increased if such fluids are used in a confined space so always ensure adequate ventilation when handling materials of this nature. Treat all such substances with care, always read the instructions and follow them implicitly.

Always ensure that the car is outside the work place in open air if the engine is running. Exhaust fumes contain poisonous carbon monoxide - even if the car is fitted with a catalytic converter, since 'cats' sometimes fail and don't function with the engine cold.

Never have the engine running with the car in the garage or in any enclosed space.

Inspection pits are another source of danger from the build-up of fumes. Never drain petrol (gasoline) or use solvents, thinners adhesives or other toxic substances in an inspection pit as the extremely confined space allows the highly toxic fumes to concentrate. Running the engine with the vehicle over the pit can have the same results. It is also dangerous to park a vehicle for any length of time over an inspection pit. The fumes from even a slight fuel leak can cause an explosion when the engine is started.

MAINS ELECTRICITY

Best of all, use rechargeable tools and a DC inspection lamp, powered from a remote 12V battery - both are much safer! However, if you do use a mains-powered inspection lamp, power tool etc, ensure that the appliance is wired correctly to its plug, that where necessary it is properly earthed (grounded), and that the fuse is of the correct rating for the appliance concerned. Do not use any mains powered equipment in damp conditions or in the vicinity of fuel, fuel vapour or the vehicle battery.

Also, before using any mains powered electrical equipment, take one more simple precaution - use an RCD (Residual Current Device) circuit breaker. Then, if there is a short, the RCD circuit breaker minimises the risk of electrocution by instantly cutting the power supply. Buy one from any electrical store or DIY centre. RCDs fit simply into your electrical socket before plugging in your electrical equipment.

THE IGNITION SYSTEM

Extreme care must be taken when working on the ignition system with the ignition switched on or with the engine cranking or running.

Touching certain parts of the ignition system, such as the HT leads, distributor cap, ignition coil etc, can result in a severe electric shock. This is especially likely where the insulation on any of these components is weak, or if the components are dirty or damp. Note also that voltages produced by electronic ignition systems are much higher than conventional systems and could prove fatal, particularly to persons with cardiac pacemaker implants. Consult your handbook or main dealer if in any doubt. An additional risk of injury can arise while working on running engines, if the operator touches a high voltage lead and pulls his hand away on to a conductive or revolving part.

THE BATTERY

Don't smoke, or allow a naked light, or cause a spark near the vehicle's battery, even in a well ventilated area. A certain amount of highly explosive hydrogen gas will be given off as part of the normal charging process. Care should be taken to avoid sparking by switching off the power supply before charger leads are connected or disconnected. Battery terminals should be shielded, since a battery contains energy and a spark can be caused by any conductor which touches its terminals or exposed connecting straps.

Before working on the fuel or electrical systems, always disconnect the battery earth (ground) terminal.

When charging the battery from an external source, disconnect both battery leads before connecting the charger. If the battery is not of the 'sealed-for-life' type, loosen the filler plugs or remove the cover before charging. For best results the battery should be given a low rate 'trickle' charge overnight. Do not charge at an excessive rate or the battery may burst.

Always wear gloves and goggles when carrying or when topping up the battery. Even in diluted form (as it is in the battery) the acid electrolyte is extremely corrosive and must not be allowed to contact the eyes, skin or clothes.

BRAKES AND ASBESTOS

Whenever you work on the braking system mechanical components, or remove front or rear brake pads or shoes:

i) wear an efficient particle mask,

ii) wipe off all brake dust from the work area (never blow it off with compressed air),

iii) dispose of brake dust and discarded shoes or pads in a sealed plastic bag,

iv) wash hands thoroughly after you have finished working on the brakes and certainly before you eat or smoke,

v) replace shoes and pads only with asbestos-free shoes or pads. Note that asbestos brake dust can cause cancer if inhaled.

Obviously, a car's brakes are among its most important safety related items. Do not dismantle your car's brakes unless you are fully competent to do so. If you have not been trained in this work, but wish to carry out the jobs described in this book, it is strongly recommend that you have a garage or qualified mechanic check your work before using the car on the road.

BRAKE FLUID

Brake fluid absorbs moisture rapidly from the air and can become dangerous resulting in brake failure. Castrol (U.K.) Ltd. recommend that you should have your brake fluid tested at least once a year by a properly equipped garage with test equipment and you should change the fluid in accordance with your vehicle manufacturer's recommendations or as advised in this book if we recommend a shorter interval than the manufacturers. Always buy no more brake fluid than you need. Never store an opened pack. Dispose of the remainder at your Local Authority Waste Disposal Site, in the designated disposal unit, **not** with general waste or with waste oil.

ENGINE OILS

Take care and observe the following precautions when working with used engine oil. Apart from the obvious risk of scalding when draining the oil from a hot engine, there is the danger from contaminates that are contained in all used oil.

Always wear disposable plastic or rubber gloves when draining the oil from your engine.

i) Note that the drain plug and the oil are often hotter than you expect! Wear gloves if the plug is too hot to touch and keep your hand to one side so that you are not scalded by the spurt of oil as the plug comes away.

ii) There are very real health hazards associated with used engine oil. In the words of Rover's MG RV8 handbook, "Prolonged and repeated contact may cause serious skin disorders, including dermatitis and cancer". Use a barrier cream on your hands and try not to get oil on them. Where practicable, wear gloves and wash your hands with hand cleaner soon after carrying out the work. Keep oil out of the reach of children.

iii) NEVER, EVER dispose of old engine oil into the ground or down a drain. In the UK, and in most EC countries, every local authority must provide a safe means of oil disposal. In the UK, try your local Environmental Health Department for advice on waste disposal facilities.

PLASTIC MATERIALS

Work with plastic materials brings additional hazards into workshops. Many of the materials used (polymers, resins, adhesives and materials acting as catalysts and accelerators) readily produce very dangerous situations in the form of poisonous fumes, skin irritants, risk of fire and explosions. Do not allow resin or 2-pack adhesive hardener, or that supplied with filler or 2-pack stopper to come into contact with skin or eyes. Read carefully the safety notes supplied on the can, tube or packaging.

JACK AND AXLE STANDS

Throughout this book you will see many references to the correct use of jacks, axle stands and similar equipment - and we make no apologies for being repetitive! This is one area where safety cannot be overstressed - your life could be at stake!

Special care must be taken when any type of lifting equipment is used. Jacks are made for lifting the vehicle only, not for supporting it. Never work under the car using only a jack to support the weight. Jacks must be supplemented by adequate additional means of support, such as axle stands, positioned under secure load-bearing parts of the frame or underbody. Drive-on ramps are limiting because of their design and size but they are simple to use, reliable and the most stable type of support, by far. We strongly recommend their use.

Full details on jacking and supporting the vehicle will be found in **Raising a car - Safely!** near the beginning of Chapter 3.

FLUOROELASTOMERS
MOST IMPORTANT! PLEASE READ THIS SECTION!

If you service your car in the normal way, none of the following may be relevant to you. Unless, for example, you encounter a car which has been on fire (even in a localised area), subject to heat in, say, a crash-damage repairer's shop or vehicle breaker's yard, or if any second-hand parts have been heated in any of these ways.

Many synthetic rubber-like materials used in motor cars contain a substance called fluorine. These materials are known as fluoroelastomers and are commonly used for oil seals, wiring and cabling, bearing surfaces, gaskets, diaphragms, hoses and 'O' rings. If they are subjected to temperatures greater than 315 degrees C, they will decompose and can be potentially hazardous. Fluoroelastomer materials will show physical signs of decomposition under such conditions in the form of charring of black sticky masses. Some decomposition may occur at temperatures above 200 degrees C, and it is obvious that when a car has been in a fire or has been dismantled with the assistance of a cutting torch or blow torch, the fluoroelastomers can decompose in the manner indicated above.

In the presence of any water or humidity, including atmospheric moisture, the by-products caused by the fluoroelastomers being heated can be extremely dangerous. According to the Health and Safety Executive, "Skin contact with this liquid or decomposition residues can cause painful and penetrating burns. Permanent irreversible skin and tissue damage can occur". Damage can also be caused to eyes or by the inhalation of fumes created as fluoroelastomers are burned or heated.

After fires or exposure to high temperatures observe the following precautions:

1   *Do not touch blackened or charred seals or equipment.*

2   *Allow all burnt or decomposed fluoroelastomer materials to cool down before inspection, investigations, tear-down or removal.*

3   *Preferably, don't handle parts containing decomposed fluoroelastomers, but if you must, wear goggles and PVC (polyvinyl chloride) or neoprene protective gloves whilst doing so. Never handle such parts unless they are completely cool.*

4   *Contaminated parts, residues, materials and clothing, including protective clothing and gloves, should be disposed of by an approved contractor to landfill or by incineration according to national or local regulations. Oil seals, gaskets and 'O ' rings, along with contaminated material, must not be burned locally.*

WORKSHOP SAFETY - GENERAL

1   *Always have a fire extinguisher of the correct type at arm's length when working on the fuel system - under the car, or under the bonnet.*

    If you do have a fire, DON'T PANIC! Use the extinguisher effectively by directing it at the base of the fire.

2   *NEVER use a naked flame near petrol or anywhere in the workplace.*

3   *KEEP your inspection lamp well away from any source of petrol (gasoline) such as when disconnecting a carburettor float bowl or fuel line.*

4   *NEVER use petrol (gasoline) to clean parts. Use paraffin (kerosene) or white spirits.*

5   *NO SMOKING! There's a risk of fire or transferring dangerous substances to your mouth and, in any case, ash falling into mechanical components is to be avoided!*

6   *BE METHODICAL in everything you do, use common sense, and think of safety at all times.*

CHAPTER 2 - BUYING SPARES

The Beetle has a well-deserved reputation for reliability, but of course, there will be occasions when you need to buy spares in order to keep your pride and joy running. There are a number of sources of supply of the components necessary when servicing the car, the price and quality varying between suppliers. As with most things in life, cheapest is not necessarily best - as a general rule our advice is to put quality before price - this policy usually works out less expensive in the long run! Your VW is a quality machine put together using quality parts and keeping it in tip-top condition demands that you continue what they started at the factory.

1. There are three places to look for reference numbers on your Beetle. The engine number is on the crankcase at the generator support flange.

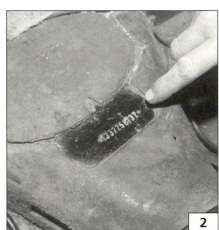

2. The chassis number is on the frame tunnel under the rear seat and...

3. ...it is also shown on the Type Identification plate on the front cross panel under the luggage compartment lid. The engine and chassis numbers should match up with the DVLC V5 form (the 'logbook').

SOURCES

VAG DEALERS

How can you identify 'quality'? It's sometimes difficult, but parts from your Volkswagen (VAG) dealer are certain to be so and, of course, they will be 'genuine' items with a comprehensive warranty (sometimes this is much longer than normal). In addition, the parts counter staff will be familiar with the vehicles, and be only too pleased to help enthusiasts locate the spares required. If required, they can use the extensive VAG microfiche system to locate an elusive part at another dealership.

Prices are occasionally reduced from the usual retail level - watch for special offers which are often listed at the parts counter.

When buying spares, have your Beetle's 'personal' details to hand - the date of registration and its chassis (or VIN) and engine numbers. These can be helpful where parts changed during production, and can be the key to a more helpful approach by some parts salespeople! You may, by now have entered this key information on the Auto-Biography pages at the front of this book, for ease of reference. The photos on these pages show you where to find the relevant information on your car.

PARTS FACTORS/MOTOR ACCESSORY SHOPS

Local parts factors and motor accessory shops can be extremely useful for obtaining servicing parts at short notice - many 'accessory' outlets open late in the evening, and on both days at weekends. However, as they tend to concentrate on more 'mainstream' models, with water cooled engines at the 'wrong' end of the car (!), you will have to be very specific about your requirements to avoid ending up with a part that is 'almost right' rather than just what you want.

Don't overlook the 'trade' motor factors outlets in the UK. One of the biggest (and a supplier of many of the parts used in this series of books) is Partco, with branches all over the country - find them in Yellow Pages.

BUYING AT THE COUNTER

If you're buying spares 'in person' rather than by post, try to avoid Saturday and Sunday mornings - weekends are often very busy for parts counters, and you may find the staff have more time to help you if you visit early on a weekday morning, or in the evening, while on your way to or from work. At these times you are also less likely to have to queue for a long time!

BUYING SPARES FROM SPECIALISTS

There are now dozens of VW specialist suppliers of which most have been in business for many years and have amassed a wealth of knowledge about the Beetle in its many variants.

The monthly VW magazines regularly carry adverts for these companies, which list the most popular spares and prices. Common to most of them is a policy of offering a choice of quality on many items. These will usually carry a note to the effect that they are O/E (original equipment) quality, or otherwise and usually the country of origin. It's true to say that some 'pattern' parts are just about as good as the originals; it's equally true to say that some certainly aren't! Some of the body panels, for example, leave something to be desired in terms of fit and finish. Which you choose will depend on the depth of your wallet and whether or not you want to stay 'original'. However, we would always recommend buying the best quality braking, steering and suspension products you can, regardless of price, because your life depends on them.

ORDERING SPARES BY POST

Most specialists offer a postal service, with payment being by credit card. The points to check are a) the cost of carriage, b) whether VAT is included and b) if there is a cut-off point where you don't pay carriage, or where it is cheaper. For example, it could be that orders over £20 are not subject to a £5 carriage charge. If your order comes to £18, you'd be better off adding a set of points or plugs or something of that nature to it, rather than pay £5 for 'nothing'.

SHOW TIME

The number of VW 'events' grows yearly and as a source of service and other parts, they are well worth attending, especially the bigger shows, which attract a big presence from the specialists who run some incredible offers. Go armed with a list of parts you need and those you're likely to need in the foreseeable future - you're almost certain to recoup your entrance fee many times over.

For example, Beetle owners will know that exhausts fail on a regular basis, usually well within two years (for standard mild steel items). These are usually so cheap at these shows that it's worth buying one 'for stock'! Such events are also an ideal place for meeting fellows of like-minds and discussing any servicing problems you have - it's a racing certainty that someone will have had the problem before you and be able to offer the solution.

BUYING SECONDHAND

These shows are just one place you could consider buying spares from an 'autojumble'. Overall, these tend to comprise private owners selling off used or unwanted stock and dealers clearing out their parts shelves. Naturally, you need consider very seriously what it is you're buying. Purchasing any safety items - braking, steering, suspension - without being absolutely sure of their provenance is dangerous indeed, and not something we would recommend. Even if you're helping a VAG dealer unload some surplus stock, the odds are it has been standing for some years. Make sure that safety-related parts are still serviceable and are not, for example, covered in a fine coating of rust.

That's not to decry buying secondhand altogether. Buying, say, a distributor, or carburettor which you know to be 'low mileage' units, to replace your worn out components makes great sense. Equally, trim panels and other interior parts can often be obtained at a fraction of the new cost.

CLUBS

There are probably more club for VWs (and VW based vehicles) than any other marque. Most will be able to offer general spares information whilst the bigger ones often have a specialist tool hire service, to save you buying expensive tools you'll only use once every ten years. We would recommend that you join an enthusiastic, established club and make the best of the benefits they offer. Their details are carried in the VW magazines.

CHECKS ON RUNNING GEAR COMPONENTS

Always take very great care when purchasing 'hardware' for the steering, suspension and braking systems, which are obviously vital for safety.

Although many outlets sell 'reconditioned' components on an 'exchange' basis, the quality of workmanship and the extent of the work carried out on such units can vary greatly. Therefore, if buying a rebuilt unit, always check particularly carefully when buying. It has to be said that, wherever possible, reconditioned units are best obtained from VAG dealers, or from reputable specialist suppliers. Always talk to fellow owners before buying - they may be able to direct you to a supplier offering sound parts at reasonable prices. When buying, always enquire about the terms of the guarantee (if any!).

In any event, the following notes should help you make basic checks on some of the commonly required components:

BRAKES

(Purchase NEW parts ONLY): Look for boxes bearing genuine VAG labels.

STEERING

Ball joints, king pins, steering boxes, rack and pinion steering units, etc, - buy new, again rejecting any moisture-damaged stock.

Stub axles are available from some suppliers on an 'exchange' basis. Ensure that the inner surfaces of the king pin bushes appear to have been properly reamed, and have uniform, smooth surfaces. With a new king pin inserted, the stub axle should rotate about the pin smoothly, without any undue slack or free play evident. Steering units may be available as exchange items. Ensure that you rotate the operating shaft fully from lock to lock, feeling for any undue free play, roughness, stiffness, or 'notchiness' as you do so. Reject any units showing signs of any of these problems.

SUSPENSION

Used shock absorbers really aren't worth buying on a used basis - standard units for all Beetle models are available incredibly cheaply from the specialist suppliers. Don't forget that shock absorbers should always be replaced in pairs and preferably in complete sets of four.

HOWEVER, we would strongly advise against buying secondhand brake, suspension, and steering components, unless you know the source of the parts, and really are sure that they are in first class condition. Even then, be sure that you see the vehicle they have been taken from, and avoid any such parts from accident-damaged cars.

In every case, ensure that the components you are buying are compatible with your particular vehicle, and carry out basic checks to ensure that they too are not badly worn.

TYRES

For the ultimate in long life, roadholding and wet grip, brand new radial tyres from a reputable manufacturer offer the best solution, especially where the car is used all year round, on an 'everyday' basis. Traditionally, Beetles are very easy on tyres, a situation created by a low power output at the rear and a light loading at the front. Buy good quality (that word again...) tyres, look after them well, and they'll last many years.

You'd have to be crazy about originality to want to fit crossplies, especially if you've driven a Beetle so-fitted in a cross wind!

Remoulds are available at lower initial cost, but life expectancy is not as long as with new tyres.

SECOND HAND TYRES

Secondhand tyre outlets are becoming increasingly common lately, most selling used tyres imported from the continent, where tyre laws are more stringent than in the U.K. However, if you purchase such covers, you are taking a risk in that you have no knowledge of the history of the tyres or what has happened to them, how they have been repaired, and so on. A report conducted by the RAC revealed that a very high percentage of tyres in their test sample had very dangerous faults, such as damaged walling. Their advice, and we would agree, is to stick to top quality, unused tyres from a reputable manufacturer. They may cost a little more, but at least you will have peace of mind, and should be able to rely on their performance in all road and weather situations. After all, your life - and those of other road users - could depend on it!

CONCLUSION

Finally, if you want to buy quality and save money, you must be prepared to shop around. Ring each of your chosen suppliers with a shopping list to hand and your car's personal data from the Auto-Biography at the front of this book in front of you. Keep a written note of prices - including VAT, delivery etc - whether the parts are proper 'brand name' parts or not and - most importantly! - whether or not the parts you want are in stock. Parts expected 'soon' have been known never to materialise. A swivel pin in the hand is worth two in the bush. (Bad pun!)

Volkswagen parts specialists, Autobarn of Pershore join with us in recommending the use of original Volkswagen parts when servicing and maintaining your Beetle. Joint proprietor Peter Stephens says, "Genuine VW parts are the main way to be sure you are getting top quality parts for your car. Our experience in fitting the parts and using the cars has shown us that the best value for money in terms of life span and performance is gained by using original VW replacement parts. The hard truth is that VW parts are expensive but their costs can be appreciated when you think of the thousands of dealers in their European network which must be serviced with a variety of supplies which is second to none. Even so, recently there has been evidence that changes are afoot and some of the new prices coming out of the local dealers for various components have probably been the lowest in their history!"
Without a doubt Volkswagen have the best record in the world (along with Porsche perhaps) for supplying parts for their older cars and it is said that 90 percent of all parts for main line Beetle models are still available. If your local main dealer does not have the parts you want in stock, they can invariably be obtained from Germany within 3 days. Some service! In addition, Volkswagen parts branded as Quantum, and these cover regular servicing commodities, and are available at more competitive prices.

CHAPTER 3
SERVICE INTERVALS, STEP-BY-STEP

Everyone wants to own a car that starts first time, runs reliably and lasts longer than the average. And there's no magic about how to put your car into that category; it's all a question of thorough maintenance! If you follow the Service Jobs listed here or have a garage or mechanic do it for you - you can almost guarantee that your car will still be going strong when others have fallen by the wayside... or the hard shoulder. Mind you, we would be among the first to acknowledge that this Service Schedule is just about as thorough as you can get; it's an amalgam of all the maker's recommended service items plus all the 'Inside Information' from the experts that we could find. If you want your car to be as well looked after as possible, you'll follow the Jobs shown here, but if you don't want to go all the way, you can pick and choose from the most essential items in the list. But do bear in mind that the Jobs we recommend are there for some very good reasons:

◆ *body maintenance* is rarely included in most service schedules. We believe it to be essential.

◆ *preventative maintenance* figures very high on our list of priorities. And that's why so many of our service jobs have the word "Check..." near the start!

◆ *older cars* need more jobs doing on them than new cars - it's as simple as that - so we list the jobs you will need to carry out in order to keep any car, older or new, in fine fettle.

USING THE SERVICE SCHEDULES

At the start of each Service Job, you'll see a heading in bold type, looking a bit like this:

☐ **Job 31. Adjust spark plugs.**

Following the heading will be all the information you will need to enable you to carry out that particular Job. Please note that different models of car might have different settings. Please check *Chapter 8, Facts and Figures*. Exactly the same Job number and heading will be found in the *Service History* Appendix, where you will want to keep a full record of all the work you have carried out. After you have finished servicing your car, you will be able to tick off all of the jobs that you have completed and so, service by service, build up a complete Service History of work carried out on your car.

You will also find other key information immediately after each Job title and in most cases, there will be reference to an illustration - a photograph or line drawing, whichever is easier for you to follow - usually on the same page.

If the Job shown only applies to certain vehicles, the Job title will be followed by a description of the type of vehicle to which the Job title applies. For instance, Job 18 applies to "CARS UP TO 1965 ONLY" - and the information in bold tells you so.

Other special headings are also used. One reads **OPTIONAL,** which means that you may wish to use your own discretion as to whether to carry out this particular Job or whether to leave it until it crops up again in a later service. Another is **INSIDE INFORMATION.** This tells you that here is a Job or a special tip that you wouldn't normally get to hear about, other than through the experience and 'inside' knowledge of the experts at Macvolks, who helped in compiling this Service Guide. The third is **SPECIALIST SERVICE,** which means that we recommend you to have this work carried out by a specialist. Some jobs, such as setting the tracking or suspension are best done with the right measuring equipment while other jobs may demand the use of equipment such as an exhaust gas analyser. Where we think you are better off having the work done for you, we say so!

We are grateful to Iain MacLeod of servicing specialists, Macvolks VW for his kind assistance with this chapter. Almost all of the work was photographed there.

Throughout the Service Schedule, each 'shorter' Service Interval is meant to be an important part of each of the next 'longer' Service Interval, too. For instance, under *500 Mile Mechanical and Electrical - Around the Car*, Job 11. you are instructed to check the tyres for wear or damage. This Job also has to be carried out at 1,500 miles, 3,000 miles, 6,000 miles, 9,000 miles, and so on. It is therefore shown in the list of extra Jobs to be carried out in each of these 'longer' Service Intervals but only as a Job number, without the detailed instructions that were given the first time around!

> *SAFETY FIRST!*
> *The other special heading is **the one that could be the most important one of all!** SAFETY FIRST! information must **always** be read with care and **always** taken seriously. In addition, please read the whole of **Chapter 1, Safety First!** before carrying out any work on your car. There are many hazards associated with working on a car but all of them can be avoided by adhering strictly to the safety rules. Don't skimp on safety!*

The 'Catch-up' Service

When you first buy a used car, you never know for sure just how well it's been looked after. Even one with a full service history is unlikely to have been serviced as thoroughly as one with a Porter Publishing Service Guide history! So, if you want to catch-up on all the servicing that may have been neglected on your car, just work through the entire list of Service Jobs listed for the *36,000 Miles - or Every Thirty Six Months* service, and your car will be bang up to date and serviced as well as you could hope for. Do allow several days for all of this work, not least because it will almost certainly throw up a number of extra jobs - potential faults that have been lurking beneath the surface - all of which will need putting right before you can 'sign off' your car as being in tip-top condition.

The Service History

Those people fortunate enough to own a new car, or one that has been well maintained from new will have the opportunity to keep a service record, or 'Service History' of their car, usually filled in by a main dealer. Until now, it hasn't been possible for the owner of an older car to keep a formal record of servicing but now you can, using the complete tick list in *Appendix 4, Service History*. In fact, you can go one better than the owners of those new cars, because your car's Service History will be more complete and more detailed than any manufacturer's service record, with the extra bonus that there is space for you to keep a record of all of those extra items that crop up from time to time. New tyres; replacement exhaust; extra accessories; where can you show those on a regular service schedule? Now you can, so if your battery goes down only 11 months after buying it, you'll be able to look up where and when you bought it. All you'll have to do is remember to fill in your Service Schedule in the first place!

When using car ramps:

(I) Make absolutely certain that the ramps are parallel to the wheels of the car and that the wheels are exactly central on each ramp.

(II) *Always* have an assistant watch both sides of the car as you drive up. Drive *up to* the end 'stops' on the ramps but never over them!

Apply the hand brake firmly, put the car in first or reverse gear (or 'neutral' in the case of Automatic Stick Shift models only).

> *RAISING A CAR - SAFELY!*
> *You will often need to raise your car off the ground in order to carry out the Service Jobs shown here. To start off with, here's what you must never do - never work beneath a car held on a jack, not even a trolley jack. Quite a number of deaths have been caused by a car slipping off a jack while someone has been working beneath. On the other hand, the safest way is by raising a car on a proprietary brand of ramps. Sometimes, there is no alternative but to use axle stands. Please read all of the following information and act upon it!*

(III) Chock *both* wheels remaining on the ground, both in front and behind so that the car can't move in either direction. (A home-made wooden chock, cut at an angle so that it wedges under the tyre will be fine).

INSIDE INFORMATION: Wrap a strip of carpet into a loop around the first 'rung' of the ramps and drive over the doubled-up piece of carpet on the approach to the ramps. This prevents the ramps from skidding away, as they are inclined to do, as the car is driven on to them.

On other occasions, you might need to raise the car with a trolley jack - invest in one if you don't already own one; the car's wheel changing jack is often too unstable. Place a piece of cloth over the head of the jack if your car is nicely finished on the underside. Ensure that the floor is sufficiently clear and smooth for the trolley jack wheels to roll as the car is raised and lowered, otherwise it could slip off the jack.

(IV) Place the jack beneath the front frame head plate when raising the front of the car and place the axle stands near the front of the floorpan, under the area of the front cross bracing. Leave the jack in situ, but let the weight of the car rest firmly on the axle stands (note the plural, don't use just one when you're raising the car like this).

(V) At the rear of the car, place a suitably flat and strong piece of wood across the top of the jack head and raise the car under the transmission, as shown here.

(VI) Place the axle stands under the torsion bars at either side. If, for any reason, you can't use the location points recommended here, take care to locate the top of the axle stand on a strong, level, stable part of the car's underside. Never use a movable suspension part because the part can move and allow the axle stand to slip, or use the floor of the car, which is just too weak.

Just as when using ramps - only even more importantly! - apply the handbrake firmly once the car is fully raised by the jack (but NOT before!), put the car in first or reverse gear (or 'neutral', in the case of an Automatic Stick Shift) and chock both wheels remaining on the ground, both in front and behind.

Be *especially* careful when applying force to a spanner or when pulling hard on anything, when the car is supported off the ground. It is all too easy to move the car so far that it topples off the axle stand or stands. And remember that if a car falls on you, YOU COULD BE KILLED!

Caution is needed when working on the car whilst it is supported on an axle stand or a pair of axle stands. These are inherently less stable than ramps and so you must take much greater care when working beneath them. In particular, ensure that the axle stand is on flat, stable ground, never on ground where one side can sink in to the ground.

Whenever working beneath a car, have someone primed to keep an eye on you! If someone pops out to see how you are getting on every quarter of an hour or so, it could be enough to save your life!

Do remember that, in general, a car will be more stable when only one wheel is removed and one axle stand used than if two wheels are removed in conjunction with two axle stands. You are strongly advised not to work under the car with all four wheels off the ground, on four axle stands. The car could then be very unstable and dangerous to work beneath.

When lowering the car to the ground, remember first to remove the chocks, release the handbrake and place the transmission in neutral.

500 MILE/WEEKLY SERVICE

500 Miles, Weekly, or Before a Long Journey

These are the regular checks that you need to carry out to help keep your car safe and reliable. They don't include the major Service Jobs but they should be carried out as an integral part of every 'proper' service.

500 Mile Mechanical and Electrical - The Engine Bay

☐ **Job 1. Check engine oil level.**

1A. The shallow sump of the air-cooled engines makes it vital that the car should be standing on level ground while the oil level is checked. Ideally, the engine should be cold, but if it's just been running, allow a couple of minutes for all the oil to run down into the sump. The dipstick is situated to the right of the generator/alternator pedestal.

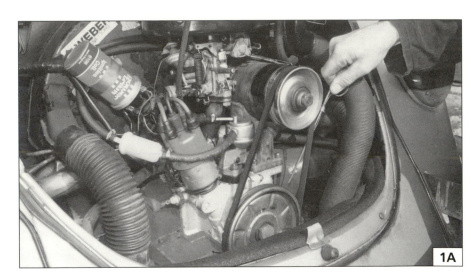

1B. Pull the dipstick out, clean it and reinsert it. Remove again and check that the level is between the 'high' and 'low' marks. The difference between them is approximately 1.25 litres.

1C. Top up if required, making sure that the dipstick has been replaced. Note that using a funnel ensures that the oil doesn't go all over the engine. Using oil (not *burning* oil!) is no great cause for concern as the engine was designed to use oil from Day One - expect to replace between 3/4 to 2 pints per 1000 miles as a matter of course.

INSIDE INFORMATION: Never overfill the engine, as any excess could find its way past an overloaded oil seal.

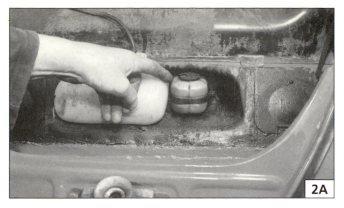
2A

500 Mile Mechanical and Electrical - Around the Car

☐ **Job 2. Check brake fluid level.**

2A. First, locate your brake fluid reservoir! Various types, - metal and plastic - and positions have been used, but on all models, it is located under the bonnet. On this 1962 car, it is positioned behind the spare wheel and has a prise-off cap. You can see the fluid content through the plastic reservoir. If no level marking is shown, the reservoir should be at least 3/4 full.

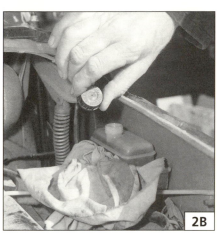
2B

2B. On this car, the reservoir is mounted on its own bracket on the left hand side of the car. It's not the easiest place to get to. Notice that it has been wiped clean before the cap was removed and also that a rag has been left there to catch any drops or spills - brake fluid will damage painted surfaces if allowed to come into contact. Wash off any accidental spillage immediately with hot soapy water.

2C. On this kind of reservoir, there's a filter which sits in the top of the filler neck. If it's not totally clean, rinse it through with white spirit (replacing the cap while you do so to prevent accidental ingress of dirt) and then put it back in the reservoir.

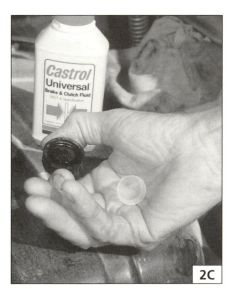
2C

2D. Now you see why the cloth was left there - it's not easy getting to this kind of reservoir!

INSIDE INFORMATION: Check the ground on which the car has been parked, especially beneath the engine bay and inside each road wheel, for evidence of oil, clutch or brake fluid leaks. If any are found, investigate further before driving the car.

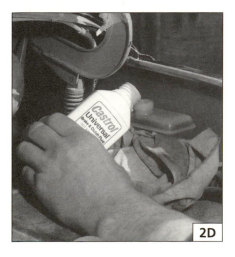
2D

SAFETY FIRST!
i) If brake fluid should come into contact with the skin or eyes, rinse immediately with plenty of water.
ii) It is acceptable for the brake fluid level to fall slightly during normal use, but if it falls significantly below the bottom of the filler cap neck, it indicates a leak or an internal seal failure. Stop using the car and seek specialist advice immediately.
iii) If you get dirt into the hydraulic system it can cause brake failure. Wipe the filler cap clean before removing.
iv) You should only ever use only new brake fluid from an air-tight container. Old fluid absorbs moisture and this could cause the brakes to fail when carrying out an emergency stop or other heavy use of the brakes - just when you need them most and are least able to do anything about it, in fact!

☐ Job 3. Check windscreen washer reservoir level.

3. Check the windscreen washer level. It is located on a side panel (later models) or in/behind the spare wheel. It's advisable to mix in proprietary washer cleaner, which also acts as a 'anti-freeze' during bad weather. (Note - never use engine anti-freeze.) The washer system is pneumatic and relies on the spare tyre for a goodly supply of pressure. When the pressure drops below around 28 psi, the washers are unlikely to work. It's a good idea to inflate the spare to the maximum recommended for high speed or high load running. Then, not only will you have enough pressure to operate the washers, you'll also be OK if you have a puncture. It's always easier to carry a tyre pressure gauge with you and let some air out than put some in!

☐ Job 4. Check windscreen washers.

4. Check the operation of the windscreen washers. If one of them fails to work, check that pipes have not come adrift and then check the jet: clear it with a pin. Jets are adjustable by inserting a pin and twisting the jet inside its rubber housing. Check that the spare tyre is at the correct pressure and able to power the washers. Make sure that the pipes from the tyre to the reservoir and from the reservoir to the jets are not trapped or split.

☐ Job 5. Check windscreen wipers.

Check that the wiper blades are not torn, worn or damaged in any way. Give each blade a wipe clean with methylated spirit (industrial alcohol). You should replace wiper blades at least once a year to be sure of optimum performance at all times.

5A. Changing wiper blades varies according to the model. Early cars had simple screw-on blades.

5B. Later cars changed to the more conventional type which clip onto the wiper arm.

5C. Here's how to go about changing them. First, lift the wiper arm away from the windscreen and hold in the retaining button (5C.1), slide the wiper blade towards the screen for a little way (5C.2), then move the blade sideways and slide it free of the arm (5C.3).

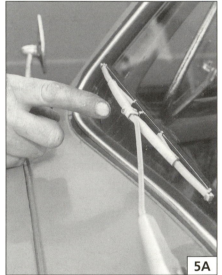

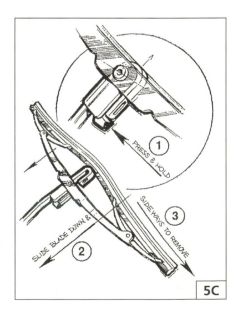

6A

☐ Job 6. Check headlamps/sidelamps.

Check that the headlamps are operative on both main and dipped beam.

6A. Bosch and Hella have been the major providers of headlamps to VW over the years. Non-sealed beam headlamps are probably the easiest to remove, the screw at the 6 o'clock position releasing either the entire headlamp assembly (early models) or just the rim on later cars.

6B. Remove the bulb holder from the rear of the reflector by turning it anti-clockwise. Pull the bulb and connection apart. When fitting a new bulb, do not handle the glass as this will leave a deposit which may ultimately cause a discolouration. If the bulb glass is inadvertently touched with your fingers, wipe it clean with methylated spirit. Refit the bulb/connector assembly so that the notches and lugs line up. DO NOT touch screws other than the securing screw at the base of the headlamp rim - the two others are for beam adjustment (see later). (Illustration, courtesy Volkswagen)

6C. Sealed beam headlamps are instantly recognisable because there is only one screw visible on the rim. When this is removed, access is given to...

6D. ...the beam adjustment screws, at roughly the 2 o'clock and 7 o'clock positions. Take care not to confuse them with the headlamp securing screws which have to be removed to release the unit. If the bulb fails in a sealed beam lamp the whole unit must be replaced. The wiring fits onto three terminals on the back of the lamp. Release the curved wire springs and separate the unit from the rim. Before replacing the unit, check that the fault is not being caused by unsound wiring or that corrosion is not causing bad connections.

6E. These are the adjustment screws on earlier models. (Illustration, courtesy Volkswagen)

SPECIALIST SERVICE It is not possible to set headlamps accurately at home. In *Chapter 7, Getting Through The MoT*, we show how to trial-set your headlamps before going to the MoT Testing Station (in the UK) but this method is not good enough, unless you are going to have the settings checked by a garage with proper headlamp beam checking equipment.

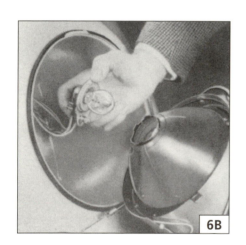

6B

Check front sidelamps

The front sidelamps are situated in the back of the headlamp reflector except in the case of sealed beam unit lights, where the holder is situated in the lower part of the main casing. Remove the main connector then the bulb and bulb holder. Where the bulb has failed, fit a new one in a reversal of this procedure.

6C

6D

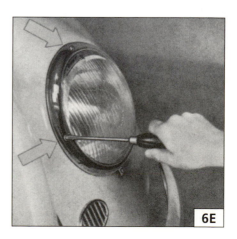

6E

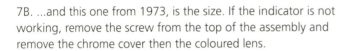

Job 7. Check front indicators.

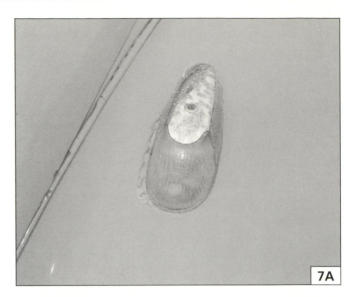

7A

7A. Since their introduction at the start of the '60s, the design of the front indicators has varied little over the years. The main difference between this one from the early sixties...

7B. ...and this one from 1973, is the size. If the indicator is not working, remove the screw from the top of the assembly and remove the chrome cover then the coloured lens.

7B

7C. The bulb may now be removed by pressing in firmly, turning anti clockwise and withdrawing from the holder. If the element is not broken, it's probable that rubbing down the bulb and bulb-holder terminals will solve the problem, as they tend to corrode with age.

INSIDE INFORMATION: If a bulb refuses to budge, try gripping with a piece of cloth - it provides a lot more grip and reduces the risk if the bulb glass breaks. If the bulb comes free of its brass ferrule, carefully break the glass away and push in one side of the ferrule with a screwdriver (lights/indicators turned off!). Spray releasing fluid behind the bulb base and leave for a while. Then work the base free by gripping the side that you have pushed in, using a pair of pliers.

SEMAPHORE SIGNALS
Very early models featured semaphore arms which have an easily-removed bulb inside the orange plastic. Several different types of fittings have been used.

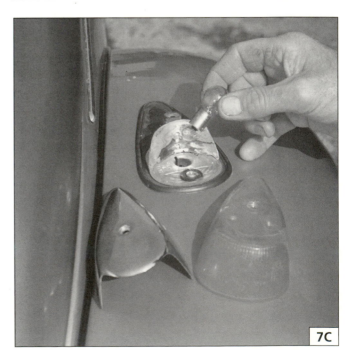

7C

□ **Job 8. Check horn.**

8. On all models, the horn is situated under the left front wing. It's right at the front of the car and takes a battering from the elements. If the horn fails to work, examine the wiring from the fuse to the horn and from there via the horn button to earth. The horn takes a heavy electrical current and demands that the connections are clean and tight - 6v owners should be particularly aware of this. There is an adjusting screw in the centre of the horn. Turning this slightly one way or the other may solve your problem, but do not turn much more than 1/4 of a turn, in case the contact points are burned out. (When checking your horn, have some consideration for your neighbours, and remember that (in the UK) the Highway Code states that you must not sound your horn between 11.30pm and 7.00am in a built-up area or when your vehicle is stationary, unless a moving vehicle poses a danger.)

INSIDE INFORMATION: When a fault occurs with any electrical item, your first move should be to ensure that the fuse is OK. A blown fuse is best discovered now, rather than when you've dismantled half the car looking for a fault that doesn't exist!

□ **Job 9. Check rear sidelamps/indicators.**

9A. VW gradually increased the size and complexity of their rear lamps. This 1959 version was secured by a single screw and contained just stop and tail lamps. (Illustration, courtesy Volkswagen)

9B. As the '60s progressed, the presence of the indicators meant an increase in lens size and the addition of one more securing screw. By the time the 1303/S cars arrived, the rear lamp clusters were almost as big as the headlamps! Four Philips screws were used to hold it in place. With the lens off, take the opportunity to give it a good clean inside.

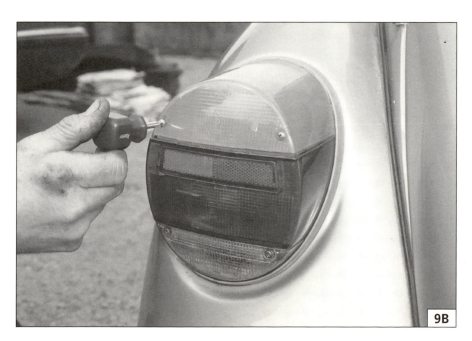

9C. To replace a bulb, remove the lens and extract the old bulb by pressing in firmly and turning anti-clockwise. Reverse this process to fit the new bulb.

The lower of the three sockets is for the reversing lamp bulb. This feature was only fitted as standard on the 1303S, though it could be added to its smaller-engined sibling quite easily. The stop/tail bulb has a bayonet fitting as it can only fit one way - check the offset pegs before fitting. You can see the damp accumulating in the bottom of the moulding, which shows that the drain section at the lower part needs cleaning. Take this opportunity to clean off rust and rust-proof.

9D. It's also important to check that the seal around the lens is in good condition. If it isn't, water will get in and cause electrical problems and rust problems, as you can see around the reversing lamp position. Also check any auxiliary lamps, such as fog lamps, that may have been fitted as original equipment (later cars) or as accessories, in which case they are still supposed to function correctly, by law.

INSIDE INFORMATION: It's a sure sign that something is wrong with an indicator when the tell-tale light on the dash flashes twice as quickly as normal. Very often, a bad earth is at fault and a quick fix can be to tap the indicator lens with the flat of your hand. Once home, you should remove the bulb and clean up all the connections with emery paper.

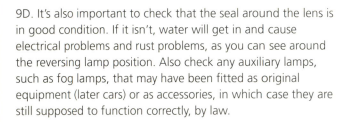

☐ Job 10. Check number plate lamp.

10. The light is secured by two screws to the underside of a protective flap on the engine lid. If it is inoperative, remove the screws and ease out the unit. Remove the bulb and replace if necessary. Take this opportunity to clean the lens.

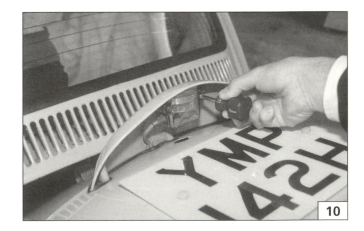

☐ Job 11. Check general condition of tyres.

SAFETY FIRST!
Tyres that show uneven wear tell their own story, if only you know how to speak the language! If any tyre is worn more on one side than another, consult your specialist VW dealer or tyre specialist. It probably means that your suspension or steering is out of adjustment - probably a simple tracking job but conceivably symptomatic of suspension damage, so have it checked. If a tyre is worn more in the centre or on the edges, it could mean that your tyre pressures are wrong, but once again, have the car checked. Incorrectly inflated tyres wear rapidly, can cause the car's handling to become dangerous and can even cause the car to consume noticeably more fuel. When checking your tyres, don't forget to include the spare.

11. Check the tyres for tread depth, using a quality gauge. Current UK laws state that there should be a minimum of 1.6mm of tread across the centre 3/4 of the outer circumference of the tyre. However, it should be regarded as an absolute minimum and safe drivers will want to replace their tyres well before this. Check the tread of the tyres for sharp stones and other foreign bodies which could cause a puncture. If you see an unusual wear pattern, it points to problems with either under or over inflation of the tyres or steering and/or suspension misalignment or maladjustment.

Make a visual check on both sides of each tyre for uneven wear, cuts, bulges or other damage in the walls. Raise each wheel off the ground, using an axle stand, otherwise you won't be able to see the inside of each tyre properly, nor will you be able to check that part of the tyre that is in contact with the ground. If you find any splits or other damage, the tyre(s) should be inspected immediately by a tyre specialist who will advise whether repair is possible or replacement is the only answer.

☐ Job 12. Check tyre pressures.

12. Use a reliable tyre pressure gauge to check the tyre pressures on the car, but never after driving the car, which warms up the tyres considerably and increases their pressures. Don't forget the spare - not only might it be required in case of a puncture, but also it powers the windscreen washers. Remember that prolonged high speed driving and/or carrying a full load of passengers or luggage requires the tyre pressures to be higher than normal.

☐ Job 13. Check security of wheel bolts.

13A. Having checked the tyres, it's always a good idea to check the wheel bolts. If you've wondered what those two holes in the side of the hub cap are for, now you know - VW supply a special wire tool which slots in and, when used as shown with the wheel wrench tommy bar, the hub caps can be removed quick as a flash. The obvious alternative is to use a flat-bladed screwdriver, though you'll have to be careful not to scratch the paint on the wheels.

13B. You need to make sure that the bolts are not loose, of course, but it's not necessary to apply huge amounts of torque - don't forget, if you have a flat tyre on the road, you'll need to be able to get the wheel off again! This last point needs particular attention if you have had new tyres fitted by a specialist where fitters with pneumatic wrenches can sometimes get a little over enthusiastic. Most standard steel wheel bolts should be tightened to around 95 lbs ft.

13B

☐ Job 14. Check battery electrolyte level.

INSIDE INFORMATION: i) When water is mixed with the acid inside the battery, it won't freeze. So, in extremely cold weather, run the car (out of doors) so that you put a charge into the battery and this will mix the fresh water with the electrolyte, cutting out the risk of freezing and a cracked battery case.

14A. The battery in the Beetle can be found beneath a cover, under the rear seat on the right hand side. Unclip the cover, take care not to damage the backrest when removing the seat itself. It is especially important to keep 6v batteries in peak condition. Unless the battery is a 'sealed for life' unit, remove the battery cap or caps and, with the car on level ground, check the level of the electrolyte: the fluid inside each battery cell. You often can't see it at first: use a flashlight and tap the side of the battery to make the surface of the electrolyte ripple a little, so that you can see it.

14A

14B. The plates inside the battery should just be covered with electrolyte. If the level has fallen, top up with distilled water, NEVER with tap water! Dry off the top of the battery. If the battery terminals are obviously furred, refer to Job 74 *(6,000 Mile Service)*. If the battery needs constant topping up but there is no obvious sign of leakage, it could be that the voltage regulator is faulty and is overcharging the battery. Have the regulator checked and, if necessary, replaced.

14C. Here's how to check the strength, or specific gravity, of the battery electrolyte. You place the end of a hydrometer into the battery electrolyte, squeeze and release the rubber bulb so that a little of the acid is drawn up into the transparent tube and the float or floats inside the tube (small coloured beads are sometimes used) give the specific gravity. (Illustration, courtesy Volkswagen)

14B

Only water evaporates out of a battery, not acid, so topping up with distilled water is invariably sufficient. If a battery goes flat because the car has been left standing for too long, use a small battery charger to top up the battery, following the instructions and disconnecting the battery on your car first. A battery that goes flat too rapidly can be checked by a garage - they may well check the specific gravity of the electrolyte in each cell in order to establish whether one or more has failed but since garages often tell you that you need a new battery anyway, it might be worth investing in a hydrometer and testing the cells yourself. Otherwise, you could try disconnecting the battery and seeing if it still goes flat. If not, suspect a wiring fault allowing the current to drain away but do be aware that some car alarms will drain a car battery in around a week. Some seem to be designed primarily for cars that are used almost every day rather than classic or special interest cars that may not be used so often.

INSIDE INFORMATION: In very cold weather, run the engine for a few minutes - in the open, not in your garage - in order that the electrolyte and distilled water mix. If you don't, it's possible that the water could freeze in the battery.

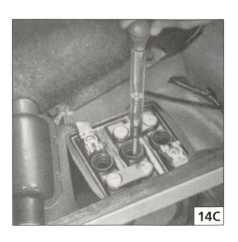

14C

500 Mile Bodywork and Interior - Around the Car

☐ **Job 15. Clean bodywork.**

15A. Wash paintwork, chrome, soft-top (on Cabrio models) and glass with water and a suitable car wash detergent, taking care not to get 'wax-wash' on the glass. Don't use washing up liquid - it will pull off the protective wax and ultimately ruin the paint surface. Finish by washing the wheels and tyre walls. Leather the paintwork dry and then polish. Use a separate leather on glass to avoid transfer of polish from paintwork.

15B. The glass - and especially the windscreen - often needs special treatment to get rid of the build up of grime, oily smears and squashed insects. Use a proprietary cleaner and wipe off with a lint-free cloth. Don't forget to clean the insides of the glass, too - it's amazing how dirty it gets!

15A

15B

Convertible Beetles
Use a soft brush to remove dust and flaking dirt from the soft top prior to washing. Do not use any form of harsh cleaning agents for cleaning the soft-top; ordinary car wash products will do the job. Never fold the soft top back whilst it is still wet.

INSIDE INFORMATION: If the weather is particularly wet or muddy, road dirt may collect beneath the leading edge of the convertible top where it fits against the windscreen surround. From time to time, open the hood and carefully wash this area.

1,500 Miles or Every Month, Whichever Comes First

1,500 Mile Mechanical and Electrical - The Engine Bay

☐ **Job 16. Check torque converter fluid level.**

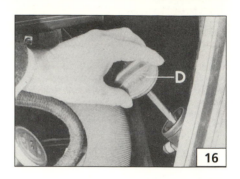
16

AUTOMATIC STICK SHIFT MODELS ONLY
16. The container holding the automatic transmission fluid for the torque converter is situated on the right hand side of the engine compartment. The filler cap has a dipstick attached to it. The level should always be between the two marks on the dipstick but never below the lower mark. If the level has dropped considerably but there is no obvious sign of leakage, it could be that the fluid is leaking into the engine - this can be checked by dipping the engine oil. If this has risen, then you have a serious problem which needs sorting NOW - it could wreck both torque converter and engine! It is most certainly a **SPECIALIST SERVICE** job. (Illustration, courtesy Volkswagen)

1,500 Mile Mechanical and Electrical - Around the Car

☐ **Job 17. Lubricate door hinges.**

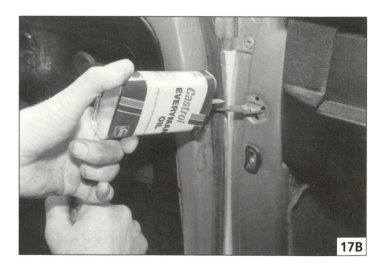
17A

17A. Beetle doors are wide, heavy objects and place plenty of strain on the hinges. Apply Castrol Everyman oil to the hinges themselves. Later models, like this 1303, have an oil chamber at the top of the hinge, covered by a plastic plug. Don't forget to replace the plug when you've finished. VW workshops also use a grease gun with a conical nozzle on the top of the hinge after removing the plastic plug.

17B. Move inside and lubricate the door stays. These can rust and seize solid quite easily, especially in damp climates.

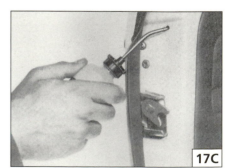
17B

17C. At the same time a few drops of oil are put into the door locks through a small hole in the end of the door which is normally sealed with a plug. (Illustration, courtesy Volkswagen)

1,500 Mile Mechanical and Electrical - Under the Car

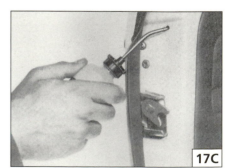
17C

The front suspension of the Beetle has become less complex over the years and the younger the car, the less maintenance is required - owners of 1302S, 1303 and 1303S models probably won't know what a grease gun is! Owners of all other Beetles, however, will have one always at the ready and filled with Castrol LM grease, for proper lubrication of your Beetle's front suspension is essential. Apply smooth strokes of the grease gun until excess grease emerges from the edges of the lubrication point. Wipe off the excess with a rag.

SAFETY FIRST!
For proper lubrication of the parts shown here, the car should be raised - make sure you do so without incident by referring to Chapter 1. In particular, make sure that you protect your eyes, as there is likely to be plenty of loose dirt and rust under the front end of any Beetle used on a regular basis. Lubricate all greasing points on one side before lowering the car and progressing to the other side.

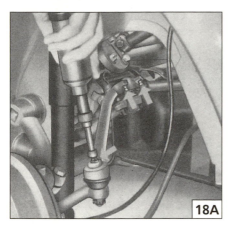

18A

18B

☐ **Job 18. Grease front suspension.**

CARS UP TO 1961 ONLY
18A. Only these very early models featured grease nipples on the tie rods as shown in this photo. (Illustration, courtesy Volkswagen)

CARS UP TO 1965 ONLY
18B. The link pin type suspension features two grease nipples per side on the king pin assembly... (Illustration, courtesy Volkswagen)

18C

18C. ...and two per side on the axle tubes. There's one on the lower tube (follow the finger!) and one directly above it on the upper tube. There are also two grease nipples per side on the torsion arm link pins.

INSIDE INFORMATION: Always wipe over the grease nipple with a cloth dipped in white spirit before applying the grease gun. This way, you'll ensure that no dirt gets into the item to be lubricated. It's also a good idea to clean the edges of the lubrication point so that you can see when enough grease has been inserted.

19A

1,500 Mile Bodywork and Interior - Around the Car

☐ **Job 19. Touch-up paintwork.**

19A. Treat stone chips or scratches to prevent or eliminate rust. Some proprietary aerosol sprays come complete with a piece of emery paper, a small amount of body stopper and a small brush, enabling you to treat any damaged areas in the best way. If you're treating an area which has already started to rust...

19B. ...remove the rusty surface, taking care not to scratch the surrounding area, ...

19C. ...and then use an anti-rust agent...

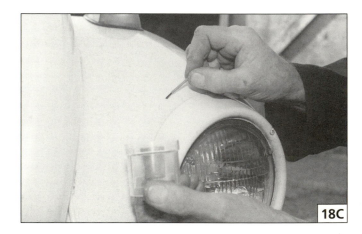

19D. ...before applying the touch-up paint. Use a small brush for small stone chips and the aerosol for larger areas.

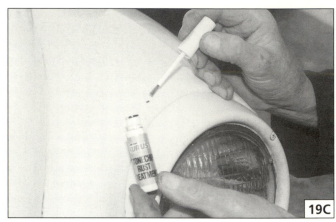

☐ **Job 20. Aerial/antenna.**

20. Clean the sections of an extending, chrome plated aerial mast. Wipe a little releasing fluid (not oil - it will attract dirt) onto the surface and work in and out a few times. This applies even more if you have a non-retractable aerial, which spends its whole life out in the elements.

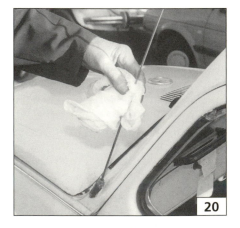

☐ Job 21. Clean interior.

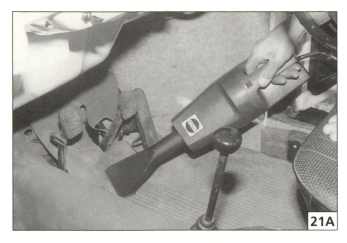

21A

21A. Use a vacuum cleaner to remove dust and grit from the interior trim and carpets. Only the best dedicated in-car vacuums are good enough to get the ground-in grit out of your carpets and it's often best to use your domestic cleaner. Consider also using the high-power vacuums found at many service stations.

Proprietary upholstery cleaners can be surprisingly effective and well worthwhile if the interior has become particularly grubby. Very bad stains, caused by grease, chocolate or unidentified flying brown stuff are best loosened with white spirit or methylated spirit before bringing on the upholstery cleaner - but first test a bit of upholstery that you can't normally see, just in case either of the spirits removes upholstery colour.

Use an anti-static spray cleaner on vinyl trim (or leather - lucky you!) and metal surfaces.

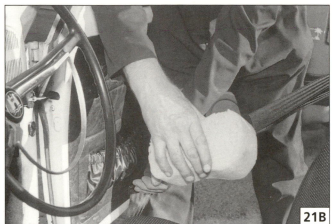

21B

21B. Seat belts should *only* be washed with warm water and a non-detergent soap. Allow them to dry naturally and do not let them retract, if they're the inertia reel type, until completely dry.

☐ Job 22. Improve visibility!

22. After thoroughly cleaning the windscreen and other glass in Job 15C, clean the wiper blades with spirit wipe to remove grease and contaminants.

1,500 Mile Bodywork - Under the Car

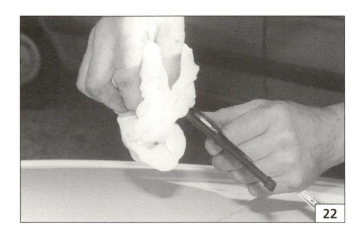

22

> **SAFETY FIRST!**
> **Wear goggles when clearing the underside of the car. Read carefully the information at the start of this chapter on lifting and supporting the car.**

☐ Job 23. Clean mud traps.

Hose the underside of the car. If it's particularly muddy, a trip to the nearest petrol station with a Jet Wash is called for. It costs peanuts, especially when compared with the price of welders' time spent patching up your car's rotten metal. Allow the car to dry before putting it in the garage. Scrape off any dry mud that's left - wear gloves because mud can force itself painfully behind your finger nails!

23A. The area around the jacking points is particularly prone to collecting mud and moisture like it's going out of fashion. Not only does this encourage rot which damages the jacking points themselves, it also starts to rot the sills above them.

23A

23B. At the rear of the front wheel arches is a place where water attacks remorselessly. As you can see on this example, a patch has already had to be welded into place. This could be your car if you don't keep it clean and rustproofed!

Just about everywhere under the rear wheel arch is a danger area. At the rear, the bumper hangers rot like mad, and the area around the chassis mounting point is notorious for gathering mud, moisture and rust. Make sure that the front of the arch is clean, especially around the end of the heater channel/sill.

Just to prove a point, it's very common to find Beetles patched up in this area. (This is particularly bad work, as it has been tack welded rather than seam welded and thus is not up to the standard required by the current UK MoT regulations.)

3,000 Miles - or Every Three Months, Whichever Comes First

3,000 Mile Mechanical and Electrical - The Engine Bay

First carry out Jobs 1 and 16

☐ **Job 24. Clean out air cleaner and refill.**

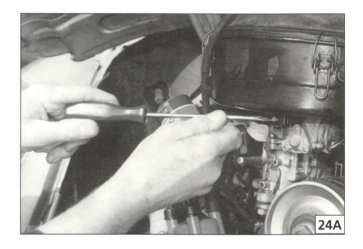

EARLY MODELS ONLY
Note: The paper air cleaners fitted to late model Beetles don't need attention until the 18,000 mile service.

24A. Undo the screw at the securing screw at the base of the cleaner and remove the various hoses - these varied in number over the years. Don't tilt the cleaner as you lift it from the car-burettor or you could spill the oil and don't upend the top, otherwise dirty sludge will drain into the filter.

24B. Prise the clips open and lift off the top cover. Empty out the old oil (NOT down the drain!) and clean out the sludge in the bottom using white spirit or paraffin. While you're doing this, let the filter soak for a while in solvent. When it's clean, let it drip dry before refilling to the line marked around the lower half of the cleaner using Castrol GTX. Fit the two halves together - careful of your fingers with those clips! - and replace the filter assembly back on the carburettor.

☐ **Job 25. Lubricate carburettor control linkage.**

The various linkages on the carburettor should be examined to ensure that they move freely as intended, but without any sign of slackness. Lubricate moving parts using Castrol Everyman oil.

1 Top cover screw
2 Top cover
3 Filter screen
4 Lower pump body
5 Spindle retaining clip
6 Cover plate
7 Pump operating lever
8 Pump operating rod

26A

☐ **Job 26. Clean fuel pump filter (where applicable).**

SAFETY FIRST!
Never work on any part of the fuel system when the engine is hot - or even warm!

26A. On some fuel pumps it is possible to remove the top cover and remove the filter screen. If yours is like this, clean the screen thoroughly in white spirit, dry and replace. If the gasket is looking the worse for wear, replace as a matter of course.

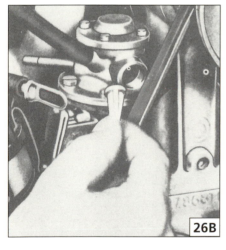

26B

26B. Later models have a tubular fitter in the side of the pump body. (Illustration, courtesy Volkswagen)

26C. Even later model cars featured sealed unit filters like the one on this 1303. These units cannot be serviced which is one of the reasons that...

26D. ...many owners take to fitting aftermarket in-line filters, like this one - recommended!. These can be checked and replaced quite easily when they become dirty or blocked. Some are designed to allow fuel to pass in one direction only - make sure that you get the arrow the right way round!

INSIDE INFORMATION: *Iain always uses small stainless steel Jubilee clips to secure fuel lines, however tight they may seem when 'pushed-on'. You can't be too safe with petrol. Because of the high temperatures in a Beetle's engine compartment, you should only use the correct rubberised fuel vacuum hoses and not the plastic type.*

26C

26D

☐ **Job 27. Adjust idle speed.**

FUEL INJECTION CARS ONLY

Only adjust the idle setting on a warm engine. If you have a multi-function meter, connect it up so that it will show engine RPM. Start the engine and locate the idle screw, which is on the side of the intake air distributor. It stays where it is set because it has either a spring or locknut holding it in place. If it's the latter, use a suitable spanner to back it off. Turn the screw clockwise to INCREASE the RPM and anti clockwise to DECREASE it. There will always be a slight delay before the engine responds. If you're using a meter, the idle speed should be around 850 RPM. If not, back off the idle screw until the engine is almost stalling (or until the red light on the dash starts to flicker) and then turn it in a quarter of a turn. Tighten the locknut if applicable.

☐ **Job 28. Check pipes and hoses.**
Carry out a visual check on all flexible and rigid pipes and hoses in and around the engine bay for leaks.

☐ **Job 29. Check fan belt for wear and tension.**

INSIDE INFORMATION: The Beetle won't run without the fan belt and it can easily snap. Always carry a spare in your toolkit - in the car!

The Beetle drive belt not only drives the generator or alternator, but also the cooling fan. It's vital to your engine's well-being and needs far more attention than the same item on a water-cooled car.

29A. The generator pulley comprises two halves and adjustment is effected by changing the number of spacer washers in between, to effectively change the diameter of the pulley. (Illustration, courtesy Volkswagen)

29B. Check the belt tension by putting firm thumb pressure on it at a mid-point between the upper and lower pulley. The deflection should be around 10 mm (0.4 in). Check the inside of the belt for cracking or for a shiny, polished surface. If *any* wear is found REPLACE!

29C. Remove the belt by locking the pulley using a screwdriver in the edge of the inner flange against the top generator bolt. Then you can use a socket to remove the pulley nut and clamp ring. This allows the outer half of the pulley to be removed. If the belt needs tightening, remove one or more spacer washers. If the belt is too tight (unlikely), then insert one or more spacer washers. Additional washers are fitted on the outer edge of the pulley, which is where you should put any washers you removed during the course of the adjustment. Reverse this sequence to replace the pulley and try the tension again. It's a good idea to rotate the crankshaft - using a spanner on the crankshaft pulley to help the belt to 'settle' properly.

If you use all the spacers and you're still having trouble getting the tension right, the belt is worn out and stretched beyond usability. REPLACE IT immediately - use the spare from your toolkit and make a note to replace that the next time you go past your local VAG dealership. Whatever you do, NEVER run your engine without the fan belt. (Illustration, courtesy Volkswagen)

30A

☐ Job 30. Check HT circuit.

30A. Check the condition of the distributor cap and rotor and the securing of wiring connections to the distributor. Lever the tops of the cap clips with a screwdriver. When you remove the cap, leave the plug leads in place to prevent them getting mixed up.

Check inside the distributor cap to ensure that there are no signs of 'tracking' between the cap contacts. This will appear as a thin black line visible on the inside or outside of the cap between the contacts. These lines are paths which let the spark run to earth instead of down the HT lead where it should be going. You probably won't notice the effect of a hairline crack in the dry, but a spot of damp, drizzly weather will have your engine misfiring like the devil as the moisture drains off that precious HT. Make sure it's clean and dry.

30B

If the cap looks OK, give it a good wipe inside and out with a clean cloth, and clean all the plug leads as well. Check each one for signs of corrosion at the end contacts and deterioration of the insulation. If in doubt fit a new set (not just one!).

30B. Check the rotor tip for burning or brightness. If it's bright, it suggests that the distributor bushes have worn out and that means new distributor time - or reconditioned, if you prefer. If the distributor rotor can move about allowing its tip to brush against the contacts inside the distributor cap, the distributor's accuracy is also way out of line, which means that your car will run badly, uneconomically and may fail the emissions part of the MOT test. If this has been happening, the contacts will also be bright and you can expect to see quite a bit of brass dust inside the distributor cap. Black dust in any quantity suggests that the top (carbon) contact has worn away - it should protrude from the centre of the cap and move in and out freely under light spring pressure.

☐ Job 31. Adjust spark plugs.

SAFETY FIRST:
Do not change or adjust your plugs with a hot engine - not only will you burn your fingers, but also, you'll run the risk of ruining your precious aluminium cylinder heads.

Your spark plugs lead a hard life, having to produce a very high voltage spark under high compression in the cylinders over a vast range of temperatures and firing up to 50 times per second! Despite this, some owners never bother to even look at their plugs until the engine develops a misfire. Regular plug check-ups will not only pre-empt any such problems, it will also ensure that your car runs smoother and more economically.

The reason that many owners avoid this job is because the plugs are hidden out of the way in positions that require at least another three joints in each wrist! It's a job that gets harder the younger the car is, but the fact that it's an awkward task is no excuse for not doing it.

Owners of twin-port cars have more work to do than most, as at least some of the pipework/hoses has to be removed to allow access to the cylinder heads. Owners of cars fitted with twin carbs have a real headache here - many opt to remove the carbs in order to reach the front two plugs (nos 1 and 3)! It's not actually necessary with a little ingenuity, but it's certainly not fun. Depending on the model you have, you'll have more or less dismantling to do before you start work proper.

It's simplest to work on one plug at a time, unless you specifically want to compare all four at once. If it's the latter, use masking tape and a pen to mark which plug lead goes where to prevent mixing them up later on.

31A. We've removed the left hand air hose mainly for picture clarity, but it also allows more space to manoeuvre. The plug leads are screwed into the plug caps, which is why you never pull on the leads when removing the plugs.

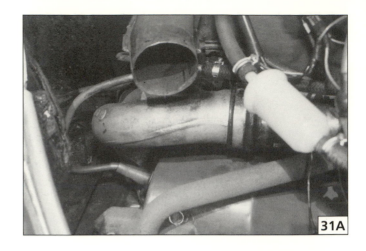

31A

31B. Check that the leads are a tight fit. If they aren't, unscrew them, clean up the lead and the cap and retighten. If the lead and cap still won't tighten up properly, you should be thinking of fitting a new set of leads (don't fit leads in anything less than full sets of five, including the coil HT lead). Check all the leads over their length to ensure that there is no sign of burning or cracking, which could cause misfires or other problems. Also check the condition of the rubber seal around the spark plug cap. If it's not good, replace it, for they help prevent loss of cooling air - vital when there's no radiator to help things along.

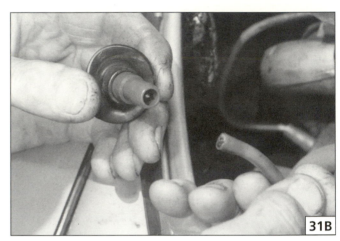

31B

31C. Remove the plugs using a proper plug socket which has a rubber insert to hold the plugs and prevent them dropping on the floor and breaking. You'll also find that a short extension is useful.

31D. Push the lead and cap to one side and position the plug spanner and extension on the plug. *Then* fit the ratchet, it's much easier than manoeuvring the whole socket/ratchet assembly in the confined space. If the plug is tight, be wary firstly of cross threads (as mentioned earlier) and of skinning your knuckles on the bulkhead - it's easy to do!

31C

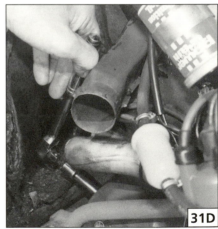

31D

31E. Once the plugs are out you can examine them and get an idea as to how the engine is running. Check out the photographs on page 65 to see how yours compare. Clean them up with a brass bristle wire brush applied vigorously!

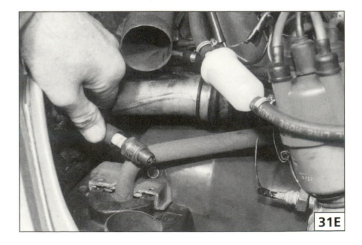

31E

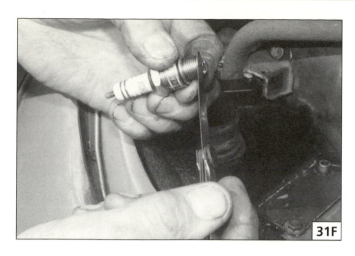

31F. Check the gap with a feeler gauge - the end of the gauge should just go in, making contact and meeting just the smallest resistance from both sides, but without being forced in any way. Lever the longer electrode away to open the gap - but take great care not to move or damage the centre electrode or its insulation and tap the electrode on a hard surface to close it up again. If in doubt, throw the plugs away and buy new. Running with damaged or worn out plugs is false economy - although having said that, don't just change them for the sake of it. Look for evidence of electrode erosion, insulator staining, damage - or just old age.

31G. INSIDE INFORMATION: Iain MacLeod at Macvolks always recommends treating the plug threads to a coating of copper-based grease, but don't use so much that the grease can find its way up the body of the plug and conduct electricity. It will help guide them smoothly along those delicate threads and prevent any problems next time you need to remove them.

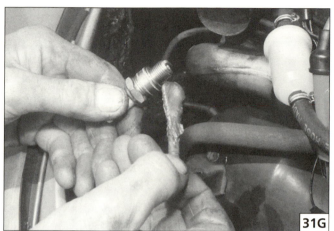

Take your time when fitting the new or re-gapped plugs. You can't see where you're putting the plug, so all you can do is rely on your inbuilt mechanical sympathy. NEVER fit plugs to a hot engine. Fit the plug into the plug socket then using your thumb and forefinger, gently twist the plugs into the threads. DON'T force them! Use your fingers to tighten them as far as you can. Then, fit the socket/extension to the plug, followed by the ratchet and tighten up. They do not need to be eye-wateringly tight - remember that easily-damaged cylinder head and the fact that it will probably be you who has to undo them again! Just a quarter to half a turn after the plug touches its seal (new plugs) or 3/4 turn (re-used plugs) will suffice. After all, they're not going to go anywhere between services, are they?

31H. Refit the leads, making sure the right lead goes to the right plug. If you do manage to get them mixed, don't panic. You'll know you've got it wrong when the car won't start or runs like it's got two and a half cylinders. Use the diagram shown here to sort out which goes where.

DISTRIBUTOR
VIEWED FROM ABOVE

ENGINE VIEWED FROM ABOVE

② ① ③ ④

NO 3 CYLINDER   NO 1 CYLINDER

NO 4 CYLINDER   NO 2 CYLINDER

31H

Job 32. Clean contact breaker points.

Remove the distributor cap and pull off the rotor arm. To check whether the surfaces of the contacts are flat and clean, push the moving contact point back against the spring. If one has a point and the other a pit, it won't be possible to judge the gap accurately with a feeler gauge. In this case, the points should be renewed. If the surfaces are flat but dirty, use a small file to clean them up.

Having established that the contact faces are clean and flat, turn the engine (use a spanner or the crankshaft pulley nut) until the cam follower or the spring contact is resting on the highest point on one of the four cam lobes.

32A. A 0.016 in (0.4 mm) feeler gauge should just slide into the points gap - if it is a tight or loose fit, adjustment is required.

32B. Slacken the screw securing the mounting plate - make sure you use the correct sized screwdriver, otherwise you'll chew the screw head up and give yourself more problems. There's a notch in the fixed plate. Insert the screwdriver and ease the plate whichever way is required. When you've got the right gap, tighten the screw and check the gap one more time. If it's still not right, repeat the procedure until it is.

32C. For a really accurate points setting, you should check the dwell angle. In essence, the four lobe cam has four periods of 90 degrees (total 360 degrees). The points will be open and closed for a proportion of each period. The dwell angle is the closed period and can be expressed as a percentage or, more usually, as degrees. Your Beetle should be between 44° to 50°, with wear limits of 42° to 58°. If the dwell reading is too high, then the points are too closed; too low and the points are too far open.

Ideally, use a multi-function device including rev. counter, volts, ohms and, of course, dwell angle. By linking it to a power source (in this case, we used a spare battery) and connecting the blue wire to a distributor lead, we were able to get the dwell/points settings of this 1303 spot-on. Such accuracy can only lead to better performance using less fuel. This is the Gunson Autoranger.

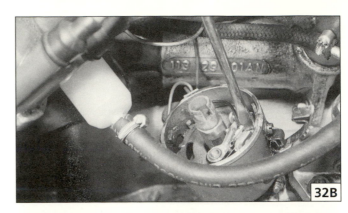
32B

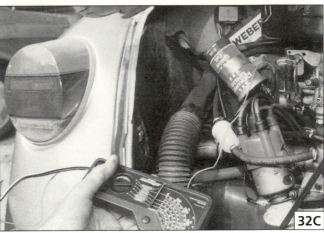
32C

☐ Job 33. Check ignition timing.

INSIDE INFORMATION: It's possible to static time all engines except dual port motors equipped with a vacuum retard distributor. How do you know if you've got a VRD? If there are two hoses running to the distributor rather than one, you have! Engines so-fitted must be timed using a strobe light, though it's as well to do this on all engines.

33A. All timing relates to TDC - Top Dead Centre. It's either spot-on (0°) or it's before (BTDC) or after (ATDC). Check out *Chapter 8, Facts & Figures* to see exactly what setting your particular engine requires and, if you're using a stroboscopic timing light, whether or not the vacuum hoses should be on or off. This diagram shows what the markings mean if your crankshaft pulley has 3 notches. If it has two, the left one is 7.5° advance and the right one 10° advance. If you've just the one notch, then time it to that - it's set for whatever your engine requires.

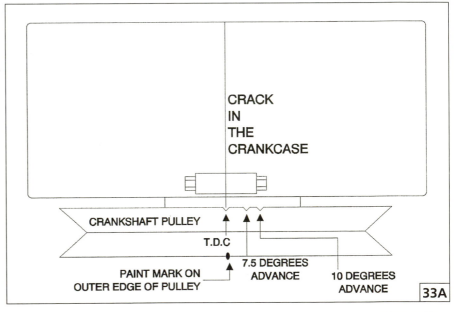

CRACK IN THE CRANKCASE

CRANKSHAFT PULLEY

T.D.C

PAINT MARK ON OUTER EDGE OF PULLEY

7.5 DEGREES ADVANCE

10 DEGREES ADVANCE

33A

Static timing

33B. To static time your engine you'll need a 12v test light (or 6v if your car demands it). Remove the distributor cap and look around the edge of the distributor base for a notch. Turn the crankshaft pulley until the rotor arm is lined up with this notch, at which point No. 1 cylinder (at front right) should be at TDC - at the end of the compression stroke.

33B

Now look at the notches in the crankshaft pulley - they should be somewhere near the crankcase centre line. Line up the appropriate pulley notch for your engine with the crankcase centre line. Now check the points. They should just be opening and this is where you need the test light. Connect one of the leads to the coil terminal which has the thin wire coming from it to the distributor. Connect the other wire to a good earth (ground). Switch on the ignition and turn the crankshaft pulley clockwise, keeping an eye on the notches, crankcase centre line and light bulb. When the notch and join are correctly aligned, the bulb should light. If there's a difference, turn the crankshaft pulley back a little (anti clockwise) and then forward until the notch lines up again. Then slacken off the distributor clamp nut and turn the distributor until the light comes on. Tighten the clamp nut and run the alignment check once more.

33C

Stroboscopic timing

> **SAFETY FIRST!**
> **Stroboscopic timing requires the engine to be running - take great care that parts of the timing light or parts of you don't get caught up in the moving parts! Also, take care to keep hands and clothing well away from the fan belt.**

33C. This method is easier and more accurate. The timing light is a device which enables you to see the timing mark on the crankshaft pulley as the engine is running. Mark it first using a dab of white paint or typist's correction fluid.

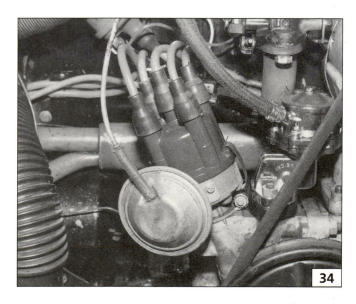

33D

33E

33D. Connect the timing light to the No. 1 plug lead as shown in the maker's instructions. This Gunson's Timestrobe uses an adaptor to fit in the distributor cap with the plug lead in the other end.

33E. With the engine running, the gun 'fires' its light at the pulley, illuminating the notch. If the notch lines up correctly, the timing is OK. If not, loosen the distributor clamp ring and turn the distributor slightly until the timing is correct, then tighten the clamp ring.

INSIDE INFORMATION: If when within the rev range of 1000-2000 rpm the dwell angle varies by more than plus or minus one degree, the distributor bearings are probably excessively worn and the distributor should be changed for a reconditioned unit.

34

☐ Job 34. Check distributor vacuum advance.

34. What sort of distributor do you have? If there's a circular metal drum with a pipe attached to it (as here), then you've got a vacuum version. The pipe leads to the carburettor and uses changes in the carb vacuum to advance or retard the spark timing. Check that the vacuum pipe fits snugly at both ends and shows no signs of leaking, something which can lead to burnt-out valves.

Checking using the stroboscopic timing light: If you used a strobe light for Job 33, you can use it again to check the operation of the vacuum advance. Point the light at the timing marks as described earlier and use the carburettor lever to increase the engine revs to around 2,500 - 3,000 RPM. The notch should move to the left as the engine revs rise. If they do, everything is OK.

Checking manually: If you haven't got a timing light, you can test manually. Remove the distributor cap and the vacuum pipe at the carburettor end. Wipe the end of the pipe and suck on it whilst looking down into the distributor. The plate on which the points are sitting should move slightly. If it does, the unit is working fine.

If your checks indicate problems, have your distributor checked out by a specialist. If the vacuum advance unit has failed, the distributor will have to be replaced - turn to *Chapter 2 - Buying Spares!*

☐ Job 35. Lubricate distributor cam shaft bearing and breaker arm fibre block.

Whilst the distributor cap is off, you can do some lubricating. Take great care not to get any oil or grease on the points or apply so much oil that it can splash onto them. This will cause poor starting, misfiring and poor fuel consumption. Squeeze a few drops of Castrol's Everyman oil to the centre cam spindle and the contact breaker pivot pin. Let a little trickle past the base of the cam to lubricate the automatic advance/retard mechanism. A smear of light grease should be applied to the cam lobes.

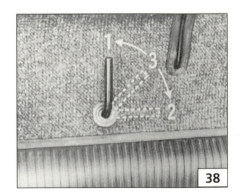

☐ Job 36. Clean auto transmission control valve filter.

AUTOMATIC STICK SHIFT CARS ONLY
The control valve is mounted on the bulkhead on the left hand side of the engine bay. Unscrew the air filter, remove and clean thoroughly in white spirit. Allow to dry and replace.

3,000 Mile Mechanical and Electrical - Around the Car

First carry out Jobs 2 to 14, and 17.

☐ Job 37. Lubricate pedal cluster.

EARLY MODELS ONLY
37. Early models featured a grease nipple which fed grease to the clutch/brake pedal shaft. Apply grease here in the usual way. (Illustration, courtesy Volkswagen)

1 Master cylinder pushrod
2 Brake pedal return spring
3 Cotter pin
4 Bush
5 Pedal bearing
6 Bush
7 Pedal shaft
8 Grease nipple

INSIDE INFORMATION: This feature was discontinued after some years, with the result that the pedal shaft could rust solid after a time. The only way to solve this problem is to dismantle the whole assembly and grease it by hand. Alternatively, many owners have found it a good idea to take their pedal assembly to a machine shop and have a grease nipple fitted.

☐ Job 38. Lubricate petrol reserve tap.

38. The motorcycle-style petrol reserve tap was a facility fitted to Beetles well into the 1970s. It's slightly to the left of the clutch pedal and a drop of Castrol Everyman oil will prevent this seizing up and breaking off. (Illustration, courtesy Volkswagen)

☐ Job 39. Check starter inhibit switch.

AUTOMATIC STICK SHIFT CARS ONLY
An important feature of automatic stick shift Beetles is the starter inhibit switch, fitted to the transmission. This prevents the car being started when a gear is engaged. To check, put the car in 'L' (low) gear and attempt to start the engine - it should not start until the gear lever is pulled back to the neutral position. If it does, check the wiring to the switch fitted at the front of the transmission. If this proves to be sound, the switch will need replacing. In the meantime, take great care to ensure that the gear lever is always in neutral before starting the vehicle.

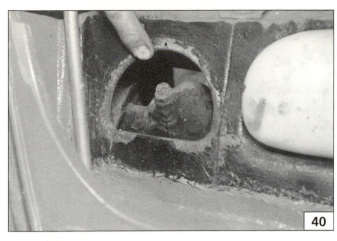

40

☐ Job 40. Check steering box oil level.

MODELS UP TO 1965 ONLY

40. The steering box is hidden behind a small panel behind the spare wheel. Remove the panel and undo the filler plug. The oil level should be just up to the lower edge of the filler plug hole. Later steering boxes are grease-filled and are recognisable by twin plastic plugs in the top of the box.

> **SAFETY FIRST!**
> *Have any work or adjustments on steering box or rack checked over by a specialist before using the car. Tight steering can cause accidents!*

☐ Job 41. Check steering mechanism.

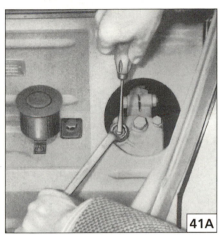

41A

Steering play which cannot be linked directly with wear in other steering and/or suspension components can sometimes be solved by making adjustments at the steering box. With the wheels in the straight ahead position, turn the steering wheel and measure how far it turns before resistance is felt - the play. Any more than 1 in. (25 mm) calls for adjustment. When you raise the front wheels remember the safety rules as itemised in Chapter 1.

41A. **Worm and sector steering box:** Turn the front wheels to the straight ahead position and loosen the lock nut and sector shaft adjusting screw on top of the steering gear case.

To adjust the worm shaft end play, loosen the adjusting sleeve clamping screw and tighten the adjusting sleeve clockwise until the worm shaft end play is taken up. Tighten the adjusting sleeve clamping screw.

To adjust sector shaft end play, tighten the adjusting screw clockwise as far as it will go and then back it off 1/8 turn.

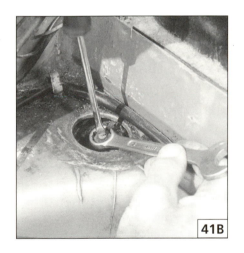

41B

Once adjustments have been carried out, tighten the locknut. Raise both front wheels and check the steering, turning it from lock to lock, to ensure that there are no tight spots and that it is not binding. If these problems are manifest, then the adjustment is too tight and the adjuster should be backed off slightly. (Illustration, courtesy Volkswagen)

41B. **Worm and roller steering box:** This kind of box was fitted to later model Beetles and can be found under the spare wheel in the luggage compartment. With the steering in the straight ahead position, loosen the locknut with a ring spanner (as shown here) and turn the adjuster until it is barely touching the thrust washer - you'll feel this as you turn. Tighten the locknut and check the steering from lock to lock to make sure that there are no tight spots.

If the steering play is still present, adjust the worm and roller tolerance. Raise the front wheels and turn the wheels to first one full lock and then the other. Loosen the roller shaft adjuster locknut and turn the adjuster anti clockwise. When you can feel the worm contacting with the roller, stop turning and tighten the locknut.

Rack and pinion steering gear: A very few late model Beetles (1975-78) were produced with rack and pinion steering mechanisms. The access hole is on the luggage compartment floor under the spare wheel. Adjustment requires the steering to be in the straight ahead position. Loosen the locknut and back off the adjusting screw. Tighten the adjusting screw until it only just touches the thrustwasher. (you'll be able to feel this happening). At this point, hold the adjusting screw with the screwdriver while you tighten the locknut - make sure the adjusting screw doesn't get turned at the same time.

With the car back on the ground, check the steering play. Turn the steering wheel left and right, making sure that the free play (at the edge of the wheel) does not exceed 1 in (25 mm). If it does, run through the procedure above but on the problematic side only. A road test should show that the steering self-centres as VW intended. If it doesn't, then the roller shaft adjustment is too tight and must be slackened off immediately, otherwise expensive damage could occur.

To get the steering absolutely spot-on, a visit to a specialist is required to set the toe-in correctly.

3,000 Mile Mechanical and Electrical - Under the Car

First carry out Job 18.

SAFETY FIRST! and SPECIALIST SERVICE:
Obviously, a car's brakes are among its most important safety related items. Do not dismantle your car's brakes unless you are fully competent to do so. If you have not been trained in this work, but wish to carry out the work described here, we strongly recommend that you have a garage or qualified mechanic check your work before using the car on the road. See also the section on BRAKES AND ASBESTOS in Chapter 1, for further important information.

☐ Job 42. Check cable brakes.

CABLE BRAKE MODELS ONLY:
All standard Beetles (i.e. not deluxe versions) were fitted with a mechanical cable braking system until 1961. These tend to need more adjustment than the later hydraulic systems. Ideally, all four wheels should be clear of the floor, which obviously needs more care and planning than usual to ensure that you are working perfectly safely.

42A

42B

42A. The procedure for all wheels is the same, though the rear wheels may need to be removed for easier access. Release the handbrake and loosen the lock nuts and cable adjusting nuts on the brake backing plate and turn both clockwise. (Illustration, courtesy Volkswagen)

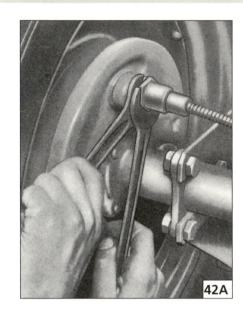

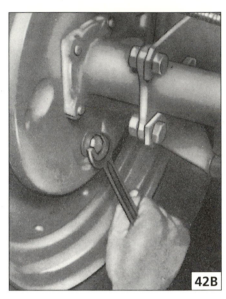

42B. Turn the brake shoe adjusting nut until the brake drum can no longer be turned by hand. Now tighten the back brake cable adjusting nut until there is very little clearance between the brake cable and the brake backing plate, then tighten the locknut.

Again, loosen the brake shoe adjusting nut, until the brake drum can just be turned freely. A light tap against the nut will place the brake shoes and adjusting cone in the right position. Repeat these operations on the other wheels. Check that the handbrake operates equally on all four wheels. (Note: not just two of them!). Pull up the handbrake by two notches and check that all four brakes feel as though they are operating equally. Pull up the handbrake by one more notch at a time and check again, at each 'click'. It should be impossible to turn any of the wheels at the fourth notch.

If there is a noticeable difference, release the handbrake and readjust at the brake backplates as follows: loosen the brake shoe adjusting nut on the wheel with most resistance; ***don't*** tighten the one with most resistance.

SPECIALIST SERVICE. It is imperative that you have the operation of the brakes checked by a garage with rolling road brake check equipment - at any MoT testing station in the UK. If necessary (i.e. if the garage is not a Beetle specialist) take this book with you so that the mechanic can follow the brake adjustments described here.

You must now adjust the handbrake. See Job 48D.
(Illustration, courtesy Volkswagen)

☐ Job 43. Check front wheel bearings.

Raise the front wheels, hold each wheel in turn at the top and bottom and apply a push-pull effort. You can feel play in a bearing, but make sure you can differentiate between play in this and in other parts of the suspension. Turn the wheel through 180 degrees and try the same test.

43A

43A. If you have too much play, remove the road wheels and the hub covers using a screwdriver or tyre lever.

On the inside of the left-hand wheel hub, remove the cotter pin securing the speedometer cable.

43B.

43C.

43B. Each bearing is held by a clamp nut. Because these are not tightened to any great degree, they are split and are secured by an Allen head screw.

Early cars were secured by a large locking nut and a tab washer which secured the nut by being bent up over the flats. Loosen this screw until the clamp nut can be turned. IMPORTANT NOTE: The clamp nut on the left hand side has a LEFT-HAND thread. In other words, you turn it anticlockwise to tighten and clockwise to remove - the opposite way to normal.

INSIDE INFORMATION: Iain Macleod at Macvolks reckons that, having got to this stage, it's a good idea to treat the outer bearing to a little more grease. This is what we show here. If you're only adjusting, then go directly to caption 43D.

43C. Remove the clamp nut altogether, followed by the large thrust washer and then the bearing itself. Waggle the brake drum or disc a little if the bearing is reluctant to leave home. Take care not to get any grit or dirt in the bearing as you clean it and the thrust washer with a lint-free cloth. If you use a solvent cleaner, the bearing MUST be totally dry before applying the new grease.

43D. Apply Castrol LM grease in and around the bearing. Don't worry about putting too much on - if you do, it will simply spill out as you fit the bearing.

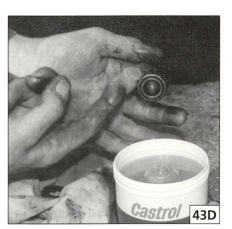
43D.

In order to adjust the bearing, refit the bearing and thrust washer and tighten the clamp nut to around 15 lbs ft, TURNING THE WHEEL while you do it to ensure that the bearing is seating correctly. Back it off again until the nut is free and then tighten it until the thrush washer can just be moved when pushed with a screwdriver. Rock the wheel as described earlier to check for play. There should be between 0.001 to 0.005 in. (0.03 to 0.12 mm) of play, though you should aim for the lower figure. It's important not to have the clamp nut too tight, otherwise the wheel will not turn freely and the bearing will wear out in no time at all.

SPECIALIST SERVICE: If you discover that bearing play is due to inboard bearing trouble then, as it requires special tools and knowledge, it's a job for a specialist.

☐ **Job 44. Check brake pads.**

SAFETY FIRST! and SPECIALIST SERVICE:
Obviously, a car's brakes are among its most important safety related items. Do not dismantle your car's brakes unless you are fully competent to do so. If you have not been trained in this work, but wish to carry out the work described here, we strongly recommend that you have a garage or qualified mechanic check your work before using the car on the road. See also the section on BRAKES AND ASBESTOS in Chapter 1, for further important information. Always replace disc pads in sets of four - never replace the pads on one wheel only.

DISC BRAKE BEETLES ONLY
The brakes adjust themselves automatically as the pads wear down and so manual adjustment is not required. Wear on the pads is the reason that the brake fluid level will go down slightly between services, even though there's no sign of leakage.

44A.

GENERAL INFORMATION - Applicable to all systems
44A. It is important to check that there is plenty of 'meat' on the pads. This is a new pad which shows just now much friction material you start with. You can see the pads while they're still in the calliper. The manufacturers recommend that the minimum permissible brake pad thickness before the pads are renewed should be 1/10 inch (approx 2 mm) but you should allow for the fact that you won't be checking the brakes again for a further 3,000 miles or three months if the pads are approaching this limit. It's very common for one pad to wear down more quickly than the other and you should always take the thickness of the most worn-out pad as your guide.

44B. When the pads on both wheels have been changed, bring the pads onto the disc by pressing the brake pedal. Check the hydraulic fluid level and top up if necessary. Check the clearance between pads and disc. If it is too great (more than 0.2mm) then the inner piston seal may be sticking.

INSIDE INFORMATION: It is sometimes possible to solve the problem of a seized piston by removing the pads and then pressing the brake to move the piston out. Then use a thick piece of wood (not metal, which would damage the piston) to force the piston back in. After a few movements, it should be freed off. If it doesn't, then it points to having the calliper overhauled - **SPECIALIST SERVICE** - or replaced.

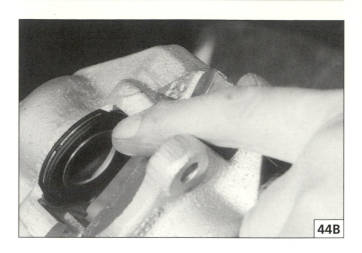

Be careful not to apply too much brake pedal pressure, otherwise you could pop out the non-sticking piston - it's best to have an assistant watching for this. Alternatively, you could put a clamp across the one that does move and press the brake pedal again, but then take extra care not to pop the piston out! **IMPORTANT NOTE:** If seizure is due to corrosion, the piston seal will now leak and the safest option is to replace the calliper or have it rebuilt - **SPECIALIST SERVICE**.

BRAKE TYPES

VW used two manufacturers as suppliers for their disc brake equipment - Teves and Girling. However, it's highly likely that, on removing your front wheels, you will find that the original parts have been replaced using 'pattern' components. This is no particular cause for concern, provided that the products used are of excellent quality. In fact, the one shown in the first section is such an item. It is based on the Teves system, though there are other variants.

TEVES TYPE SYSTEMS INCLUDING NON-STANDARD/PATTERN COMPONENTS

44C. This diagram shows the later of two standard fitment Teves (ATE) versions. Earlier models featured a different spreader spring and two (rather than one) retaining pins.

1 Clamp ring
2 Seal
3 Piston
4 Seal
5 Calliper retaining bolts
6 Bleeder valves
7 Calliper outer housing
8 Noise damping plates
9 Friction pads
10 Spreader spring
11 Pad retaining pin
12 Calliper inner housing

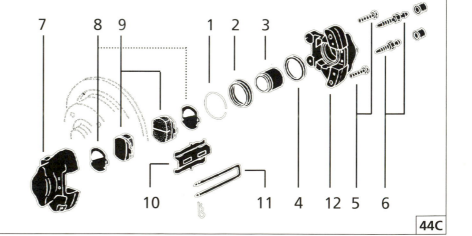

REPLACING THE DISC PADS

INSIDE INFORMATION: During the course of pad removal or installation, the pistons will be pushed back forcing brake fluid back along the system. To prevent problems, remove the cap from the brake fluid reservoir and place a rag around it (brake fluid will ruin paintwork). If the fluid level is already on the high side, you'll need to remove some of the fluid. A plastic container (with plastic nozzle) could be used.

44D. Use long-nose pliers to remove the split 'R' pins from the ends of the retaining pins. Place them somewhere safe because you'll need them for the new pads and you can't drive your car (safely) without them. Original Teves pins were held in place by the friction of a split bush on one end and so no split pins were required.

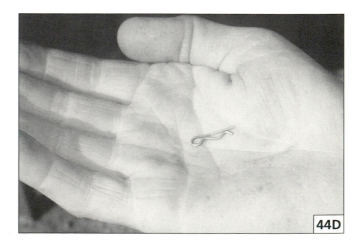

44E. Use a punch to drive out the retaining pins and remove the spring retainer plate. The pads will come out easier if you use a tyre lever (or similar) to ease them back against the pistons. Remember that doing this will result in brake fluid being pushed back down the system with the possibility of the reservoir overflowing - see earlier *INSIDE INFORMATION*.

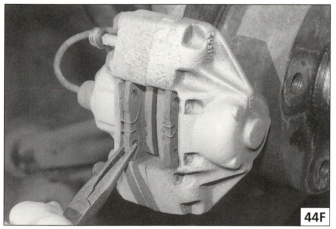

44F. Remove the pads, the pad spreader plate and piston retaining plate - some have a portion cut away on the piston side. If you are replacing the original spring retaining plate, try not to turn the piston as it makes reinstallation easier. Clean the calliper aperture - don't forget the health warning regarding asbestos dust and make sure you wear a mask while doing this. Check the seal to make sure it has not gone brittle with age.

44G. Most new pads come complete with a new piston retaining plate, which should always be fitted. On original Teves callipers, make sure that the wide side of the plate goes upwards. If you use a punch to drive in the retaining pins make sure it's almost the same diameter as the pins, otherwise they could be damaged.

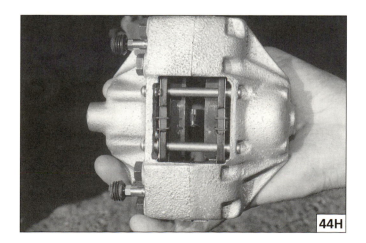

44H. This is what you should end up with, perfect symmetry with clips, clamps and pads in place, but on the car, of course!

SAFETY FIRST!
When fitting new brake pads, use only asbestos-free friction materials.

GIRLING TYPE CALLIPERS

44. This is the Girling type calliper fitted by the factory to some models. Getting to the pads is quite an involved procedure. Use long-nose pliers to take out the locking pin and them remove the 'U' pin which holds the pads in place, followed by the central spreader spring. Before removing the two calliper mounting bolts, bend back the locking plates. Make sure that the calliper is adequately supported to prevent strain or damage to the brake hose as the bolts are removed. Remove the pads by turning them through a right angle to get them out of the calliper. Then remove the noise damping plates in the same way. Clean the calliper and check as described earlier. Fitting new pads is a reversal of the removal procedure and requires some tricky manoeuvring so it's important that the friction surfaces don't get oiled-up or chipped around their edges. Use new locking places before tightening up the calliper bolts to the required torque places before tightening up the calliper bolts to their required torque (see *Facts and Figures, Chapter 8)*. Fit a new spreader spring and the retaining pin/locking clip in a reversal of the removal procedures.

1	Piston retaining plate	7	Seal
2	Spreader spring	8	Calliper inner housing
3	Cheese head screws	9	Piston
4	Calliper outer housing	10	Seal
5	Friction pads	11	Bleeder valve
6	Clamp ring	12	Pad retaining pin

44

Alternative Spreader Plate Arrangement

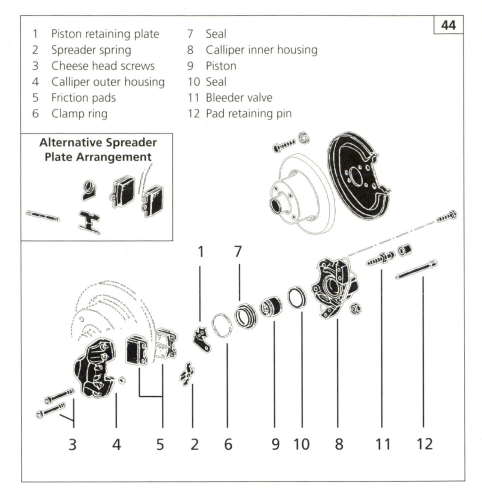

SAFETY FIRST:
The calliper securing bolts are likely to be very tight and require a great deal of torque to remove/replace. Make sure that the car is extremely stable, otherwise, you could bring it down on yourself.

Also, note carefully that new brake pads won't work as effectively as they should until they have "bedded-in". Moreover, they can become glazed if the brakes are applied very hard within the first few hundred miles of running after fitting new bake pads. AP Lockheed advise that for the first 150-200 miles (250-300 km), therefore, you should avoid braking hard unless you have to, such as in an emergency, and allow extra braking distance because of the fact that the brakes won't work quite as efficiently. You may also have noticed that the brake discs will have become scored and grooved and the new brake pads have to take the shape of the brake discs before they will work to maximum efficiency.

☐ **Job 45. Check hydraulic front drum brakes.**

HYDRAULIC BRAKE MODELS ONLY

SAFETY FIRST! and SPECIALIST SERVICE:
Obviously, a car's brakes are among its most important safety related items. Do not dismantle your car's brakes unless you are fully competent to do so. If you have not been trained in this work, but wish to carry out the work described here, we strongly recommend that you have a garage or qualified mechanic check your work before using the car on the road. See also the section on BRAKES AND ASBESTOS in Chapter 1, for further important information.

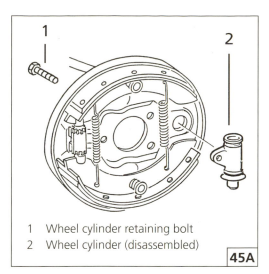

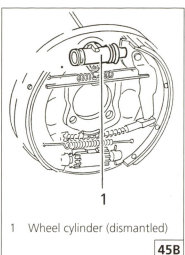

1   Wheel cylinder retaining bolt
2   Wheel cylinder (disassembled)

45A

1   Wheel cylinder (dismantled)

45B

45A. There are two types of front drum brake, though the basic checking, adjustment and replacement procedure is the same for both. Many early cars had the wheel cylinder and the adjusting wheels at the 10 o'clock and 2 o'clock positions (not illustrated) within the drum while others were at 3 o'clock and 6 o'clock. The access hole for checking the shoe wear and for adjusting the shoes is in the brake drum. Both checking and adjusting can be carried out from the outside. (Illustration, courtesy Volkswagen)

45B. The later type of drum was similar except that the whole arrangement was turned through 90 degrees - the cylinder was at the top and the adjusting wheels were at the 6 o'clock position. The holes for checking the shoe condition and for reaching the adjusting wheels are either in the drum or in the back plate, according to model, and it may be necessary to get at least part way under the car. (Illustration, courtesy Volkswagen)

45C

45D

45C. Jack up one of the front wheels, following the safety rules in Chapter 1. The first check is on the condition of the brake shoes. There should ideally be around 1/8 in. of friction material left. If it is 1/16 in. or less, replacement is in order. Don't forget that each drum contains two shoes - both need to have an acceptable amount of friction material left. For some models, check through the hole in the drum; in others check through the relevant holes in the backplate, as shown here.

45D. To adjust the brakes (i.e., to move them closer to the drums) use a screwdriver through the relevant access hole to turn one of the adjusting wheels. Turn the toothed adjuster wheel until the road wheel cannot be turned. Then back off the adjuster three notches and ensure that it turns freely. Repeat the operation with the other adjuster wheel - there are two per wheel. This photo shows the two adjuster wheels from the inside, that is, with the drum removed. As you can see, as the threaded wheel is turned, the brake shoes are forced out further towards the drum - a simple, but effective arrangement. Lubricate the adjuster threads sparingly with specialist brake grease.

INSIDE INFORMATION: *If any shoe or shoes need considerable adjustment (because they have been allowed to go unadjusted for too long) then they will have to 'bed in' again to a different radius and this will call for further adjustment after a short interval. This is why regular brake adjustment is necessary to ensure top braking efficiency at all times. The linings will last longer as it will ensure that the whole surface area is used evenly all the time.*

Having completed adjusting one wheel, it is good practice to operate the brake pedal once or twice and then adjust again. Sometimes the shoes move fractionally off centre during adjustment. The extra time required is well worth the trouble.

If a shoe still rubs against the drum a little even after being backed off more than three notches, leave it, provided it is only superficial. However, if the binding is quite severe then it is possible that the lining is unevenly worn. In such instances, remove the drum and take a look. Replace the shoes if necessary.

Replacing the brake shoes

SAFETY FIRST!
*Make sure that you never handle brake friction surfaces with oily or greasy hands. Read **Chapter 1, Safety First** before commencing work. Replace worn brake shoes only with asbestos-free friction materials.*

45E. Remove the front wheel bearings as described in Job 43 and then pull off the drum. If it sticks, you may have to back off the adjusting wheels slightly to ease the brake shoes off the drum - see procedures already described.

45E

Brush out the backplate to get rid of the dust and loose rust, but wear a face mask to prevent the inhalation of brake dust. (See *Chapter 1, Safety First)* Examine carefully for any sign of leakage from the wheel cylinders or wheel bearings.

45F. Use a pair of pliers to remove the slotted cup washer from the spring in the centre of each shoe. Take care on removal, so that the spring doesn't bounce all round the workshop or worse, into your eyes. Push in against the spring (45F.1) and twist (45F.2). Again, use the pliers to remove the end of the spring nearest the adjuster wheels from the shoes. The shoes can then be eased out of the adjuster mechanism and then from the wheel cylinder.

Check around the inside of the brake drums. They should shine and be very smooth. If there is any sign of deep score marks, they should be replaced.

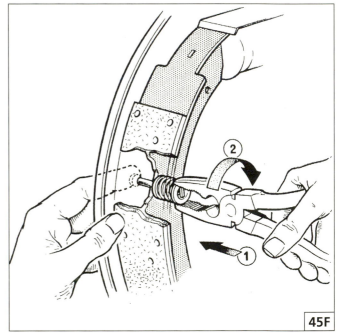

45F

45G. INSIDE INFORMATION: Use a strong rubber band wrapped around the wheel cylinder to prevent the pistons popping out while you're working on the shoes.

Remove the adjuster wheel mechanisms, clean thoroughly and treat to a small dab of brake grease (not ordinary grease) in order to optimise their operation.

Replace the shoes in a reversal of the removal procedure making sure that you replace any rubber bungs. Fit and adjust the wheel bearing as described in Job 43 and then press the footbrake to centralise the shoes in the drum before adjusting them as described earlier in this Job number.

45G

☐ **Job 46. Check hydraulic rear brakes.**

HYDRAULIC BRAKE MODELS ONLY

SAFETY FIRST! and SPECIALIST SERVICE:
Obviously, a car's brakes are among its most important safety related items. Do not dismantle your car's brakes unless you are fully competent to do so. If you have not been trained in this work, but wish to carry out the work described here, we strongly recommend that you have a garage or qualified mechanic check your work before using the car on the road. See also the section on BRAKES AND ASBESTOS in Chapter 1, for further important information.

46A. The rear brake shoes can be checked through holes in the backplate arrowed here - remove the rubber bungs first - or in the brake drum, according to model. There are four holes here, the second two of which are for access to the adjuster wheels which are positioned at the bottom of the backplate. Use a screwdriver to turn each adjuster wheel in turn until the shoe is hard against the drum and prevents the wheel from turning. Then back the adjusters off three notches, making sure that the brake drum turns freely. There will be some 'drag' from the transmission, so it is important not to confuse that with brake binding.

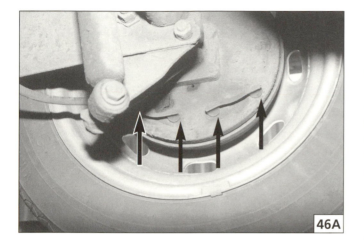
46A

Replacing the brake shoes

46B. Start by removing the hub cap and then the axle shaft nut split pin. Make sure you have a replacement - if you haven't don't start the job until you've bought one, because it's not good practice to reuse old ones and it's extremely dangerous to run without one!

46C. Leave the car on the ground, with the handbrake on and in gear. Removing the axle shaft nut requires a 36mm socket (and that's very big!) and a piece of strong tube to act as an extension for the socket tommy bar. Because of the enormous torque of this nut, you should look to have an effective bar length of 1.5 metres or more, (4 to 5 ft.).

46B

46D. With the nut removed, the drum can follow. You'll need to back off the adjusters (accessed from the rear) and if the drum is reluctant to leave, a few gentle taps with a rubber mallet should encourage it. If it's really sticking, you'll need to obtain a hub puller.

46C

46D

46E. Clean off the back plate (remember to wear a mask to prevent inhaling dangerous substances- see *Chapter 1, Safety First*) and take a good look at what goes where - it's a good idea to make a diagram. Note the adjusters at the 6 o'clock position and the wheel cylinder at the top. If there is any sign of leakage from the axle shaft oil seal, it's a **SPECIALIST SERVICE** job - it's dangerous to drive a car with such a fault, as the oil could get onto the brake friction surfaces and reduce or negate the braking effect.

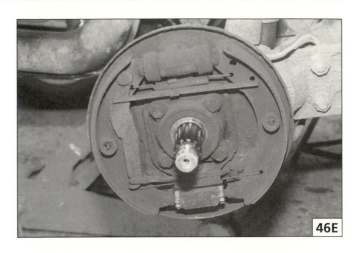

46F. The adjusters lead a hard life and a *very small* squirt of Castrol's Easing Fluid should help them spin more easily. Ultimately, remove them altogether, clean them up and apply a dab or two of brake grease.

Use a pair of pliers to remove the slotted cup washer from the spring in the centre of each shoe as described in Job 45. Use the pliers to remove the end of the retractor spring nearest the adjuster wheels from the shoes and the handbrake cable from the lever. The shoes can then be eased out of the adjuster mechanism and then from the wheel cylinder as a complete unit. The handbrake operating lever (which links the shoes just below the wheel cylinder) should be unclipped for fitting to the new shoes.

INSIDE INFORMATION: Use a strong rubber band wrapped around the wheel cylinder to prevent the pistons popping out while you're working on the shoes.

Replace the shoes and handbrake cable mechanism in a reversal of the removal procedure making sure that you replace any rubber bungs. Press the footbrake to centralise the shoes in the drum before adjusting them as described earlier in this Job number.

46G. Before refitting the drum, clean the axle shaft splines with a lint-free cloth and apply a coating of Castrol LM grease. IT IS VITAL that the axle shaft nut be torqued up to a massive poundage, 217 lbs ft, to be precise. This takes an enormous amount of effort and it may be that you are unable to do this at home in which case, regretfully, this entire job becomes **SPECIALIST SERVICE.** Make sure that you line up the hole for the new split pin. It's unlikely you'll have an industrial-style torque wrench like this one at Macvolks. Do not stint on this operation, as it is vital to your safety.

SELF ADJUSTING REAR BRAKES ONLY

46H. Some Beetle models feature self-adjusting rear brakes, though these are the exception rather than the rule. The adjustment method is purely mechanical, relying mainly on springs. As the foot brake is operated, a return spring pulls the adjusting lever and the adjusting wheel moves on the connecting link. This effectively increases the length of the link, thus moving the shoes nearer to the drum in accordance with the amount of wear. Manual adjustment is not required, though you should still check the condition of the shoes. Replacing the shoes follows the basic principles outlined in 44B, though there are certain differences. If the drum is reluctant to come off, turning the handbrake adjustment back may help. In addition, it is possible to insert a screwdriver through the inspection hole and manually push the brake lever so that the shoes move away from the drum.

FOOT BRAKE ADJUSTMENT

After the new shoes have been fitted, it is necessary to reset the mechanism. Screw the connecting link into the sleeve until the adjusting wheel butts up against the sleeve. Refit the brake drum and then press the brake pedal several times until the pedal travel is constant.

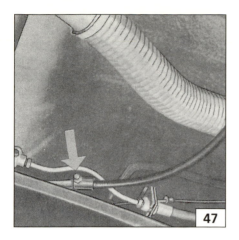

☐ Job 47. Lubricate handbrake cables.

47. A good idea which has been dispensed with is the fitting of a grease nipple to the handbrake cables. Early models had them - they're fitted close to the rear brake drums. If your car is so-fitted, apply a few strokes of the grease gun to each side and a dab of grease to the ends of the cables at the brake lever end, under the rubber boot on the centre tunnel. If you have a later model, you can only carry out the second part of that instruction. (Illustration, courtesy Volkswagen)

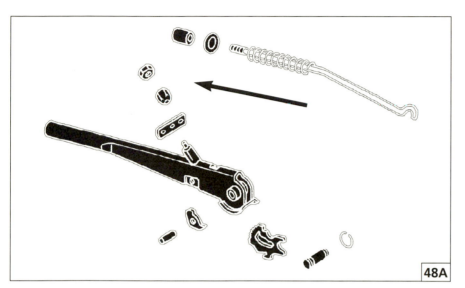

☐ Job 48. Check handbrake travel.

SAFETY FIRST!
Don't work beneath a car supported on axle stands with someone else sitting in the car trying the hand brake. It's too risky that their movements will cause the car to fall off the axle stands. Make sure that you are well clear of the raised car when someone's inside it. Read carefully the information at the start of this chapter on lifting and supporting the car.

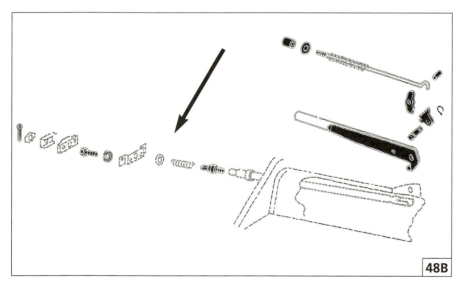

Once the rear brake shoes have been correctly adjusted the handbrake can be checked - there's little point in adjusting it otherwise. If both back wheels can be jacked off the ground together it will save some time, but remember the safety warnings. The handbrake ratchet sometimes wears and allows the lever to release itself. In addition, the release mechanism sometimes seizes in the lever and stops the ratchet from holding. Lubricate with Castrol easing oil but if that fails, you'll have to renew the ratchet and/or the mechanism. Seek specialist advice if necessary.

48A. On all models produced after 1955, the method of adjustment is by means of screws mounted on a bracket (arrowed) on the handbrake lever itself. On some models, the rubber boot over the lever has to be removed to get to the adjusters, on later versions, you can reach the adjusters through small holes. There are two cables, one for each rear wheel.

48B. On pre-1955 models, the end cover of the head frame has to be removed to allow access to the adjusters (arrowed) on the cross beam. The basic procedures are essentially the same.

48C. Press the footbrake a few times and pull the handbrake on four notches. At this, the rear wheels should both be locked so that they cannot be turned by hand. If they can be turned, undo the locknuts and tighten the adjusting screws as far as you can but while still permitting the rear wheels to turn by hand. Then try the handbrake - at two notches, the wheels should be binding and by four notches, they should be locked. Make sure that equal braking effort is being applied to both rear wheels (measured by how much effort it takes to turn them at the 2 notches point). If you're getting uneven braking, slacken off the cable effecting the most braking effort - DON'T tighten up the other one! Once you've finished, tighten the locknuts, lower the car and refit the rubber boot (where necessary). Also, make sure that with the handbrake released, both rear wheels are free to turn without binding.

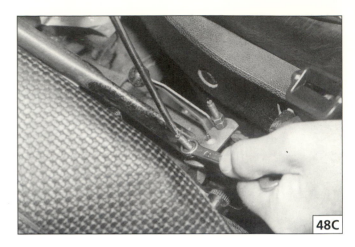

SELF-ADJUSTING REAR BRAKES ONLY

48D. In normal circumstances, it is not necessary to adjust the handbrake - only after new linings or a new handbrake cable has been fitted. You'll need a willing helper, as one of you will need to be underneath the car. Drive the rear of the car onto ramps; don't use axle stands. After fitting the new brake shoes, adjust the foot brake as already described in Job 46H, then release the handbrake and adjust the cable tension at the handbrake lever. Whoever is under the rear of the car should be looking through the hole in the backplate of the wheel and watching the brake lever. Tensioning should stop when the lever moves off the stop for the secondary shoe (48D.7). (Illustration, courtesy Volkswagen)

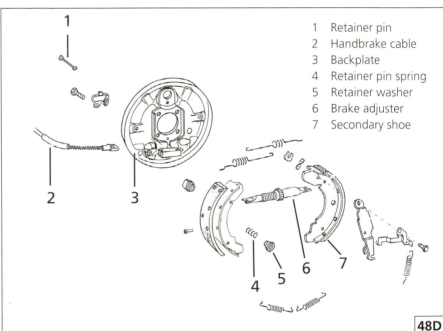

1 Retainer pin
2 Handbrake cable
3 Backplate
4 Retainer pin spring
5 Retainer washer
6 Brake adjuster
7 Secondary shoe

Job 49. Change engine oil.

Regular oil changing is one of the ways to ensure that your Beetles engine reaches the very high mileages so prevalent in the air-cooled world. Regard 3,000 miles as a maximum and if yours leads a hard life, with lots of stop/start motoring or is driven in particularly hot/dusty conditions, changing the oil every 1,500 miles is in order.

SAFETY FIRST!
Old engine oil is now known to be a possible cause of cancer. ALWAYS wear plastic or rubber gloves when draining or handling old engine oil.

49A. Operate the engine until it has reached its normal working temperature. For preference, a 5 mile trip to the shops to buy a paper will cause less engine wear than just letting it idle. You'll need something to catch the oil old, and an empty 5 litre plastic oil can is perfect if you cut a hole in the side. Whatever you use, it should be able to hold at least 2.8 litres (5 pints). Remove the drain plug if you have one (earlier models) and... (Illustration, courtesy Volkswagen)

49B. ...allow the oil to drain out for ten minutes. Remember that the oil will be quite warm, so take some care.

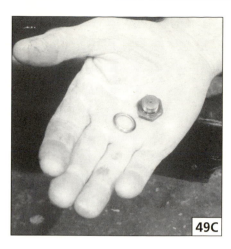

49C. The drain plugs are magnetic and should be cleaned of any metal swarf which may have accumulated. Note the washer - this should be discarded and a new one fitted. Later models did not have a drain plug, in which case, proceed to the next step.

Don't pour the old oil down the drain - it's both illegal and irresponsible. Your local council waste disposal site will have special facilities for disposing of it safely.

49D. Remove the dome nuts holding the surrounding plate to the crankcase (if you haven't already done so) to remove the oil filter screen.

INSIDE INFORMATION: Don't panic if you drop the nuts and washers into the drain can. When the draining operation is complete, use a magnet, or magnetised screwdriver to fish them out.

49E. This collection is what you should end up with. Thoroughly clean the screen, plate and drain plug in paraffin or a suitable solvent. Take note of how clean Iain MacLeod got his - yours should be the same, just like new! Fit new gaskets when you replace the screen and plate and use new copper washers for the dome nuts and, where required, for the drain plug. Reusing the old gaskets and/or washers is simply asking for an oily garage floor.

49F. And this is the order in which they all go back together. (Illustration, courtesy Volkswagen)

49G. The six nuts which hold the screen in place are dome nuts, the important point being that they should only ever be torqued up to 6 lbs ft - no more! If they are overtightened, they will tend to pull the stud out next time the screen is cleaned.

49H. Fill the engine with 4.4 pints (2.5 litres) of Castrol GTX. When it has had time to settle, check the engine oil level and top up if necessary. As you can see, Iain used a funnel, as it's almost impossible to fill the engine without slopping oil all over the place. Wait for 5 minutes or so (to give time for the oil to run into the sump) and then check the oil level. Run the engine for a few minutes and check that everything is oil-tight. Switch off, wait another five minutes and perform a final oil level check.

INSIDE INFORMATION: If you find a white foamy substance around the oil filler cap it can't be the usual trouble - water mixing with the oil - because your Beetle is air-cooled! It's likely to be oil and/or water vapour which has condensed, something which is especially prevalent in damp climates. Simply wipe it over with a rag and feel good about not having to mess about with radiators, water hoses and anti-freeze.

49H

Job 50. Check valve to rocker clearance.

Getting your valve clearances right is very important, though it will become a true labour of love, unless you *really* enjoy grubbing around on the floor under your car! The photos here show the Macvolks spare engine on its display stand, the better to illustrate what's going on. If you have clearances that are too great, the valves will close early and open late - and not fully at that. If the clearances are too small, however, there's the possibility that the valves will not close completely, resulting in a loss of compression. Apart from loss of performance, getting them wrong can also result in damage to both the valves and the valve seats. Check the specifications for your particular model in *Chapter 8 - Facts and Figures.*

SAFETY FIRST!
In the real world, you'll have to raise the car and work at an awkward angle. Obey the rules with regard to raising and supporting the car safely (Chapter 1, Safety First!) and make sure you protect your eyes with goggles.

INSIDE INFORMATION: You must only set your valve clearances with the engine STONE COLD. Iain MacLeod suggests that you set up the car (on ramps or whatever you choose) the evening before you're going to do the job, so that the engine does not have to be started at all before commencing.

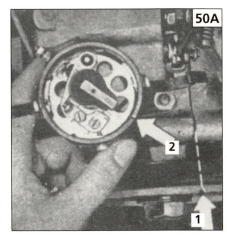
50A

50A. You must set the clearances for the inlet and exhaust valves for each cylinder when the piston for that cylinder is at the top of its firing stroke. Start by setting No.1 cylinder at TDC (Top Dead Centre) by lining up the notch in the crankshaft pulley with the crankcase centre line, (50A.1) and with the distributor rotor arm pointing towards the notch in the edge of the distributor (50A.2). (Illustration, courtesy Volkswagen)

50B. Ease off the rocker cover spring clip using a large screwdriver or similar. Take care not to trap your fingers. Be aware that you'll probably get oil dripping out as you remove the cover, so don't lie right underneath it and have something ready to catch the drips.

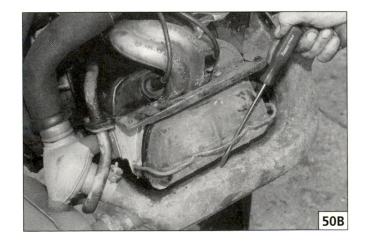
50B

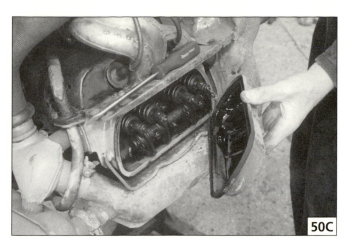

50C. Remove the rocker cover and the gasket. It's a good idea to place the rocker cover underneath the valves to catch any oily drips. Throw the old gasket away - refitting it is a way to guarantee an oil leak. Make sure you are completely orientated with which cylinders are which - No.1 is at the right front; the valve nearest the front is the exhaust valve - the next one along being the inlet valve.

50D. Start with the No.1 cylinder exhaust valve, using the feeler gauge to check the current clearance - there's no point in adjusting it if it's right already!

50E. If it needs adjusting, use a ring spanner to loosen the locknut and use a screwdriver to turn the adjusting screw in or out, depending on whether you need more or less clearance (it's 'in' for less, 'out' for more). Use the feeler gauge to check at regular intervals and TAKE YOUR TIME - it's a tricky task to perform and there's precious little room to manoeuvre. Check, check and check again is the motto. When you're absolutely sure that the No.1 exhaust valve is spot-on, hold the adjusting screw steady with the screwdriver while you tighten the locknut. It's easy to upset the clearance as you do this, so check yet once more before going any further. If you have accidentally changed the clearance it's back to square one.

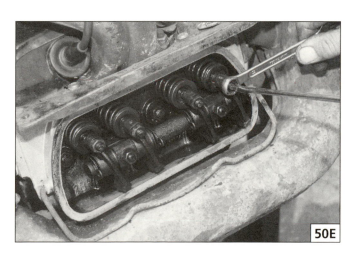

50F. If you've got it right, you can repeat the procedure on No.1 inlet valve. When that's right, you can come up for air, a quick coffee and prepare to check the clearances on the rest of the valves. Rotate the crankshaft pulley BACKWARDS (anti-clockwise) 180 degrees - half a turn - and watch the rotor arm which should turn through a quarter of a turn. At this point the clearances for No.2 cylinder can be set. Turn the pulley through a further 180 degrees (backwards, don't forget) to set-up No.3 cylinder and once more through 180 degrees for No.4.

When you've finished, replace the rocker cover with a new gasket. Start the engine and let it run for a few minutes while you feel good and get ready to go on to the next Job.

INSIDE INFORMATION!: If you can't undo the locknut with a ring spanner, try loosening it with a socket. If the heads have been chewed up by a non-caring previous owner, you'll have to remove the two 13 mm nuts which secure the rocker assembly and remove the whole thing so you can work on it on the bench. If you still have problems, it should be taken to a machine shop for specialist attention.

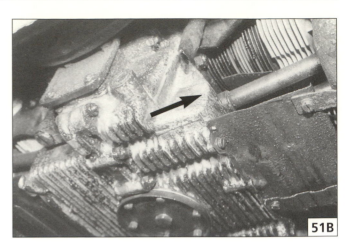

51A

51B

Job 51. Check for oil leaks.

51A. Having removed and replaced the rocker covers, it's a good time to check for oil leaks - there and under the whole of the engine and transmission. A fine film of oil on the crankcase is not unusual - it tends to come from the mist from the breather. However, this engine has leaked oil onto the heat exchangers which is not healthy, as fumes could end up in the car.

51B. Closer inspection shows plenty more oil around the pushrod tubes and the cylinder barrels (arrowed). Reusing gaskets or incorrect or insufficient torque settings on vital fastenings are two possible reasons. Whatever the cause, oil leaks of this nature need sorting sooner, rather than later.

51C. If the oil cooler appears to be leaking, check the rubber grommet at the base of the cooler. Also, remove the oil pressure relief valve (shown here) to ensure that the plunger is not sticking. From top to bottom, the component parts are: Valve plunger, valve spring, gasket, retaining plug. (Illustration, courtesy Volkswagen)

Job 52. Check CV joints for tightness.

AUTOMATIC STICK SHIFT AND 1302/1302S/1303/1303S MODELS ONLY
On some later model cars, the axle shafts feature CV (Constant Velocity) joints at each end. You'll need a suitable splined key or socket attachment to suit the socket head securing screws - don't attempt to turn them without *exactly* the right tool. Check that the screws are tight - around 25 lbs ft. Take the opportunity to make sure that none of the rubber gaiters are split - apart from being an MoT failure point, it's also potentially dangerous and expensive.

Job 53. Check clutch adjustment.

MANUAL TRANSMISSION CARS ONLY

53A. Adjustment of earlier cars (as shown here) requires two ring spanners, a pair of pliers or a self-grip wrench and three hands! Later models featured a wing nut instead of the two locking nuts and are much easier to adjust. For all, however, it is necessary to crawl right under the middle of the car alongside the transmission and the usual attention must be paid to the safety rules. (Illustration, courtesy Volkswagen)

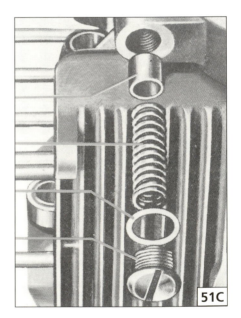

51C

53B. Free-play at the clutch pedal (a) should be 10 to 20 mm (3/8 to 3/4 in.). In use, the cable stretches and the free-play increases. Release the lock nut to reduce free-play. Work the pedal several times, recheck the free-play then tighten the lock nut. Apply grease to the thread on the end of the cable and to the grease nipple on the cable outer, if fitted, at the tunnel end.

INSIDE INFORMATION: If free-play can't all be taken up, it is the first sign that the clutch plate is worn. Have it replaced now, before it lets you down! (Illustration, courtesy Volkswagen)

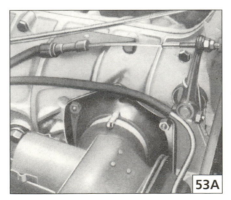

53A

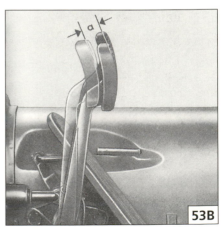

53B

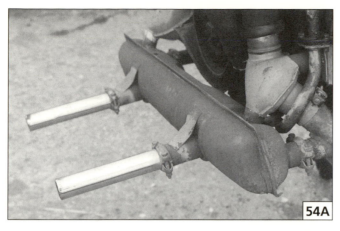

54A

Job 54. Check exhaust/heat exchangers.

54A. The Beetle exhaust became progressively more complex over the years and, particularly on later cars, there is a myriad of connections which need to be gas tight, as you can see here - with the engine out of the car for clarity. One of the simplest tests is to grab hold of the tailpipes (cold engine!) and try to waggle the exhaust. If it is solid (ie not rusted) and secured in the correct manner, there should be no adverse movement. In general, you can expect an exhaust to last around 2 years.

54B

54B. SAFETY FIRST!
The Beetle heats its interior by passing hot exhaust gases through heat exchangers on the side of the engine, as seen here. It's important that they are in good condition, otherwise poisonous fumes could enter the cabin. Check that they are solid and securely mounted. Also, when carrying out the following check take note that the heat riser pipe will probably be extremely hot. Take great care and use your discretion. Also take great care not to get hands or clothing trapped by the moving fan belt and pulleys when the engine is running.

The engine will only work at its most efficiently if the heat risers (or heat riser, depending on model) is allowing the heat from the exhaust system to heat the inlet gases leading to proper fuel vaporisation.

Run the engine, out of doors, and touch the heat riser pipe VERY BRIEFLY at each end with your fingers. If the heat riser pipe is clear, both ends of the pipe will feel hot but if the pipe is clogged, either one end or both will feel relatively cold.

Please note that this procedure will not work where the vehicle is equipped with dual heat riser pipes such as some Californian Beetles and the exhaust system will have to be removed so that the heat riser pipes can be checked manually.

A blocked heat riser is best cleared with compressed air which may be SPECIALIST SERVICE but if you have your own compressor, be sure to wear goggles. You can also loosen much of the carbon blocking the heat riser by poking a stiff wire up each end of the heat riser pipe rather like a pipe cleaner. Tapping on the sides of the heat riser pipe - but not so hard that you cause damage - will also help to loosen the accumulated deposits.

3,000 Mile Mechanical and Electrical - Road Test

Job 55. Clean controls.

Clean the door handles, controls and steering wheel, they may well have become greasy from your hands while you were carrying out the rest of the service work on your car. Start up the engine while you are sitting in the driver's seat.

Job 56. Check instruments.

Before pulling away, and with the engine running, check the correct function of all instruments and switches.

Job 57. Accelerator pedal.

Check the accelerator pedal for smooth operation. If the throttle does not operate smoothly, turn off the engine and check the cable itself for a cracked or broken casing, kinks in the casing, or fraying at the cable ends, especially where the ends of the cable 'disappear' into the cable 'outer'. If you find any of these faults, replace the throttle cable.

Job 58. Handbrake function.

Check the function of the handbrake as described under Job 48. But this time, add a further check. An experienced mechanic will be able to engage first gear and let in the clutch just a little at a time until the clutch 'bites' and strains against the handbrake - not too much - just enough to let him know that the brakes are working, and without travelling more than three or four feet (1 metre) or so. If you're not an experienced driver or mechanic and there's some risk that you might strain the car's mechanical components, try turning the engine off, pulling the handbrake on, putting the gearbox in neutral, getting out of the car - only do this on level ground! - and see if you can push the car with the handbrake on. If, in the first test, the car moves blithely away, unhindered by the effect of the handbrake, or in the second, if the car moves at all, you've got major problems with the rear brakes. The most likely reason is that the brakes are oiled with transmission oil, because of a failed oil seal, or because the brake hydraulic wheel cylinder is leaking brake fluid onto the brake shoes. Both require SPECIALIST SERVICE, unless you are an experienced mechanic and in both cases THE CAR SHOULD NOT BE DRIVEN until repairs have been carried out.

☐ **Job 59. Brakes and steering.**

SAFETY FIRST!
Only carry out the following tests in daylight, in clear dry conditions when there are no other road users about and no pedestrians. Use your mirrors and make sure that there is no traffic following you when carrying out the following brake tests.

Only a proper brake tester at an MoT testing station will be able to check the operation of the brakes accurately enough for the MoT test, but you can rule out some of the most obvious braking problems in the following way: drive along a clear stretch of road and, gripping the steering wheel fairly lightly between the thumb and fingers of each hand, brake gently from a speed of about 40 mph. Ideally, the car should pull up in a dead straight line without pulling to one side or the other. If the car pulls to the left (when being driven on the left-hand side of the road) or to the right (when being driven on the right-hand side of the road, such as in the USA), it might be that there is no problem with your brakes but that the camber on the road is causing the car to pull over. If you can find a stretch of road with no camber whatsoever, you may be able to try the brake test again or failing that, find a one-way street where you can drive on the "wrong" side of the road and see if the pulling to one side happens in the opposite direction. If it does not, then you've got a problem with your steering or brakes. Before assuming the worst, check your tyre pressures and try switching the front wheels and tyres from one side of the car to the other. If the problem doesn't go away, seek SPECIALIST SERVICE.

3,000 Mile Bodywork and Interior - Around the Car

First carry out Jobs 15, and 19 to 22

☐ **Job 60. Check windscreen.**

Check the windscreen for chips, cracks or other damage - see *Chapter 7, Getting Through The MoT* for what is, and is not, acceptable according to UK regulations.

☐ **Job 61. Wiper blades and arms.**

Check the operation of the windscreen wipers and correct position of 'sweep'. Particularly on early cars, check the physical security of the arms - it's not unknown for them to fly off!

☐ **Job 62. Check rear view mirrors.**

Check your rear view mirrors, both inside and outside the car, for cracks and crazing. Also ensure that the interior rear view mirror is soundly fixed in place since they can come loose and when they do, the vibration can get so bad that you can't tell whether you're being followed by a long distance truck or one of the boys in blue!

☐ **Job 63. Chrome trim and badges.**

Rust can easily start to form behind badges and in the holes where badges are mounted. Apply water dispersant behind chrome trim and badges.

3,000 Mile Bodywork - Under the Car

Read and note carefully the SAFETY information in the Introduction to this chapter on raising and supporting the car above the ground.

First, carry out Job 23

☐ **Job 64. Inspect underside.**

When dry, inspect the underside of the car for rust and damage. Renew paint, underbody sealant and wax coating locally as necessary. Look for loose underseal in particular, especially that of the old-fashioned bitumen type. It goes brittle and comes loose, allowing water to get behind it and form a breeding ground for corrosion. Scrape off any such loose underseal and paint on wax coating in its place, when dry.

6,000 Miles - or Every Six Months, Whichever Comes First

6,000 Mile Mechanical and Electrical - The Engine Bay

First carry out Jobs 1 and 16, then 24 to 36 as applicable

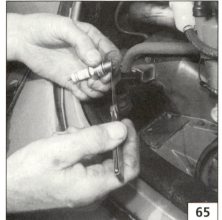

65

☐ **Job 65. Replace spark plugs.**

65. Fit a set of new spark plugs - the NGK reference for all standard Beetle models is B5-HS. The Beetle uses 'short reach' plugs which have a relatively short thread length. Spark plug references denote the heat range the plug has been designed to work in. Make sure that the gaps are as specified before installing. Some owners leave spark plugs in place for longer, but there is always the risk that the insulation will break down and lower the performance of the plug even though it may appear perfect in every other way. We recommend that you renew plugs now, but whatever your feelings, NEVER leave plugs in place for more than 12,000 miles, even with the regular cleaning and adjustment described in the 3,000 mile servicing intervals.

Plug changing in the Beetle can be a tricky operation and is covered fully in Job 31. The key point is that the soft aluminium cylinder heads are easily damaged and so the engine should be cold before you start work.

INSIDE INFORMATION: If you are trying to remove a plug which gets ever tighter as you turn it, there's every possibility that it is cross threaded. Once out, it probably won't go back in again. Tighten it up again and take it to a machine shop or specialist who, if nothing else, will be able to solve the problem by adding a thread insert to your cylinder head, should the worst happen.

☐ **Job 66. Renew contact breaker points.**

66A. In normal use, contact breaker points invariably deteriorate causing a steady and indiscernible drop off in performance. They're such inexpensive items that it is best to renew them at 6,000 miles, although not necessarily at six months, since it is purely the usage that causes them to deteriorate. Several of the part numbers are referred to later in this and subsequent sections. (Illustration, courtesy Volkswagen)

66B. Remove the distributor cap and take out the securing screw holding the points in place. It's easy to drop this screw, so it's a good idea to magnetise your screwdriver first. Pull off the wire at the single terminal connector clip. The complete points assembly (66A.4) may then be lifted off the pivot post.

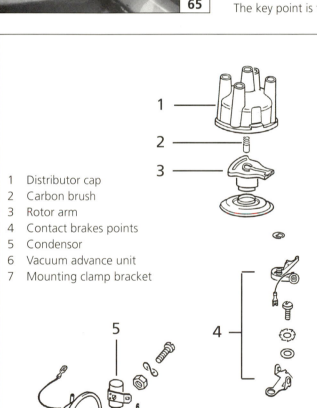

1   Distributor cap
2   Carbon brush
3   Rotor arm
4   Contact brakes points
5   Condensor
6   Vacuum advance unit
7   Mounting clamp bracket

66A

66B

66C. When buying new points, take along your engine number to ensure you get the right type - there are plenty to go at. Make sure that you keep the contact faces away from grease or oil - wipe clean with a little petrol on a rag before fitting.

66D. Another inexpensive item and one that is well worth fitting every time the points are renewed, is the condenser. (66A.5) Note that the fixing screw that holds the condenser in place is even smaller and easier to lose than the screw for fixing the points in place.

Before offering up the new points, remember to lubricate the distributor as shown in Job 35. Refit the points and adjust as described in Job 32.

SPECIALIST SERVICE: Have a specialist with the appropriate equipment check the voltage drop between the coil CB terminal and earth (ground).

66C

66D

 **Job 67. Check cylinder compressions.**

Cylinder compression test
Because of the flat-four engine design of the Beetle, not all compression testers are suitable for getting down into those awkward-to-reach plug holes. Check before you buy!

67. Remove all four plugs and the central coil lead. Insert the compression tester and turn the engine over six to 10 times. You should have around 100 psi on all four cylinders. Whatever they read, they should be within 10 psi of each other. Drastic differences mean that something is amiss and demands your immediate attention. No.3 cylinder will usually be a little down on the others because it runs hottest.

INSIDE INFORMATION: If one (or more) cylinders is showing a much lower reading, put a teaspoonful of oil into the cylinder and run the test again. If it is still low, the inference is that the valves and/or seats are burnt. If the reading rises, the valves are OK but the cylinders and piston rings are worn.

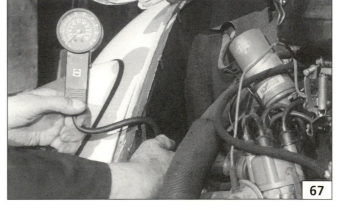

67

Job 68. Check exhaust emissions.

68. Though many Beetles may be too old to need accurate emissions testing at MoT time (depending on latest regulations), you're wise to keep an eye on what comes out of your exhaust, as it gives a very definite indication of the state of your engine. The Gunson's Gastester MKII is a surprisingly accurate device for use by the DIY servicer and can be used as part of the arsenal of tuning gear now available. It shows a reading of the percentage of CO (carbon monoxide) in the exhaust gases. If you look closely, you can see that this 1303 is running at a very healthy 4.5%.

SAFETY FIRST!
By definition, running this check means having your engine running for some time. DO NOT perform this check in your garage or any confined space - exhaust gases, are dangerous and can KILL within minutes!

SPECIALIST SERVICE: If you don't have such a machine (many clubs own them and offer their use for a small fee) have a properly equipped garage carry out an exhaust emissions check, especially for carbon monoxide (CO) and unburned hydrocarbons.

68

☐ **Job 69. Adjust carburettor idle speed.**

Beetles were only equipped with a single carb from the factory, though many owners have deemed it necessary to add an extra one. Balancing and tuning twin carbs is and art form and extremely time-consuming. You're not advised to try it without specialist equipment, such as a carburettor balancer, a tachometer, an exhaust gas analyser and plenty of time!

Don't tinker with your carburettor for the sake of it - remember the old adage - if it ain't broke, don't fix it! For the most part, this is likely to be true. If the results of your exhaust emissions test (Job 68) and/or the condition of your plugs indicates that the mixture is OK (with light grey/brown deposits with no obvious damage to the electrodes) then leave your carburettor alone. The two basic adjustments open to you are the idle speed and the mixture.

Before touching your carburettor, you should ensure that the spark plugs, points, valve clearances and timing are absolutely right and that the filter oil has been changed (or air filter, if necessary - see 18,000 mile service).

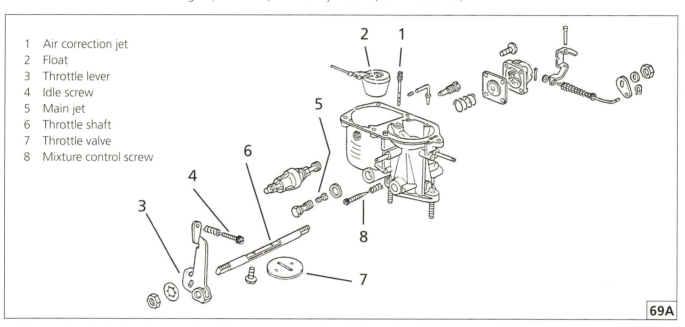

1 Air correction jet
2 Float
3 Throttle lever
4 Idle screw
5 Main jet
6 Throttle shaft
7 Throttle valve
8 Mixture control screw

69A

Adjusting idle speed and mixture

69A. **Pre-1971 models:**
Over the years, many different carburettors have been used, though all standard variants have been of Solex manufacture. The reference number will be shown on the side of the float chamber. In general, PICT, PICT-1 and PICT-2 carbs were fitted to pre-'71 Beetles and are adjusted as follows: (Illustration, courtesy Volkswagen)

69B. Locate the Idle Speed Screw. It's at the top of the throttle lever, facing toward the back of the car. Turning it clockwise INCREASES the idle speed, turning it anti-clockwise DECREASES it. If you have a tachometer (either in the car or on a portable meter), adjust the engine speed to around 850 RPM.

69C. Now locate the Volume Control Screw - it's on the left-hand side of the carb and has a spring on it. Screw this clockwise (the screw will go in) until the engine revs start to stutter then back it off until the engine is running at its fastest. Then, it's back to the Idle Screw. Adjust it until you've got the correct tickover speed and that's the job done.

69B

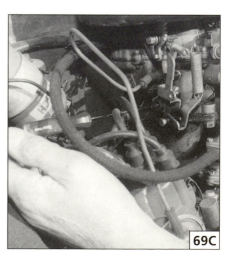

69C

6,000 MILE SERVICE

69D. **Post 1971 models:**
After 1971, the Solex PICT-3 and PICT-4 carburettors were used. Unlike earlier models, there are three screws for adjustment (the Throttle Stop Screw, the By-pass Air Screw and the Idle Mixture Adjustment Screw), but only two should be used.

INSIDE INFORMATION: It is most important that the intake manifold and carburettor are fully secure before attempting to tune the carburettors and that the gaskets are in good condition. Try running the engine - TAKE CARE OF THE MOVING FAN BELT AND PULLEYS! - and spray carburettor cleaner around all of the flanges. Any change in the idling speed of the engine while you are spraying indicates a probable leak which calls for stripping and further investigation before attempting to set the carburettors.

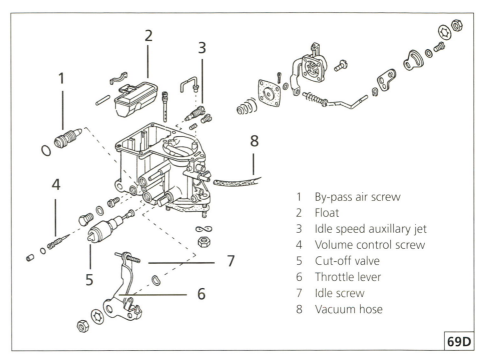

1	By-pass air screw
2	Float
3	Idle speed auxillary jet
4	Volume control screw
5	Cut-off valve
6	Throttle lever
7	Idle screw
8	Vacuum hose

69D

The Throttle Stop Screw is on the back of the carb and should be fitted with a plastic cap. This is the one you DON'T need to touch unless a previous owner has tried to adjust the carb using it and has not reset it correctly. To check, make sure that the Throttle Stop Screw only just brushes the Fast Idle Cam (with the choke OFF) and that it does not hold the throttle open at all. If this is not the case, you are the victim of a tinkerer and you'll have to correct his or her efforts before you start work.

Use the by-pass Air Screw to adjust the idle speed. This can be found on the left-hand side of the carb. (This is very small, so use the correct screwdriver - using the wrong tool for the job could butcher the screw head and completely prevent further adjust-

ment.) Then adjust the mixture as already described. Finally, reset the idle speed again using the By-pass Air Screw.

INSIDE INFORMATION: If you adjust the By-pass Air Screw (all models) but it has no effect on the running of the engine, the odds are that the carburettor is of a big age and has started to fill up with gunge in its important little places. There are proprietary carburettor cleaners (which are added to the fuel) but if that doesn't work, the carb will have to be removed and thoroughly cleaned - beyond the scope of this book, but at least you know what's required.

Run-on valve

69E.INSIDE INFORMATION: What happens when, with the engine set-up just perfectly, every time you bring the car to a halt, the engine dies? You adjust the idle speed but to no avail. The odds are that the run-on valve has died on you. Remove the lead (tape it up for safety - sparking electrics and petrol do not mix) and unscrew it. You can't mend it if it's gone awry, just replace it. (Illustration, courtesy Volkswagen)

69E

☐ **Job 70. Check automatic choke.**

The usefulness of the Beetle automatic choke is a contentious matter and one on which owners seldom agree. To some it's a perfect piece of engineering, to others it is a fuel-wasting and engine-ruining complication. It *can* be disconnected altogether, which will make starting a little more difficult and will mean the engine will need to be warmed through before you start off, otherwise it will tend to stall at every junction you stop at until the engine thoroughly warms up - a dangerous business so we don't recommend disconnection.

70. If you leave it wired up, it's important to make sure that it is correctly set-up. Take a lint-free rag and wipe it clean - it sits on the right-hand side of the carburettor. You

70

should be able to see three marks on the carburettor body and one on the choke element. Iain MacLeod at Macvolks always puts a drop of typist correction fluid or similar on it for easy identification. When the carb is new and/or running perfectly, the mark on the element should line-up with the centre of the three marks. As wear takes place, it may be necessary to adjust the position slightly, by loosening the three securing screws and turning until the desired position is reached. When adjustment requires movement outside the range of the three marks, there's extreme wear and replacement is required. This is not likely for many hundreds of thousands of miles.

Job 71. Replace fuel filter.

AFC FUEL INJECTION CARS ONLY

Only carry this out with a cold engine and apply the 'no smoking' rule. This filter can't be cleaned so you'll need a new one before you start. Remove the top pipe first (the one that goes to the fuel tank) and be ready to mop up any fuel with a rag. Plug the fuel pipe with a pencil or clean screwdriver. Alternatively, you could use brake pipe clamps. Remove the lower hose (to the fuel pump) and then the filter itself. When fitting the new filter, make sure that the arrow is pointing toward the fuel pump, i.e. in the same direction as the fuel will flow.

Job 72. Check all fuel connections.

Make a physical check of all fuel lines and connections in the engine bay. Bend the lines in order to expose hairline cracks or deterioration which may not be immediately obvious. Start the engine and (taking the usual precautions) check that there are no fuel leaks. Replace damaged parts, but only work on your fuel system when the engine is cold.

Job 73. Check warm air control flap.

Since 1961, the Beetle air cleaner has featured a counterweighted warm air inlet and control flap. This takes warm air directly from the engine into the air cleaner when required. If the air into the carburettor is too cold, the fuel/air mixture will not vaporise correctly. At low throttle openings or at idle, the mixture can stick to the sides of those long inlet manifolds and lead to fuel starvation and the famous Beetle flat spots. Check to ensure that it is free to operate in the correct manner.

6,000 Mile Mechanical and Electrical - Around the Car

First carry out Jobs 2 to 14, 17, and 37 to 41

Job 74. Check battery and terminals.

Remove the battery (situated under the right-hand side of the rear seat) and clean the terminals if necessary. They tend to accumulate a white 'fur' when left unprotected. Cover the terminals with a copper-based grease or petroleum jelly. Wipe the battery casing and make sure there are no cracks - acid spillage can cause metal corrosion. Check in the battery tray to ensure that there is no sign of this. If there is, clean the surface using ammonia then apply an anti-rust treatment and a thick coating of hammer finish paint before replacing the battery.

Job 75. Check headlamp alignment.

It is possible to adjust your own headlamps, though not with enough accuracy to pass an MoT test - unless by fluke! As such, headlamp alignment should be left to the specialists, but here is a method of setting up the aim in an emergency (when you've had to replace a headlamp, for example). See headlamp alignment chart on page 93.

Place the unloaded car in a level position facing your garage door or a wall. It needs to be in a shaded position or the procedure carried out on a cloudy day. Draw two cross lines on the door as per the diagram.

The longitudinal centre line (car axis) must hit the centre of the screen exactly between the two cross marks. Switch on the main beams and check the beams at the cross marks. Adjust using the adjuster screws on the top or side of the headlamp assemblies.

It should be noted that Bosch and Hella headlamps adjust in opposite directions, as shown here:

BOSCH HEADLAMPS
Vertical adjustment - turn upper screw:

| Clockwise | Beam swings down |
| Anti-clockwise | Beam swings up |

Horizontal adjustment - turn right-hand screw:

| Clockwise | Beam swings to left |
| Anti-clockwise | Beam swings to right |

HELLA HEADLAMPS
Vertical adjustment - turn left-hand screw:

| Clockwise | Beam swings up |
| Anti-clockwise | Beam swings down |

Horizontal adjustment - turn right-hand screw:

| Clockwise | Beam swings to right |
| Anti-clockwise | Beam swings to left |

☐ **Job 76. Check automatic stick shift switch contacts.**

AUTOMATIC STICK SHIFT CARS ONLY

Check the electrical contacts at the base of the gear lever by pulling up the rubber boot and loosening the locknut at the lower part of the sleeve. Back the shift sleeve off to reveal the contacts. The gap, measured with your feeler gauge should be between 0.010 to 0.016 in. (0.25 to 0.4 mm). Achieve this by screwing the sleeve until the contacts touch and then backing off slightly. After adjustment, the elongated hole in the sleeve must run fore and aft. Retighten the assembly, replace the rubber boot and road test to ensure that the gear changing operation works correctly.

6,000 Mile Mechanical and Electrical - Under the Car

First carry out Jobs 18, and 42 to 54

☐ **Job 77. Check brake pipes and fuel lines.**

SAFETY FIRST!
Make sure you follow the safety instructions detailed in Chapter 1 when working under your car.

77A. Check the condition of all brake pipes. Remember that there are metal lines running down the car which join flexible rubber hoses at the front and rear. As well as damage from stones etc., the metal lines are prone to rusting, so you need to apply a wire brush to clean them off. Excessive rusting is an MoT failure point. Apply some anti-rust wax.

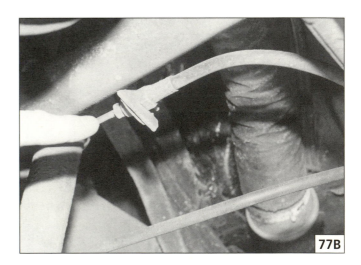

77B. Pay particular attention to the flexible brake hoses at the front (steering) end of the car. Get hold of each hose and bend it to expose any hidden cracks or splits. At the first sign of either, the hose should be replaced.

77C. Fuel lines, too, should be checked in the same way, starting at the fuel tank under the bonnet. In later cars, the fuel filler is on the outside of the car and the hoses and breather shown here are all prone to deterioration over a period of time. Check for leaks and splits as above.

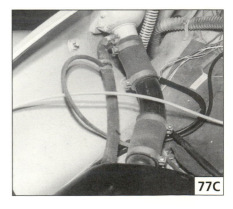

You can learn a lot about the condition of an engine from looking at the spark plugs. The following information and photographs, reproduced here with grateful thanks to NGK, show you what to look out for.

1. Good Condition

If the firing end of a spark plug is brown or light grey, the condition can be judged to be good and the spark plug is functioning at its best.

4. Overheating

When having been overheated, the insulator tip can become glazed or glossy, and deposits which have accumulated on the insulator tip may have melted. Sometimes these deposits have blistered on the insulator's tip.

6. Abnormal Wear

Abnormal electrode erosion is caused by the effects of corrosion, oxidation, reaction with lead, all resulting in abnormal gap growth.

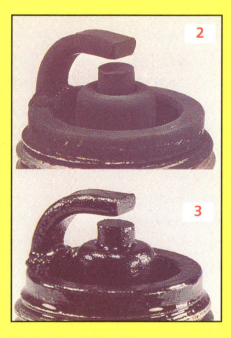

2. Carbon Fouling

Black, dry, sooty deposits, which will eventually cause misfiring and can be caused by an over-rich fuel mixture. Check all carburettor settings, choke operation and air filter cleanliness. Clean plugs vigorously with a brass bristled wire brush.

3. Oil Fouling

Oily, wet-looking deposits. This is particularly prone to causing poor starting and even misfiring. Caused by a severely worn engine but do not confuse with wet plugs removed from the engine when it won't start. If the "wetness" evaporates away, it's not oil fouling.

5. Normal Wear

A worn spark plug not only wastes fuel but also strains the whole ignition system because the expanded gap requires higher voltage. As a result, a worn spark plug will result in damage to the engine itself, and will also increase air pollution. The normal rate of gap growth is usually around 'half-a-thou.' or 0.0006 in. every 5,000 miles (0.01 mm. every 5,000 km.).

7. Breakage

Insulator damage is self-evident and can be caused by rapid heating or cooling of the plug whilst out of the car or by clumsy use of gap setting tools. Burned away electrodes are indicative of an ignition system that is grossly out of adjustment. Do not use the car until this has been put right.

☐ Job 78. Check front dampers.

Make a visual check of the front dampers to ensure that they are securely mounted and that they are not leaking. If hydraulic oil is present on the outside of the damper, then replacement is called for - note, in pairs only - NEVER replace only one damper. Make sure that you can differentiate between oil and rain water splashed up from the road. If you're unsure, clean the damper thoroughly and take the car for a 5 mile drive in the dry. Any fluid then on the damper has to be leaking hydraulic fluid. (See also Job 82)

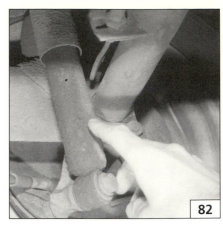

82

☐ Job 79. Check front springs.

1302/1303 SERIES CARS ONLY

Make a visual check on the front coil springs, looking for secure mounting and for cracks in the spring itself. Extreme care is required, as they are under a lot of pressure. Make sure you check right up to the top of the spring. (See also Job 83)

☐ Job 80. Check steering components.

Check the condition of the track rods, torsion arm link pins, steering swivels and steering ball joints for signs of excessive wear or leaks.

☐ Job 81. Check front wheel alignment.

SPECIALIST SERVICE: The wheel alignment should be checked by the local garage on specialised equipment.

☐ Job 82. Check rear dampers.

82. Run the same checks as in Job 78. Again, any problems with dampers requires that they be replaced in pairs.

☐ Job 83. Check rear springs.

1302/1303 SERIES CARS ONLY

Run the same checks as in Job 79.

☐ Job 84. Check heater control cables and levers.

The Beetle draws air into the cabin via the heat exchangers along channels running alongside the sills. Flaps on the heat exchangers determine how much, if any, heat enters the car. These cables should be lubricated under the car in the positions shown in the diagrams.

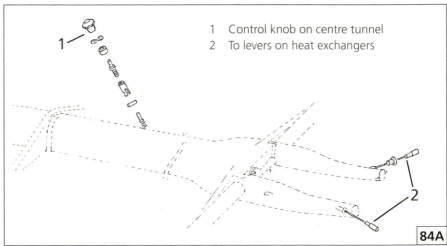

1 Control knob on centre tunnel
2 To levers on heat exchangers

84A

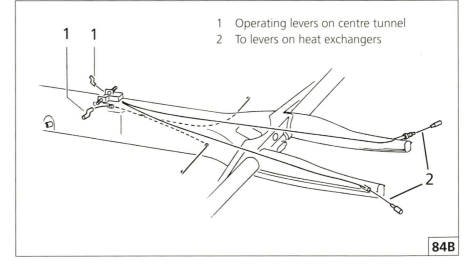

1 Operating levers on centre tunnel
2 To levers on heat exchangers

84B

84A. Early Beetles featured a circular control knob on the central tunnel. (Illustration, courtesy Volkswagen)

84B. Later cars utilised twin levers mounted on the central tunnel. (Illustration, courtesy Volkswagen)

84C. The cables feature a nipple which connects to the lower part of the control lever adjacent to the engine. Its position under the car makes it prone to rusting and both cables and levers should be lubricated regularly to prevent the possibility of seizure/breakage.

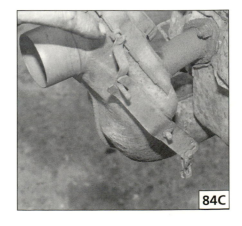

84C

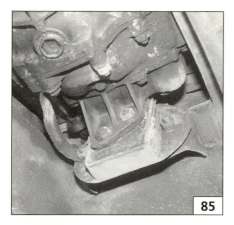

85

☐ Job 85. Check power unit mountings.

85. Check the condition of the engine mountings and the transmission mountings (shown here) to ensure that they are sound. Serious deterioration requires renewal.

☐ Job 86. Check drive shaft/CV joint gaiters.

All Beetles feature axle tubes except Automatic Stick Shift models and 1302/1303 cars. All cars are fitted with rubber boots/gaiters which MUST be sound. Cracks, splits or tears are dangerous, could cause expensive transmission failures and are MoT failure points.

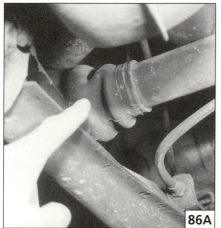

86A

86A. The axle tubes are hollow and carry oil from the transmission to lubricate the outer wheel bearing. Clearly, a leak from the rubber boot (there's one at either end of the axle shafts) could spell disaster.

86B. The axle shaft on this 1303 is a single piece, but the gaiters still serve a purpose - holding in the grease which lubricates the CV joints. Again, check carefully for any damage whatsoever, replacing where necessary. Unless you are well qualified, it's a SPECIALIST SERVICE job.

☐ Job 87. Check transmission oil level.

MANUAL TRANSMISSION ONLY

To check the transmission oil level, you'll have to get right underneath the car. The car must be on the level - it's not enough just to jack up the rear of the car. Ideally, it should be supported by four axle stands. This is not something to be undertaken lightly, and you must take even more care than ever that the car cannot fall on you - see the safety rules in Chapter 1.

86B

87A. Locate the level plug which is on the left-hand side of the transmission casting, about half way up (87A.A). The only way to check the level is to remove the plug and top up with Castrol Hypoy light SAE EP80 oil, which comes in handy plastic packs featuring a long nozzle, ideal for this kind of transmission, where the filling has to be performed 'uphill'. This is thick oil and should only be added slowly. When excess oil spills over from the drain plug, allow the last few drips to escape before replacing the plug. Overfilling the transmission adds to the risk of blowing (expensive) oil seals. (Illustration, courtesy Volkswagen)

INSIDE INFORMATION: Place the sealed container of oil in hot water to thin it down before using. Wipe the container dry.

87B. **AUTOMATIC STICK SHIFT ONLY**
Check the gearbox oil level in a similar way to that of the manual transmission. Also check the torque converter ATF level. The level should be between the upper and lower levels but NEVER below the lower mark. (Illustration, courtesy Volkswagen)

☐ Job 88. Check clutch adjustment.

AUTOMATIC STICK SHIFT CARS ONLY

In order to check if your clutch needs adjustment, drive at around 40/45mph in 2nd gear and, without depressing the accelerator, change down to 1st. This should be a smooth transition and take around 1 second. If it takes longer and/or there are signs

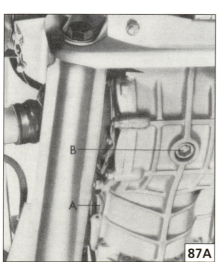

87A

87B

of 'snatch' as the clutch bites, adjustment is required. The adjustment screw is situated in the control valve. Remove the valve cap and turn the screw between 1/4 and 1/2 turn. Turning clockwise DECREASES the speed of engagement, anti-clockwise INCREASES the speed of engagement. After adjustment, perform the test outlined above to ensure that it is now working correctly.

CHAPTER THREE

6,000 Mile Mechanical and Electrical - Road Test

Carry out jobs 55 to 59

6,000 Mile Bodywork and Interior - Around the Car

First carry out Jobs 15, 19 to 22 and 60 to 63

☐ **Job 89. Lubricate luggage lid release and hinges.**

Use Castrol Everyman oil to lubricate the luggage lid release and its cable. A dab of grease on the striker is also a good idea, though too much could result in it getting onto clothing as the bonnet is operated. Use the same oil to lubricate the bonnet hinges. These support a lot of weight and must not be allowed to run 'dry'.

☐ **Job 90. Lubricate door locks and striker plates.**

Use Castrol Everyman oil to lubricate the striker plates. Though oil can be used in the locks, the best way is to dip the key into graphite powder and then insert it into the lock. This ensures that the innermost workings of the lock are lubricated. Make sure that you wipe the key thoroughly afterwards.

90

☐ **Job 91. Lubricate engine lid lock.**

Use either Castrol Everyman oil or the graphite technique described in Job 90 to lubricate the engine lid lock.

☐ **Job 92. Check seats and seat belts.**

Check the condition and security of seats and seat belts. Shake each seat to check its security, pull hard on each length of belt webbing near where each section is fitted to the car and test each buckle. Check inertia reel belts. With most types, you can test by tugging; if you pull hard and quickly on the belt, the reel should lock; with others, the lock may only work under braking. Carry out a careful road test, in the daylight, under dry road conditions and with no other traffic or pedestrians around.

93

☐ **Job 93. Check floors including spare wheel well.**

Lift the carpets to check for water accumulation beneath them. Pay particular attention to the footwells at either side (water drips down inside the 'A' pillars and rots holes for the water to enter), under the rear seat and in the spare wheel well. Find and eliminate sources of water leaks before the smell of rotting carpet drives you to it - by which time the problem of rotting steel will have joined the list.

94

Check the seals around the doors and the bonnet and engine bay.
Leaks are best found with the inside of the car dry and, if it's feasible, the carpets taken out. Have someone play a hose on an area of the car at a time whilst you go leak hunting.

6,000 Mile Bodywork - Under the Car

First carry out Jobs 23 and 64

☐ **Job 94. Rustproof underbody.**

Renew wax treatment to wheel arches and underbody areas. Refer to Chapter 5, Rustproofing, for full details.

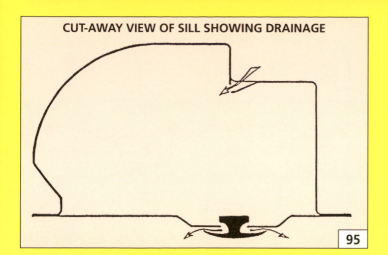

CUT-AWAY VIEW OF SILL SHOWING DRAINAGE

95

☐ **Job 95. Clear all drain holes.**

95. Check and clear the drain holes in the sills, doors and spare wheel well. From the 1968 model year, Beetle sills received two small openings in the door step and two rubber drainage valves beneath. Research by Autobarn of Pershore has shown that if any of these holes are blocked - including the top ones - corrosion becomes more likely to occur. (Illustration, courtesy Autobarn)

12,000 Miles - or Every Twelve Months, Whichever Comes First

12,000 Mile Mechanical and Electrical - The Engine Bay

First carry out Jobs 1 and 16, 24 to 36, and 65 to 73 as applicable

☐ **Job 96. Change in-line fuel filter.**

Though most Beetles seem to be fitted with an in-line fuel filter, they were never fitted by the factory as standard (only to the Types 3 and 4). The cars that tend to have them fitted mostly are the later models fitted with fuel pumps with non-serviceable filters. Regardless, if you have such a filter on your car it should be replaced every 12,000 miles. Remember the safety rules when working with your fuel system - do not smoke or allow others to do so and work only with a cold engine. Before removing the filter, secure the fuel pipes at either end by using clamps intended for brake hoses. Don't use self-locking grips or similar, as their teeth could bite into the fuel line and cause a leak. As a last resort, use a Philips screwdriver to push down the hose and prevent leakage. The filter will simply pull off and the new one should be a push fit into the fuel lines. It is very important that the arrow on the filter matches the direction of the fuel flow - otherwise the fuel won't flow!

INSIDE INFORMATION: Iain MacLeod at Macvolks always recommends fitting small, stainless steel worm drive clips to any pipework - that way, you know that it will not come adrift.

12,000 Mile Mechanical and Electrical - Around the Car

First carry out Jobs 2 to 14, 17, 37 to 41, and 74 to 76

☐ **Job 97. Test dampers.**

'Bounce' test each corner of the car in turn in order to check the efficiency of the dampers. If the car 'bounces' at all, the dampers have had it. They should be replaced in pairs as an axle set, NEVER as individual units. Efficient dampers can make an enormous difference to your car's safety and handling.

98

☐ **Job 98. Alarm remote control transmitters.**

98. Replace the battery in each alarm remote control transmitter (if fitted). Usually, these are snap-together items which contain either a watch-type nicad battery or a 12v lighter-style battery. Replacement is simple. Leave this Job at your peril, for, as the publisher once found, it is all too easy to be banished from your own car, if the battery 'dies' at an inopportune moment. Like in France. With the shops shut...

12,000 Mile Mechanical and Electrical - Under the Car

First carry out Jobs 18, 42 to 54 and 77 to 88

☐ Job 99. Check suspension rubbers.

99. Macpherson strut cars have more suspension rubbers than torsion bar suspension cars, but all have some. Check all mounting rubbers, especially on anti-roll bar countings, shock absorber mountings, track control arm bushes (Macpherson strut cars), three per side. Oil, heat and passage of time causes bushes to soften and sometimes fall right away. Handling will be vastly improved if soft bushes are renewed. Consult your workshop manual or **SPECIALIST SERVICE**. (Illustration, courtesy Volkswagen)

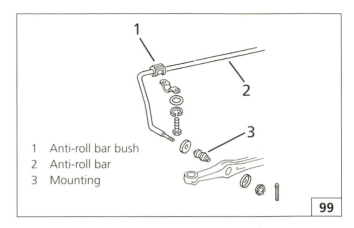

1 Anti-roll bar bush
2 Anti-roll bar
3 Mounting

99

☐ Job 100. Change automatic transmission oil.

AUTOMATIC STICK SHIFT CARS ONLY

SAFETY FIRST!
This Job requires you to be underneath the car, so take the usual safety precautions as outlined in Chapter 1, and at the beginning of this Chapter.

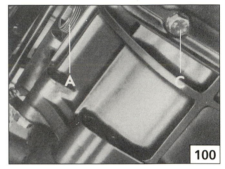

100

Drain the oil when the transmission is warm, but take care not to scald yourself! Remove the 14 screws securing the bottom cover and let the oil drain into a suitable receptacle. Let the oil drain thoroughly and after cleaning the cover with white spirit, replace it together with a new gasket. The 14 screws should be tightened evenly and to a torque of just 7 lbs ft. Fill the transmission through the filler hole (A) with 3 litres of Castrol TQD automatic transmission fluid until it starts to overflow the filler hole - make sure that all the excess has drained, as an overfull transmission could lead to blowing oil seals. (Illustration, courtesy Volkswagen)

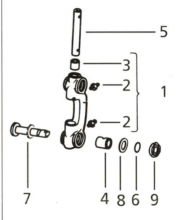

1 Link - torsion arm
2 Grease nipple
3 King pin bush
4 Torsion arm link pin bush
5 King pin
6 Dust excluder
7 Torsion arm link pin
8 Torsion arm link pin shim
9 Dust excluder - Retainer

101

☐ Job 101. Check kingpins.

EARLY CARS ONLY

101. Check the kingpins for wear. Jack the car up beneath the front suspension and place axle stands under the car for safety, without lowering the weight of the car onto the axle stands; it is important that the jack compresses the suspension. DON'T go beneath the car! Use a lever to lift and lower the road wheel and look for movement in the top and bottom of the kingpin.

☐ Job 102. Front brake callipers.

DISC BRAKE CARS ONLY

SAFETY FIRST! and SPECIALIST SERVICE:
Obviously, a car's brakes are among its most important safety related items. Do not dismantle your car's brakes unless you are fully competent to do so. If you have not been trained in this work, but wish to carry out the work described here, we strongly recommend that you have a garage or qualified mechanic check your work before using the car on the road. See also the section on BRAKES AND ASBESTOS in Chapter 1, and RAISING A CAR - SAFELY! at the beginning of this Chapter for further important information.

Examine the front brake callipers for fluid leakage. Replace the calliper if any is found. This is a SPECIALIST SERVICE job, unless you are particularly well qualified.

☐ Job 103. Check steering free play.

Check the free play at the steering wheel. See *Chapter 7, Getting Through The MoT*, for details of what is acceptable.

☐ **Job 104. Check track rod ends.**

Check for play in the inner and outer track rod ends.

☐ **Job 105. Check steering box mountings.**

Check the steering box clamp mounting bolts for security.

12,000 Mile Mechanical and Electrical - Road Test

Carry out Jobs 55 to 59

12,000 Mile Bodywork and Interior - Around the Car

First carry out Jobs 15, 19 to 22, 60 to 63, and 89 to 93

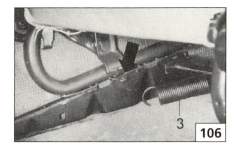

☐ **Job 106. Seat runners.**
Carefully lubricate the seat runners, preferably using non-staining silicone grease, taking care not to get grease onto the carpet or rubber mats. (Illustration, courtesy Volkswagen)

☐ **Job 107. Toolkit and jack.**
Inspect the toolkit and make sure everything you're likely to need in an emergency is present and correct. Wipe tools with an oily rag to stop them rusting and lubricate the jack, checking that it works smoothly.

12,000 Mile Bodywork - Under the Car

First carry out Jobs 23 and 64

☐ **Job 108. Steam clean underside.**

SPECIALIST SERVICE: Unless you have access to an electronic power washer, it's unlikely that your garden hose will be able to get the underside of your car really clean. That's why you should make it a once a year task to get it steam cleaned professionally. It will remove every bit of mud and caked on gunge from places you didn't even know were there. This gives you an opportunity to check for bodywork rust and rot and the security and condition of all cables, pipes and hoses.

Now carry out Jobs 94 and 95.

18,000 Miles - or Every Eighteen Months, Whichever Comes First

First carry out the regular jobs for a 6,000 mile service shown in *Appendix 4, Service History*.

18,000 Mile Mechanical and Electrical - The Engine Bay

☐ **Job 109. Change air filter.**

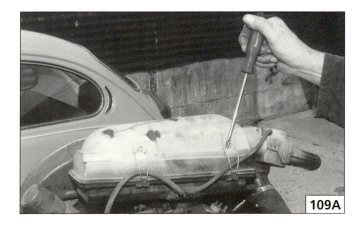

LATE MODEL CARS ONLY WITH PAPER AIR FILTER

109A. You may be able to remove just the top plastic cover of the filter assembly in order to remove the element. However, it's probable that you'll have to remove the whole unit, along with many and various hoses and pipes. As these filters were fitted to the later model Beetles, the cars are absolutely awash with emission control gear, so there's plenty to go at!

CHAPTER THREE

109B. The top half is secured by a series of metal clips, which can be undone by prising open with a screwdriver. Be careful not to trap your fingers and that there is no danger of a damaged clip flying off into your eyes. The paper element can then be removed, discarded and replace with a new one. Refit in a reversal of the dismantling procedure, making sure that all the hoses go back where they should.

109B

24,000 Miles - or Every Twenty Four Months Whichever Comes First

The Service Jobs mentioned below should be carried out in addition to the full list of *12,000 Miles - or Every Twelve Months* Service Jobs. They cover the sort of areas that experience has shown can give trouble in the longer term or, in some cases, they cover areas that may prevent trouble from starting in the first place. Some of them don't appear on manufacturers' service schedules - but these are the sort of jobs which make all the difference between a car that is reliable, and one that gives problems out of the blue.

24,000 Mile Mechanical and Electrical - The Engine Bay

☐ **Job 110. Replace fan belt.**

Replacing this item at such a relatively early time is literally a 'fan belt and braces' move! Because the fan belt is so vitally important on your air-cooled steed, it's prudent to swap it now. If the cost of a belt worries you, balance the price against that of a replacement engine! See Job 29 dealing with the adjustment of the belt for details of how the pulley is removed and how the various shims should be replaced. Make sure that the belt is tightened to the correct tension. Also carefully check the condition of the pulley halves and if they show significant signs of wear, replace them too. If they should fail in use, the effect would be the same as if the belt fails and the engine will overheat and expire in a major way!

INSIDE INFORMATION: *Some owners have been known to hit the pulley arms with a hammer in an attempt to get the various sections to line up. YOU SHOULD NEVER DO SO because the metal can fracture and the pulley can then fly apart at high revolutions. Instead, spray both pulley halves and the generator shaft itself with aerosol releasing fluid which allows the replacement belt to go on a lot more easily.*

24,000 Mile Mechanical and Electrical - Under the Car

SAFETY FIRST!
Raise the car as necessary after reading the information at the start of this chapter on lifting and supporting the car.

☐ **Job 111. Change transmission oil.**

MANUAL TRANSMISSION CARS ONLY (For Automatic Stick Shift models, see Job 100)

111A. The transmission and final drive are lubricated by the same oil. On early casings (recognisable because they are split vertically) there are two drain plugs to undo and remove, as seen in this photo. (Illustration, courtesy Volkswagen)

111B. Later cars featured a horizontally split casing and just one drain plug (B). On all versions, the filler plug is on the side of the casing and tricky to get at. With the engine and transmission oil warm, remove the drain plug(s) and allow the oil to drain totally into a suitable receptacle - take your coffee break here, because transmission oil is thicker than engine oil and it may take a while. Check the drain plugs. From 1958

111A

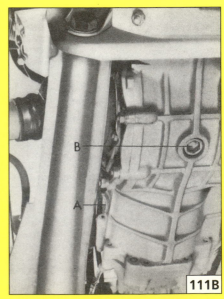

111B

111C

onwards, the drain plugs were magnetic and so you need to remove any pieces of swarf. If any plug has an excessive amount of metal pieces, it points to a possible problem - one for a transmission specialist. If your car hasn't got magnetic plugs, it's a good idea to uprate them. (Illustration, courtesy Volkswagen)

111C. When you're sure all the oil has drained, replace the drain plugs and remove the filler plug on the side. It's awkward to get oil into the box, which is why garages use special fillers like the one in this photo. However, the Castrol Hypoy Light gear oil required comes in plastic packs with a long, flexible nozzle, ideal for Beetle transmission filling. When completely empty, the transmission should take 4.4 pints (2.5 litres). Refer to Job 87 which describes the procedure for checking the oil level.

INSIDE INFORMATION: In winter, the thick oil will be time-consuming to squeeze out. Stand the bottle (sealed) in hot water for several minutes before using. (Illustration, courtesy Volkswagen)

☐ Job 112. Renew brake fluid.

Brake fluid should be drained out and replaced every two years at most - and preferably every year! This is because brake fluid absorbs moisture from the air which means that there will be a progressive reduction in braking effectiveness: under heavy braking, the absorbed moisture can turn to vapour, creating an air lock in the system and brakes can fail totally and without warning. The moisture will also allow rust to form on the inside of braking components, such as cylinders, pipes etc. The only exception to this rule is silicone fluid, which is non-moisture absorbent, provided that there is no conventional brake fluid mixed in with it.

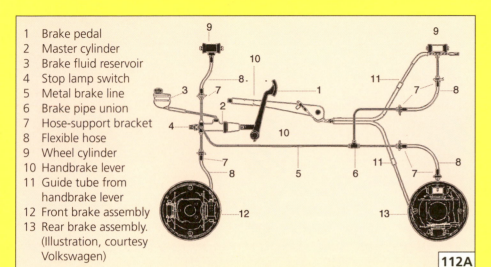

1 Brake pedal
2 Master cylinder
3 Brake fluid reservoir
4 Stop lamp switch
5 Metal brake line
6 Brake pipe union
7 Hose-support bracket
8 Flexible hose
9 Wheel cylinder
10 Handbrake lever
11 Guide tube from handbrake lever
12 Front brake assembly
13 Rear brake assembly.
   (Illustration, courtesy Volkswagen)

112A

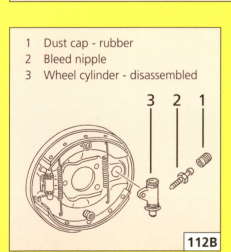

1 Dust cap - rubber
2 Bleed nipple
3 Wheel cylinder - disassembled

112B

HYDRAULIC BRAKED CARS ONLY

INSIDE INFORMATION: Using a small plastic 'squeezy' bottle or syringe, remove as much of the old fluid as you can from the master cylinder. Top up with new fluid and use it to push the old out of the system, as described below.

SAFETY FIRST! and SPECIALIST SERVICE:
Obviously, a car's brakes are among its most important safety related items. Do not dismantle your car's brakes unless you are fully competent to do so. If you have not been trained in this work, but wish to carry out the work described here, we strongly recommend that you have a garage or qualified mechanic check your work before using the car on the road. See also the section on BRAKES AND ASBESTOS in Chapter 1, for further important information.

112C

112A. This diagram shows the component parts of the hydraulic braking system. It's a single master cylinder version, but dual circuit systems are the same in essence, certainly from the point of view of bleeding the hydraulic fluid.

112B. It may also be necessary to bleed the brakes if air finds its way into the system for any reason. This shows as a 'spongy' brake pedal and a diminished braking response.

112C. You can use the old method of bleeding which requires a willing helper with a strong right leg to sit in the car. You'll need a container with some new brake fluid in the bottom - a milk bottle seems to be the favoured receptacle! Run the plastic tube from the brake nipple into the container so that the end is under the fluid level. As the nipple is undone, the helper should press the brake pedal and fluid will start to flow out. Keep going until the discoloured fluid stops coming out, replaced by a stream of clean new fluid.

36,000 MILE SERVICE

MOST IMPORTANT: Don't let the master cylinder run out of brake fluid or you'll add air into the system. Top up every few strokes. Ask the helper to press down the brake pedal hard and hold it, while you tighten the nipple. That's one wheel done, now you can progress around the car, getting ever nearer the master cylinder.

112D. Always start with the wheel furthest from the master cylinder - the left-hand rear on RHD cars. Locate the bleed nipple (112B.2) on the brake back plate. It should be protected by a rubber cover (112B.1). If not, make a note to obtain one and fit after finishing the job. Remove the rubber cover and place a piece of plastic pipe onto the end of the nipple.

You may have to apply a little Castrol Easing oil before the nipple will move. Take your time and use plenty of patience, for if you shear the nipple, it will have to be drilled out of the wheel cylinder (112B.3) or a replacement wheel cylinder will be needed. (Illustration, courtesy Volkswagen)

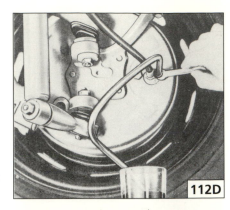
112D

112E. If you prefer an easier life, you can use a brake bleeding tool, such as Gunson's Easi-Bleed. By connecting a receptacle full of brake fluid to the brake fluid reservoir at the front and pressuring it using air from the spare wheel, there is no need for the second person to pump the brakes. As the nipple is undone, fluid/air is forced out under pressure, making this an easy one-person job. But do remember to check the master cylinder and the brake bleeding tool receptacle, and top up regularly with fresh fluid!

112E

☐ **Job 113. Check brake discs.**

DISC BRAKE CARS ONLY

SAFETY FIRST! and SPECIALIST SERVICE:
Obviously, a car's brakes are among its most important safety related items. Do not dismantle your car's brakes unless you are fully competent to do so. If you have not been trained in this work, but wish to carry out the work described here, we strongly recommend that you have a garage or qualified mechanic check your work before using the car on the road. See also the section on BRAKES AND ASBESTOS in Chapter 1, and RAISING A CAR - SAFELY! at the beginning of this Chapter for further important information.

Use a micrometer to measure the thickness of the brake discs. All disc brake cars use discs of the same thickness and diameter. When new, the discs are 0.374 in (9.5 mm) thick. The minimum thickness recommended is 0.335 in (8.5 mm). When your discs reach this stage, replacement is the answer. They are not expensive, particularly not when you consider that they could save your life! Disc replacement is a SPECIALIST SERVICE job.

INSIDE INFORMATION: If the discs are thick enough but badly scored, it is sometimes possible to have an engineering shop skim them down for you. However, we do not recommend it - new discs are not expensive and fitting replacements is always the safest answer. See Job 44 for information on removing and replacing brake pads. When it is time to check the front pads, remove them and wash and scrape out the brake callipers, with proprietary brake cleaner, to reduce the risk of brake squeal and seizure.

SAFETY FIRST!
Only use proprietary brake cleaner, never any other substance when cleaning out the brakes.

☐ **Job 114. Check brake drums.**

First read the **SAFETY FIRST!** and **SPECIALIST SERVICE** note in the previous Job. If this work is carried out in an unskilled manner, the car's braking system could fail totally. If the work is not carried out at all, the system could also fail. Examine thickness and depth of wear of rear brake drums. If excessively scored or worn thin or if any sign of cracking is found, replace. If you don't have sufficient experience to know whether the drums are excessively worn or not, take professional advice from a fully trained mechanic.

INSIDE INFORMATION: Tap the drum, suspended on a piece of string or a hook, to see if it rings true. If it produces a flat note, the drum is cracked and must be replaced. Don't use the car until you have done so.

☐ **Job 115. Brake back plates.**

First read the **SAFETY FIRST!** and **SPECIALIST SERVICE** note at the beginning of Job 112.

INSIDE INFORMATION: Strip and clean the rear brake back plates using brake cleaner (to reduce risk of brake squeal and seizure) and clean out and lubricate the brake adjuster.

24,000 Mile Bodywork and Interior - Around the Car

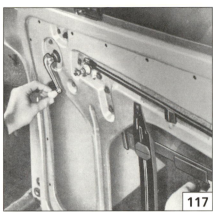

☐ **Job 116. Check lamp seals.**

116. Remove the indicator lenses at the front and the rear lamp lenses and ensure that the seals are effective. If water has been getting in to the lamps, remove the bulbs and smear a light coating of petroleum jelly inside the bulb holder to help prevent rust. Renew the seal.

☐ **Job 117. Maintain window mechanism.**

117. Lubricate the window control mechanism. Take off the door interior trim and lubricate with grease the window winder gear and in particular the channel in which the window runners move.
(Illustration, courtesy Volkswagen)

36,000 Miles - or Every Thirty Six Months, Whichever Comes First

Carry out all of the jobs listed under the earlier service headings before undertaking these additional tasks.

36,000 Mile Mechanical and Electrical - Under the Car

☐ **Job 118. Renew brake pipes, seals and hoses.**

These are jobs requiring **SPECIALIST SERVICE.** Your chosen specialist should examine all brake pipes and flexible hoses with a view to replacement where serious signs of deterioration are present. The rubber hoses in particular are prone to cracking. Whilst this does not necessarily lead to a leak, it could allow the hose to 'bulge' when the brake pedal is applied and thus lead to a loss of braking effect.

Equally, the master cylinder and the wheel cylinders and callipers (where appropriate) will need to be examined. If any sign of fluid leakage is seen - turn back the rubber dust coveron each wheel cylinder to see if any fluid has gathered inside - replace with brand new units.

☐ **Job 119. Lubricate gear change.**

After removing the floor mat, take out the two 13mm bolts that secure the gear change lever plate to the top of the tunnel. When you lift out the gear change lever and plate, be certain that you have made a note of the position of the parts that remain. Remove all the gear change parts and clean them with white spirit to wash out any old grease and embedded dirt. Any of the parts that seem to be worn should be replaced at this stage.

When you reassemble the mechanism, be sure to repack the socket with grease and this will help to cut out gear change lever rattles. Also be certain that the rubber boot which surrounds the bottom of the lever is fitted properly and is not split. This keeps abrasive dirt out of the mechanism and it is most important that it is kept in place. Note that on 1955-67 Beetles - those with a curved gear change lever - the pin on the gear change lever ball must engage with the slot in the socket.

Before road testing the car, ensure that the gear change lever operates correctly and all gears can be engaged. If not, double check your reassembly procedures.

YOU HAVE NOW COMPLETED ALL OF THE SERVICE JOBS LISTED IN THIS SERVICE GUIDE, THE 'LONGEST' INTERVAL BETWEEN ANY JOBS BEING 3 YEARS OR 36,000 MILES. WHEN YOU HAVE FILLED IN EACH OF THE SERVICE INTERVALS SHOWN HERE, YOU MAY PURCHASE CONTINUATION SHEETS TO ENABLE YOU TO CONTINUE AND COMPLETE YOUR SERVICE HISTORY FOR AS LONG AS YOU OWN THE CAR.

PLEASE CONTACT PORTER PUBLISHING AT:

The Storehouse, Little Hereford Street, Bromyard, Hereford, HR7 4DE, England. Tel: 01885 488800.

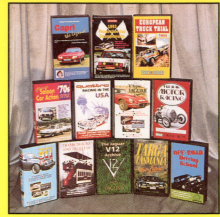
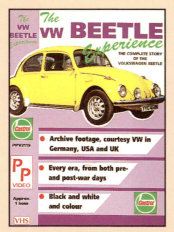
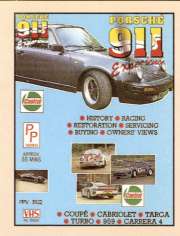

CHAPTER 4
REPAIRING BODYWORK BLEMISHES

However well you look after your car, there will always be the risk of car park accident damage - or even worse! The smallest paint chips are best touched up with paint purchased from your local auto. accessory shop. If your colour of paint is not available, some auto. accessory shops offer a mixing scheme or you could look for a local paint factor in Yellow Pages. Take your car along to the paint factor and have them match the colour and mix the smallest quantity of cellulose paint that they will supply you with.

Larger body blemishes will need the use of body filler. You should only use a filler with a reputable name behind it, such as Isopon P38 Easy Sand and that's what we used to carry out this repair.

SAFETY FIRST!
Always wear plastic gloves when working with any make of filler, before it has set. Always wear a face mask when sanding filler and wear goggles when using a power sander.

4.1

4.2

4.3

4.1 The rear of this car has sustained a nasty gash - the sort of damage for which you will certainly need to use body filler.

4.2 The first stage is to mask off. Try to find "natural" edges such as body mouldings or styling stripes and wherever you can, mask off body trim rather than having to remove it.

4.3 Isopon recommend that you remove all paint from the damaged area and for about 1 in. around the damaged area. Roughen the bare metal or surface with coarse abrasive paper - a power sander is best - and wipe away any loose particles. If you have access to professional spirit wipe, so much the better and the whole area should now be wiped down. If not, wipe over the area with white spirit (mineral spirit) and then wash off with washing-up liquid in water - not car wash detergent.

4.4 Use a piece of plastic on which to mix the filler and hardener, following the instructions on the can.

4.4

4.5 Mix the filler and hardener thoroughly until the colour is consistent and no traces of hardener can be discerned. It's best to use a piece of plastic or metal rather than cardboard because otherwise, the filler will pick up fibres from the surface of the card.

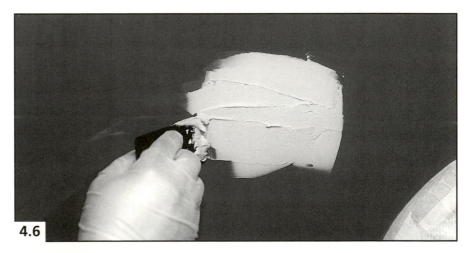

4.5

4.6 You can now spread the filler evenly over the repair.

4.7 If the damage is particularly deep, apply the paste in two or more layers, allowing the filler to harden before adding the next layer. The final layer should be just proud of the level required, but do not overfill as this wastes paste and will require more time to sand down. (Courtesy Isopon)

4.6

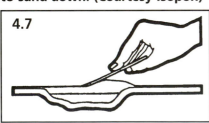

4.7

4.8 It is essential when sanding down that you wrap the sanding paper around a flat block. You can see from the scratch marks that the repair has been sanded diagonally in alternate directions until the filler is level with the surrounding panel but take care not to go deeply into the edges of the paint around the repair.

4.8

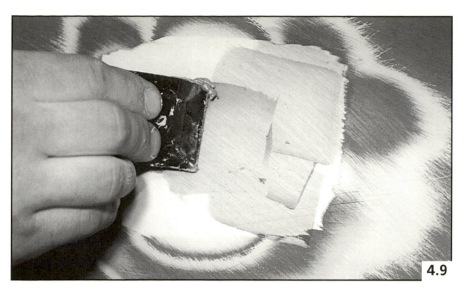

4.9 There will invariably be small pin holes even if, as in this case, the right amount of filler was applied first time. Use a tiny amount of filler scraped very thinly over the whole repair, filling in deep scratches and pin holes and then sanding off with a fine grade of sand paper - preferably dry paper rather than wet-or-dry because you don't want to get water on to the bare filler - until all of the core scratches from the earlier rougher sanding have been removed.

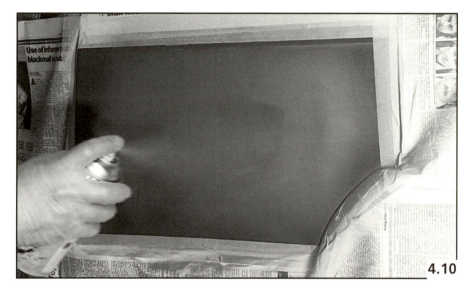

4.10 You can now use an aerosol primer to spray over the whole area of the repair but preferably not right up to the edges of the masking tape...

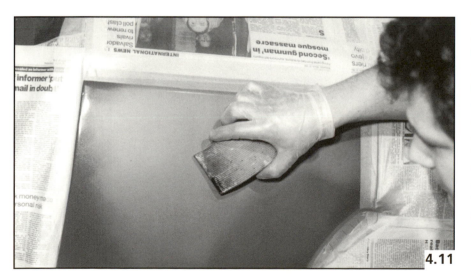

4.11 ...and you can now use wet-or-dry paper, again on a sanding block, to sand the primer paint since the Isopon is now protected from the water by the paint. If you do apply paint right up to the edge of the tape, be sure to 'feather' the edges of the paint, once it has dried off thoroughly (usually next day) so that the edges blend in smoothly to the surrounding surface, with no ridges.

SAFETY FIRST!
Always wear an efficient mask when spraying aerosol paint and only work in a well-ventilated area, well away from any source of ignition, since spray paint vapour, even that given off by an aerosol, is highly flammable. Ensure that you have doors and windows open to the outside when using aerosol paint but in cooler weather, close them when the vapour has dispersed otherwise the surface of the paint will "bloom", or take on a milky appearance. In fact, you may find it difficult to obtain a satisfactory finish in cold and damp weather.

4.12 Before starting to spray, ensure that the nozzle is clear. Note that the can must be held with the index finger well back on the aerosol button. If you let your finger overhang the front of the button, a paint drip can form and throw itself on to the work area as a paint blob. This is most annoying and means that you will have to let the paint dry, sand it down and start again.

4.12

4.13 One of the secrets of getting a decent coat of paint which doesn't run badly is to put a very light coat of spray paint on to the panel first, followed by several more coats, allowing time between each coat for the bulk of the solvent to evaporate. Alternate coats should go horizontally, followed by vertical coats as shown on the inset diagram.

4.14 If carried out with great care and skill, this type of repair can be virtually invisible. After allowing about a week for the paint to dry, you will be able to polish it with a light cutting compound, blending the edges of the repair into the surrounding paintwork.

Do note that if your repairs don't work out first time and you have to apply more paint on top of the fresh paint that you have already used, allow a week to elapse otherwise there is a strong risk of pickling or other reactions taking place. Also note that a prime cause of paint failure is the existence of silicone on the surface of the old paint before you start work. These come from most types of polish and are not all that easy to remove. Thoroughly wipe the panel down with white spirit before starting work and wash off with warm water and washing-up liquid to remove any further traces of the polish and the white spirit - but don't use the sponge or bucket that you normally use for washing the car otherwise you will simply introduce more silicones onto the surface!

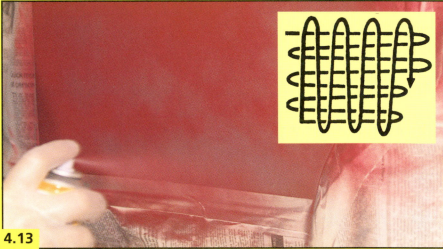

4.13

4.15 We are grateful to W. David & Sons Ltd, the makers of Isopon for their assistance with this section of the book and to CarPlan for their supply of the aerosol paints featured here. Isopon P38 is available in several different sizes of container and can easily be matched to the size of the repair that you have to carry out and all of the products shown here are readily available from high street motorists' stores.

4.14

4.15

CHAPTER 5
RUSTPROOFING

When mechanical components deteriorate, they can cost you a lot of money to replace. But when your Beetle's bodywork deteriorates it can cost you the car, if the deterioration goes beyond the point where the car is economic to repair. Many people believe that the Beetle never rusts, simply because there are still so many Beetles around. This is largely due to the fact that the hefty construction enables the car to outlast virtually everything else on the road. But if rust proofing has been neglected in the past, you may find yourself 'playing catch-up' for some time and even having to have repair sections welded in.

The car used in this section had been restored for owners, Bill and Sandy Beavis. Although it was in excellent condition for its year (1969) it already showed some of the classic Beetle rusting problems - including peeling, hardened underseal.

1A. Contrary to popular myth, the Beetle does rot. Rust around the rear bumper hanger is common.

1B. The whole of the underneath of the rear wheel arch is prone to MoT-failing rot-spots. The chassis mounting point gathers mud (and moisture) as does the section at the front of the wheel arch and, of course the jacking points.

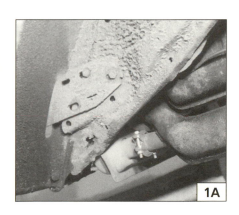

Other places you're likely to find trouble are:-
i) The spare wheel well
ii) Around front bumper hangers
iii) Under the front wheel arches
iv) The lower 'A' pillars (door pillars)
v) Inside the rear 3/4 panels (where the rear doors would be on a four-door car)
vi) Under the rear seat in the battery compartment and opposite.
vii) Sills/heater channels - inside and out
viii) All four wings, particularly around the mounting bolts.

You may have noticed several places in *Chapter 3, Service Intervals Step-by-Step* where checking the cars underbody and topping up its rust preventative treatment is called for. Here's how to carry out that preventative treatment in the first place and, of course, how to reapply it when the time comes. In this chapter, we show the basic principles of rustproofing, but please remember that different models of Beetle have 'access' holes (they weren't put there for that, of course) in different places, so it isn't possible to be too specific about which models have to have holes drilled for injecting wax and which have suitable existing holes.

Do take note of the fact that in Britain, the Automobile Association has carried out research into rustproofing materials and has found that inadequately applied materials do more harm than good. A car's body panels are forever in the process of rusting unless there is a barrier in place to keep out the air and moisture which are necessary to help the rusting process along. However, if that barrier is inefficiently applied, the rusting process seems to concentrate itself on the areas where the rustproofing is missing which speeds up the rusting and makes it worse in those areas. So do take great care that you apply the rustproofing materials used on your car as thoroughly as possible. It's not a question of quantity; more a question of quality of application - reaching every part of the car with a type of rustproofing fluid that "creeps" into each of the seams, into any rust that may have already formed on the surface and using an applicator that applies the fluid in a mist rather than in streams or blobs which unfortunately is all that some of the hand applicators we have seen seem to do.

Also, you should note that the best time to apply rustproofing materials to your car is in the summer when the warmer weather will allow the materials to flow better inside the hidden areas of the car's bodywork and, just as importantly, the underside of the car and the insides of the box sections will be completely dried out. You are always better off applying rust preventative materials when the car is dry than when it is wet simply because although products such as Dinitrol can push aside moisture to get to the metal, they cannot be expected to work through large pools of water!

RUSTPROOFING

Cover all brake friction components with plastic bags to keep them free of the rustproofing material and keep it well away from the clutch bellhousing and from exhaust and heat exchangers.

INSIDE INFORMATION: i) *All electric motors should be covered up with plastic bags so that none of the rustproofing fluids get into the motors (these include power windows and power aerials) and all windows should be fully wound up when injecting fluid inside the door panels.*

ii) *Ensure that all drain channels are clear (see Job 95 in* **Chapter 3, Service Intervals Step-by-Step***) so that any excess rustproofing fluid can drain out and also check once again that they are clear after you have finished carrying out the work to ensure that your application of the fluid has not caused them to be clogged up, otherwise water will get trapped in there, negating much of the good work you have carried out.*

☐ Job 1. Wash Underbody.

You will need to wash off the underside of the car before commencing work, scraping off any thick deposits of mud with a wooden scraper and also remove any loose paint or underseal beneath the car. A power washer is best - a garage forecourt Jet Wash will do if you haven't got your own. You'll have to leave the car for at least a couple of days and preferably a week in warm dry weather so that it dries out properly underneath.

All of the better rustproofing materials manufacturers make two types: one which is "thinner" and which is for applying to box sections and another one which is tougher and is for applying to the undersides of wheel arches and anywhere that is susceptible to blasting from debris thrown up by the wheels.

☐ Job 2. Equipment.

2. Gather together all the materials and equipment you will need to carry out the work. Bear in mind the safety equipment you will need - referred to in Safety First! - see above. The Dinitrol fluid used here comes in canisters to suit the pneumatic gun. You will also need lifting equipment and axle stands - see *Chapter 1, Safety First!* for information on raising and supporting a car above the ground and also the Introduction to *Chapter 3, Service Intervals Step-by-Step*, for the correct procedures to follow when raising your car with a trolley jack. You will need copious amounts of newspaper to spread on the floor because quite a lot of the fluid will run out of the car and you may need to park your car over newspaper for a couple of days after carrying out this treatment. Do remember that the vapour given off will continue for several days and you would be best parking the car out of doors for about a week after carrying out the work shown here.

2

Probably the best known makes of rust preventative fluid in the UK are Waxoyl and Dinitrol. The later product came out top in a survey carried out by Practical Classics magazine. Dinitrol produce a simple applicator which, though being pneumatic, requires a compressor; if you don't have one, they can be hired on a daily rate. This gun is particularly good at atomising the fluid and putting a thorough misting inside each enclosed box section. Hand pumped applicators work so poorly that - in the light of what we said earlier about the need for complete coverage - they can make matters worse, instead of better.

This work for this chapter was carried out at the Motorworld Body shop in Kidlington and relies on the expertise of Roger McNickle of Dinol GB Ltd. Take note of Roger's professional attitude and make it your own. He rustproofed the car using two products, the first being Dinitrol 3654, a cavity wax which gives up to 20 mm penetration into seams. It contains a rust inhibitor that will nullify any minor areas of corrosion. The wax always stays soft and durable so that as the car is driven and the body panels flex the wax will not crack.

Job 3. The front of the car, underbonnet.

3A. Roger started at the front and worked backwards. Here he has already treated the box sections of the bonnet itself and is getting plenty of 3654 down into the back of the 'A' pillar - a notorious place for rotting.

3B. The cavity wax is forced into seams and other tricky places at a high pressure with Roger's professional gear. It may look messy, but great patches of rotten metal look far worse! It's vital to put plenty around the wing mounting bolts, otherwise they'll seize solid, and as a result, a simple wing replacement job could take all weekend.

3C. Everywhere at the front of the car was covered, as you can see. Note that no seam has been missed, the wax creeping into them by capillary action up to 20 mm. Particular care was taken in the spare wheel well and around the front bumper hangers, inside and out. Roger went back to areas like this when he'd finished the car and wiped off the messy excess.

3D. This lip along the edge of the bonnet opening offers an ideal place for rust to start. When he'd finished here, the chrome strips along the side of the car were removed (they prise out easily but take care not to bend them) and the areas behind them treated. He also sprayed the wax into the hollow rear sections of the trim pieces.

3E. Moving further back along the car, more attention was paid to the 'A' pillars. By removing the two grommets accessible from inside the car, more wax could be forced into this rust-prone area.

Job 4. Inside the doors.

4. Doors can be treated in one of two ways - either by drilling a hole in the end of the door and spraying in 'blind' - putting a bung in the hole afterwards - or removing the trim and doing the job properly. Note the protective plastic sheeting which should be replaced once the job is finished, as it prevents moisture from entering the cabin, damaging the trim and carpets. If you find it's missing when you've removed the card trim, take the trouble to fabricate a new one. A suitably sized piece of polythene and some strips of double-sided tape will do the job. The wax was sprayed well down into the bottom of the door skin so that it could creep right down into the various seams. Take great care not to block drain holes.

Job 5. Inner sills and floorpan, under rear seat.

5. The sills on any Beetle are prime rust spots. The constant heating/cooling of the heater channels, which run down each side of the car, creates enormous amounts of moisture which rot the sills from the inside out. The hole shown here is ideal for getting the flexible pipe into. If you feel you're not getting enough coverage, don't be afraid to drill another further down the sill. Fit a bung when you've finished. The nozzle at the end had a 360° spray as well as forward so that no area could be missed. It's important to cover the sill area adjacent to the rear seat and the rear threequarter panel, too. As you can see, this has already been treated. Pull up the carpets (and sound deadening, too) and spray the floorpan. The areas under the rear seat and up into the rear luggage compartment are prone to rot, so they need treating. Remove the battery and make sure that spilled acid has not started to corrode the floorpan (see Job 74). Take careful note of the Beetle's ingenious sill drain holes (See Job 95) and ensure that they are kept clear.

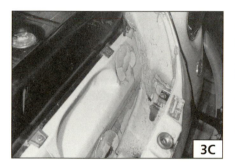

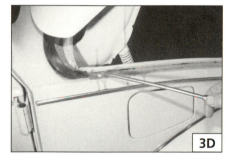

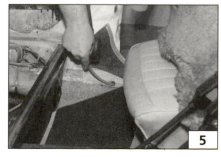

INSIDE INFORMATION: i) Modern VWs come straight from the factory with a coating of protective wax on all the undersides and in the engine bay. It doesn't look very pretty, especially after a few thousand miles worth of dirt and grime have stuck to it, but it does stop rust and rot taking a hold. It also keeps rubber items supple and stops screws from seizing solid. It's a good idea to fol-

low their example and, in order to present a 'clean face' to anyone who looks, wash the wax off with a steam cleaner or with degreaser every two or three years and apply fresh wax.

ii) Always buy any blanking grommets you may want to use - a dozen or so are usually enough - before you drill any holes in the car's underbody. Grommets are often only available in a limited range of sizes and you will find it easier to match a drill to a given size of grommet than the other way around.

SAFETY FIRST! Keep wax off manifolds and any other very hot areas and away from any electrical or brake components and out of the brake master

Job 6. The rear of the car.

6A. At the rear, the box sections on the engine lid were treated...

6B. ...as was this area above the engine bay. This place is often missed, but it is open to rusting because of all the rain water that runs down here and along the gutter.

6C. The sound deadening material was pulled away (it is secured by metal lips which bend back) and more wax was sprayed behind them

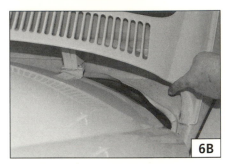

Job 7 Under the car.

7A. Under the car we found the bane of many Beetle owners - hardened underseal! Normal underseal goes on well enough and stays supple for perhaps a few months, but after that it hardens and, ultimately, cracks. This allows moisture to get behind it and stay there, quietly rotting away your precious metal. Loose underseal like this should be scraped away (wear goggles!) and then the surface wire-brushed before applying the wax treatment. Check the whole of the underside before going any further, getting rid of rust, old underseal and dirt. Roger sprayed any areas under the car showing signs of corrosion with 3654 before going on to spray over the top with a thicker black underbody wax which will never crack called '4941'.

INSIDE INFORMATION: When applying thick underseal, it's a good idea to heat it by placing the container in warm water. It is essential that all underbody seams are sprayed with the thinner 'creeping' fluid then covered with the thicker, tougher stuff otherwise the former will be washed back out again. Never heat pressurised containers!

7B. All the box sections underside, such as this area of the hollow central tunnel and rear frame fork, were injected with rustproofer. Don't forget the side running boards. They're not expensive or difficult in themselves to replace, but if they start rotting, they can take the ends of the wings or even the sills with them. If you can, it's a good idea to remove them and treat any corrosion they hide, applying a coating of wax before replacement.

7C. The 4941 surface coating will stick to any surface as long as it is clean and rust-free (even if it has already been treated with 3654). The entire surface should be covered.

7D. The areas under the wings and at the end of the sills (front and rear) were treated from underneath - with the car up on the four post ramp - and from outside, just to make sure. Special care was taken to make sure that the rear chassis mounting points were well-protected. For the ultimate treatment, it's a good idea to remove the wings and apply plenty of wax in between the seal on both sides. Replace the wings and then apply plenty more wax to the seam. This may appear excessive, but moisture needs only the smallest opportunity to start your bodywork rusting.

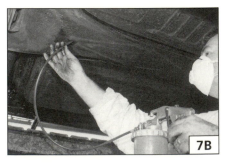

CHAPTER 6 - FAULT FINDING

This Chapter aims to help you to overcome the main faults that can affect the mobility or safety of your car. It also helps you to overcome the problem that has affected most mechanics - amateur and professional - at one time or another... Blind Spot Syndrome!

It goes like this: the car refuses to start one damp Sunday morning. You decide that there must be no fuel getting through. By the time you've stripped the fuel pump, carburettor, fuel lines and "unblocked" the fuel tank, it's time for bed. And the next day, the local garage finds that your main HT lead has dropped out of the coil! Something like that has happened to most of us!

Don't leap to assumptions: if your engine won't start or runs badly, if electrical components fail, follow the logical sequence of checks listed here and detailed overleaf, eliminating each "check" (by testing, not by "hunch") before moving on to the next. Remember that the great majority of failures are caused by electrical or ignition faults: only a minor proportion of engine failures come from the fuel system, follow the sequences shown here - and you'll have better success in finding that fault. Before carrying out any of the work described in this Chapter please read carefully *Chapter 1 Safety First!*

ENGINE WON'T START.

1. Starter motor doesn't turn.

2. Starter motor turns slowly.

3. Starter motor noisy or harsh.

4. Starter motor turns engine but car will not start. See 'Ignition System' box.

5. Is battery okay?

6. Can engine be rotated by hand?

7. Check battery connections for cleanliness/tightness.

8. Test battery with voltmeter.

9. Have battery 'drop' test carried out by specialist.

10. If engine cannot be rotated by hand, check for mechanical seizure of power unit, or pinion gear jammed in mesh with flywheel - 'rock' car backwards and forwards until free, or apply spanner to square drive at front end of starter motor.

11. If engine can be rotated by hand, check for loose electrical

connections at starter, faulty solenoid, or defective starter motor.

12. Battery low on charge or defective - re-charge and have 'drop' test carried out by specialist.

13. Internal fault within starter motor - e.g. worn brushes.

14. Drive teeth on ring gear or starter pinion worn/broken.
15. Main drive spring broken.

16. Starter motor securing bolts loose.

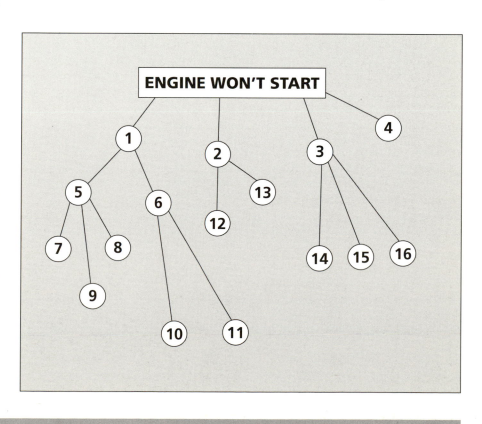

IGNITION SYSTEM.

17. Check for spark at plug (remove plug and prop it with threads resting on bare metal of cylinder block). Do not touch plug or lead while operating starter.

18. If no spark present at plug, check for spark at contact breaker points when 'flicked' open (ignition 'on'). Double-check to ensure that points are clean and correctly gapped, and try again.

19. If spark present at contact breaker points, check for spark at central high tension lead from coil.

20. If spark present at central high tension lead from coil, check distributor cap and rotor arm; replace if cracked or contacts badly worn.

21. If distributor cap and rotor arm are okay, check high tension leads and connections - replace leads if they are old, carbon core type suppressed variety.

22. If high tension leads are sound but dirty or damp, clean/dry them.

23. If high tension leads okay, check/clean/dry/re-gap sparking plugs.

24. Damp conditions? Apply water dispellant spray to ignition system.

25. If no spark present at contact breaker points, examine connections of low tension leads between ignition switch and coil, and from coil to contact breaker (including short low-tension lead within distributor).

26. If low tension circuit connections okay, examine wiring.

27. If low tension wiring is sound, is condenser okay? If in doubt, fit new condenser.

28. If condenser is okay, check for spark at central high tension lead from coil.

29. If no spark present at central high tension lead from coil, check for poor high tension lead connections.

30. If high tension lead connections okay, is coil okay? If in doubt, fit new coil.

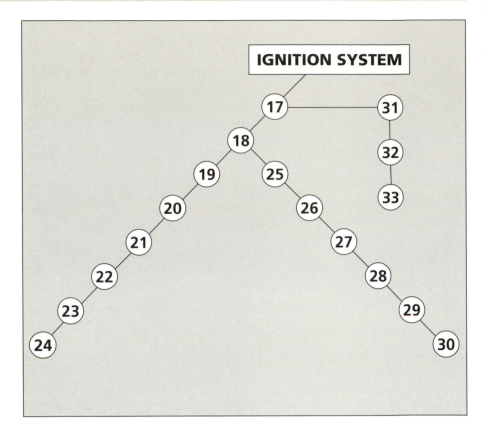

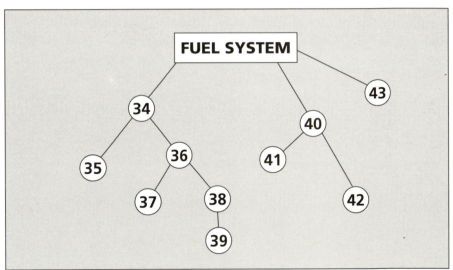

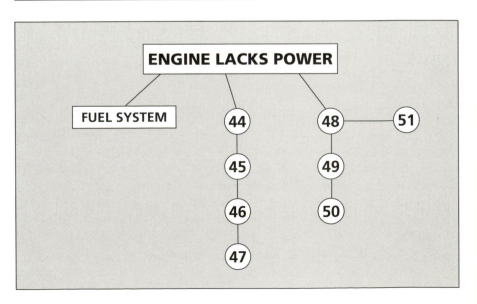

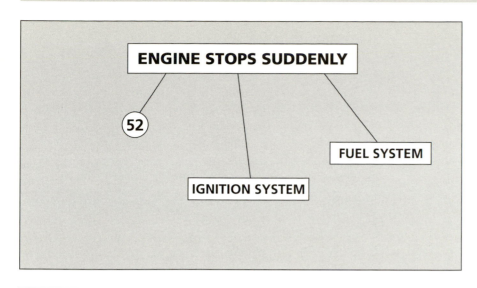

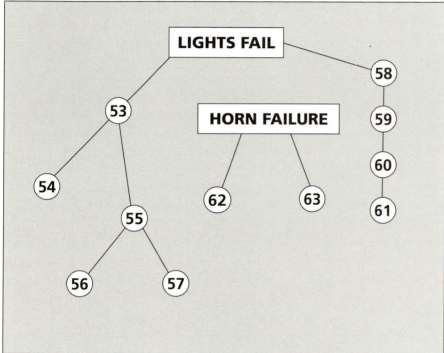

(Rock car and listen for 'sloshing' in tank, as well as looking at gauge).

35. If tank is empty, replenish!

36. If there is petrol in the tank but none issues from the feed pipe from pump to carburettor, check that the small vent hole in the fuel filler cap is not blocked and causing a vacuum.

37. Check for a defective fuel pump. With outlet pipe disconnected AND AIMED AWAY FROM PUMP AND HOT EXHAUST COMPONENTS, ETC. as well as your eyes and clothes, and into a suitable container, turn the engine over and fuel should issue from pump outlet.

38. If pump is okay, check for blocked fuel filter or pipe, or major leak in pipe between tank and pump, or between pump and carb.

39. If the filter is clean and the pump operates, suspect blocked carburettor jet(s) or damaged/sticking float, or incorrectly adjusted carburettor.
40. If fuel is present at carburettor feed pipe, remove spark plugs and check whether wet with unburnt fuel.

41. If the spark plugs are fuel-soaked, check that the automatic choke is operating as it should and is not jammed 'shut'. Other possibilities include float needle valve(s) sticking 'open' or leaking, float punctured, carburettor incorrectly adjusted or air filter totally blocked. Clean plugs before replacing.

42. If the spark plugs are dry, check whether the float needle valve is jammed 'shut'.

43. Check for severe air leak at inlet manifold gasket or carburettor gasket. Incorrectly set valve clearances.

31. If spark present at plug, is it powerful or weak? If weak, see '27'.

32. If spark is healthy, check ignition timing.

33. If ignition timing is okay, see 'Fuel System' box. (see 36).

FUEL SYSTEM.

34. Check briefly for fuel at feed pipe to carb. (Disconnect pipe and turn ignition 'on', ensuring pipe is aimed away from hot engine and exhaust components and into a suitable container). If no fuel present at feed pipe, is petrol tank empty?

FUEL SYSTEM - SAFETY FIRST!
*Before working on the fuel system, read **Chapter 1, Safety First!** Take special care to 1) only work out of doors, 2) wear suitable gloves and goggles and keep fuel out of eyes and away from skin: it is known to be carcinogenic, 3) if fuel does come into contact with skin, wash off straight away, 4) if fuel gets into your eyes, wash out with copious amounts of clean, cold water. Seek medical advice if necessary, 5) when draining fuel or testing for fuel flow, drain or pump into a sufficiently large container, minimising splashes, 6) don't smoke, work near flames or sparks or work when the engine or exhaust are hot.*

ENGINE LACKS POWER.

44. Engine overheating. Check oil temperature gauge (where fitted). Low oil pressure light may come on.

45. Thermostat not opening/closing at the correct temperatures or the cooling air flaps not operating because they've seized. Replace or free-off as necessary.

FAULT FINDING

46. If thermostat/air flaps okay, check oil level. BEWARE - DIPSTICK AND OIL MAY BE VERY HOT.

47. If oil level okay, check for slipping fan belt, cylinder head gasket 'blown', partial mechanical seizure of engine, blocked or damaged exhaust system.

48. If engine temperature is normal, check cylinder compressions.

49. If cylinder compression readings low, add a couple of teaspoons of engine oil to each cylinder in turn, and repeat test. If readings don't improve, suspect burnt valves/seats.

50. If compression readings improve after adding oil as described, suspect worn cylinder bores, pistons and rings.

51. If compression readings are normal, check for mechanical problems, for example, binding brakes, slipping clutch, partially seized transmission, etc.

ENGINE STOPS SUDDENLY.

52. Check for sudden ingress of water/snow onto ignition components, in adverse weather conditions. Sudden failure is almost always because of an ignition fault. Check for simple wiring and connection breakdowns.

LIGHTS FAIL.

53. Sudden failure - check fuses.

54. If all lamps affected, check switch and main wiring feeds.

55. If not all lamps are affected, check bulbs on lamps concerned.

56. If bulbs appear to be okay, check bulb holder(s), local wiring and connections.

57. If bulb(s) blown, replace!

58. Intermittent operation, flickering or poor light output, check connections inside lamp housings/bulb holders.

59. Check earth (ground) connections(s).

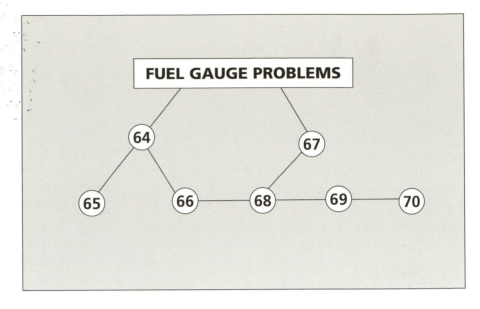

60. If earth(s) okay, check switch.
61. If switch okay, check wiring and connections.

HORN FAILURE.

62. If horn does not operate, check fuse, all connections (particularly earths/grounds) and cables. Remove horn connections and check/clean. Use 12v/6v test lamp to ascertain power getting to horn. On 6v cars, start engine - battery sometimes not charged enough to sound horn.

63. If horn will not stop(!), disconnect the horn and check for earthing of horn button or cable between button and horn unit and the wiring and contacts in the horn switch and steering column tube. The Beetle's brown wire can often short itself out at the lower end of the steering tube - check!

FUEL GAUGE PROBLEMS.

64. Gauge reads 'empty' - check for fuel in tank. Rock car from side-to-side and listen for sound of fuel 'sloshing' around inside tank.

65. If no fuel present, replenish!

66. If fuel is present in tank, check for earthing of wiring from tank to gauge, and for wiring disconnections. On many models, gauge is mechanical - check cable is sound from gauge to tank and that it is not trapped.

67. Gauge permanently reads 'full', regardless of tank contents. Check wiring and connections as in '66'.

68. If wiring and connections all okay, sender unit/fuel gauge defective.

69. With wiring disconnected, check for continuity between fuel gauge terminals. Do NOT test gauge by short-circuiting to earth. Replace unit if faulty.

70. If gauge is okay, disconnect wiring from tank sender unit and check for continuity between terminal and case. Replace sender unit if faulty.

CHAPTER 7
GETTING THROUGH THE MOT

Taking your beloved Beetle for the annual MoT test can be rather like going to the dentist - you're not sure what to expect and the result could be painful - not only to your pocket! However, it needn't be like that...

This Chapter is for owners in Britain whose cars need to pass the 'MoT' test. The Test was first established in 1961 by the then-named Ministry of Transport: the name of the Test remains, even though the name of the government department does not!

The information in this Chapter could be very useful to non-UK owners in helping to carry out a detailed check of a car's condition - such as when checking over a car that you might be interested in buying, for instance. But it is MOST IMPORTANT that UK owners check for themselves that legislation has not changed since this book was written and that non-UK owners obtain information on the legal requirements in their own territory - and that they act upon them.

PASS THE MoT!

The aim of this chapter is to explain what is actually tested on a Beetle and (if it is not obvious) how the test is done. This should enable you to identify and eliminate problems before they undermine the safety or diminish the performance of your car and long before they cause the expense and inconvenience of a test failure.

SAFETY FIRST!
The MoT tester will follow a set procedure and we will cover the ground in a similar way, starting inside the car, then continuing outside, under the bonnet, underneath the car etc. When preparing to go underneath the car, do ensure that it is jacked on firm level ground and then supported on axle stands or ramps which are adequate for the task. Wheels which remain on the ground should have chocks in front of and behind them, and while the rear wheels remain on the ground, the handbrake should be firmly ON. For most repair and replacement jobs under a car these normal precautions will suffice. However, the car needs to be even more stable than usual when carrying out these checks. There must be no risk of it toppling off its stands while suspension and steering components are being pushed and pulled in order to test them. Read carefully Chapter 1, Safety First! for further important information on raising and supporting the car above the ground.

The purpose of the MoT test is to try to ensure that vehicles using British roads reach minimum standards of safety. Accordingly, it is an offence to use a car without a current MoT certificate. Approximately 40 per cent of vehicles submitted for the test fail it, but many of these failures could be avoided by knowing what the car might 'fall down' on, and by taking appropriate remedial action before the test 'proper' is carried out. It is also worth noting that a car can be submitted for a test up to a month before the current certificate expires - if the vehicle passes, the new certificate will be valid until one year from the date of expiry of the old one, provided that the old certificate is produced at the time of the test.

It is true that the scope of the test has been considerably enlarged in the last few years, with the result that it is correspondingly more difficult to be sure that your VW will reach the required standards. In truth, however, a careful examination of the car in the relevant areas, perhaps a month or so before the current certificate expires, will highlight components which require attention, and enable any obvious faults to be rectified before you take the car for its test.

If the car is muddy or particularly dirty (especially underneath) it would be worth giving it a thorough clean a day or two before carrying out the inspection so that it has ample time to dry. Do the same before the real MoT test. A clean car makes a better impression on the examiner, who can refuse to test a car which is particularly dirty underneath.

GETTING THROUGH THE MOT

MoT testers do not dismantle assemblies during the test but you may wish to do so during your pre-test check-up for a better view of certain wearing parts, such as the rear brake shoes for example. See *Chapter 3, Service Intervals Step-by-Step* for information on how to check the brakes.

TOOL BOX

Dismantling apart, few tools are needed for testing. A light hammer is useful for tapping panels underneath the car when looking for rust. If this produces a bright metallic noise, then the area being tapped is solid metal. If the noise produced is dull, the area contains rust or filler. When tapping sills and box sections, listen also for the sound of debris (that is, rust flakes) on the inside of the panel. Use a screwdriver to prod weak parts of panels. This may produce holes of course, but if the panels have rusted to that extent, you really ought to know about it. A strong lever (such as a tyre lever) can be useful for applying the required force to suspension joints etc. when assessing whether there is any wear in the joints.

You will need an assistant to operate controls and perhaps to wobble the road wheels while you inspect components under the car.

Two more brief explanations are required before we start our informal test. Firstly, the age of the car determines exactly which lights, seat belts and other items it should have. Frequently in the next few pages you will come across the phrase "Cars first used ..." followed by a date. A car's "first used date" is either its date of first registration, or the date six months after it was manufactured, whichever was earlier. Or, if the car was originally used without being registered (such as a car which has been imported to the U.K. or an ex-H.M. Forces car) the "first used date" is the date of manufacture.

Secondly, there must not be excessive rust, serious distortion or any fractures affecting certain prescribed areas of the bodywork. These prescribed areas are load-bearing parts of the bodywork within 30 cm. (12 in.) of anchorages or mounting points associated with testable items such as seat belts, brake pedal assemblies, master cylinders, servos, suspension and steering components and also body mountings. Keep this rule in mind while inspecting the car, but remember also that even if such damage occurs outside a prescribed area, it can cause failure of the test. Failure will occur if the damage is judged to reduce the continuity or strength of a main load-bearing part of the bodywork sufficiently to have an adverse effect on the braking or steering.

The following notes are necessarily abbreviated, and are for assistance only. They are not a definitive guide to all the MoT regulations. It is also worth mentioning that the varying degrees of discretion of individual MoT testers can mean that there are variations between the standards as applied. However, the following points should help to make you aware of the aspects which will be examined. Now, if you have your clipboard, checklist and pencil handy, let's make a start...

THE 'EASY' BITS

Checking these items is straightforward and should not take more than a few minutes - it could avoid an embarrassingly simple failure...

LIGHTS:

Within the scope of the test are headlamps, side and tail lights, brake lamps, direction indicators, and number plate lamps (plus rear fog lamps on all cars first used on or after 1 April, 1980, and any earlier cars subsequently so equipped, and also hazard warning lamps on any car so fitted). All must operate, must be clean and not significantly damaged; flickering is also not permitted. The switches should also all work properly. Pairs of lamps should give approximately the same intensity of light output, and operation of one set of lights should not affect the working of another - such trouble is usually due to bad earthing.

Indicators should flash at between 60 and 120 times per minute. Rev the engine to encourage them, if a little slow (often the case on 6v cars), although the examiner might not let you get away with it! Otherwise, renew the (inexpensive) flasher unit and check all wiring and earth connections.

Interior 'tell-tale' lamps, such as for indicators, rear fog lamps and hazard warning lamps should all operate in unison with their respective exterior lamps. Owners of early models with semaphore type indicators should note that a tell-tale is not a requirement as long as one or more of the indicators on each side can be seen from the driving seat.

Head light aim must be correct - in particular, the lights should not dazzle other road users. An approximate guide can be obtained by shining the lights against a vertical wall, but final adjustment may be necessary by reference to the beam checking machine at the MoT station. Most testers will be happy to make slight adjustments where necessary but only if the adjusters work make sure before you take the car in that they are not seized solid!

Reflectors must be unbroken, clean, and not obscured - for example, by stickers.

WHEELS AND TYRES

Check the wheels for loose nuts, cracks, and damaged rims. Missing wheel nuts or studs are also failure points, naturally enough!

There is no excuse for running on illegal tyres. The legal requirement is that there must be at least 1.6 mm. of tread depth remaining, over the 'central' three-quarters of the width of the tyre all the way around. From this it can be deduced that there is no legal requirement to have 1.6 mm. (1/16 in.) of tread on the 'shoulders' of the tyre, but in practice, most MoT stations will be reluctant to pass a tyre in this condition. In any case, for optimum safety - especially 'wet grip' - you would be well advised to change tyres when they wear down to around 3 mm. (1/8 in.) or so depth of remaining tread.

Visible 'tread wear indicator bars', found approximately every nine inches around the tread of modern tyres, are highlighted when the tread reaches the critical 1.6 mm. point.

Tyres should not show signs of cuts or bulges, rubbing on the bodywork or running gear, and the valves should be in sound condition, and correctly aligned.

Cross-ply and radial tyre types must not be mixed on the same axle (i.e. the front or rear of the car), and if pairs of cross-ply and radial tyres are fitted, the radials must be on the rear axle (rear end).

WINDSCREEN

The screen must not be damaged (by cracks, chips, etc.) or obscured so that the driver does not have a clear view of the road. See *Inside the Car, Check 4.* below.

WASHERS AND WIPERS

The wipers must clear an area big enough to give the driver a clear view forwards and to the side of the car. The wiper blades must be securely attached and sound, with no cracks or 'missing' sections. The wiper switch should also work properly. The screen washers must supply the screen with sufficient liquid to keep it clean, in conjunction with the use of the wipers.

MIRRORS

If your Beetle was first used before 1 August, 1978 (ie. most of them), it doesn't need by law to have an exterior mirror in addition to its interior mirror. Later cars must have at least two mirrors, one of which must be on the driver's side. The mirrors must be visible from the driver's seat, and not be damaged or obscured so that the view to the rear is affected. Therefore cracks, chips and discolouration can mean failure.

HORN

The horn must emit a uniform note which is loud enough to give adequate warning of approach, and the switch must operate correctly. Multi-tone horns playing 'in sequence' are not permitted, but two tones sounding together are fine.

SEAT SECURITY

The seats must be securely mounted, and the sub-frames should be sound.

NUMBER (REGISTRATION) PLATES

Both front and rear number plates must be present, and in good condition, with no breaks or missing numbers or letters. The plates must not be obscured, and the digits must not be repositioned (to form names, for instance).

VEHICLE IDENTIFICATION NUMBERS (VIN)

Beetles first used on or after 1 August, 1980 are obliged to have a clearly displayed VIN - Vehicle Identification Number (or old-fashioned 'chassis number' for older cars), which is plainly legible. See *Chapter 2, Buying Spares* for the correct location on your car.

EXHAUST SYSTEM

The entire system must be present, properly mounted, free of leaks and should not be noisy - which can happen when the internal baffles fail. 'Proper' repairs by welding, or exhaust cement, or bandage are acceptable, as long as no gas leaks are evident. Then again, common sense, if not the MoT, dictates that exhaust bandage should only be a very short-term emergency measure. For safety's sake, fit a new exhaust if yours is reduced to this!

SEAT BELTS

Belts are not needed on Beetles first used before 1 January, 1965. On cars after this date - and earlier examples, if subsequently fitted with seat belts - the belts must be in good condition (i.e. not frayed or otherwise damaged), and the buckles and catches should also operate correctly. Inertia reel types, where fitted, should retract properly.

Belt mountings must be secure, with no structural damage or corrosion within 30 cm. (12 in.) of them.

MORE DETAILS

You've checked the easy bits - now it's time for the detail! Some of the 'easy bits' referred to above are included here, but this is intended as a more complete check list to give your car the best possible chance of gaining a First Class Honours, MoT Pass!

INSIDE THE CAR

☐ 1. The steering wheel should be examined for cracks and for damage which might interfere with its use, or injure the driver's hands. It should also be pushed and pulled along the column axis, and also up and down, at 90 degrees to it. This will highlight any deficiencies in the wheel and upper column mounting/bearing, and also any excessive end float, and movement between the column shaft and the wheel. Rotate the steering wheel in both directions to test for free play at the wheel rim - this shouldn't exceed approximately 75 mm. (3.0 in.), assuming a 380 mm. (15 in.) diameter steering wheel. Look, too, for movement in the steering column couplings and fasteners, and visually check their condition and security. They must be sound, and properly tightened.

☐ 2. Check that the switches for headlamps, sidelights, direction indicators, hazard warning lights, wipers, washers and horn, appear to be in good working order and check that the tell-tale lights or audible warnings are working where applicable.

☐ 3. Make sure that the windscreen wipers operate effectively with blades that are secure and in good condition. The windscreen washer should provide sufficient liquid to clear the screen in conjunction with the wipers.

☐ 4. Check for windscreen damage, especially in the area swept by the wipers. From the MoT tester's point of view, Zone A is part of this area, 290 mm. (11.5 in.) wide and centred on the centre of the steering wheel. Damage to the screen within this area should be capable of fitting into a 10 mm. (approx. 0.4 in.) diameter circle and the cumulative effect of more minor damage should not seriously restrict the driver's view. Windscreen stickers or other obstructions should not encroach more than 10 mm. (approx 0.4 in.) into this area. In the remainder of the area swept by the wiper, the maximum diameter of damage or degree of encroachment by obstructions

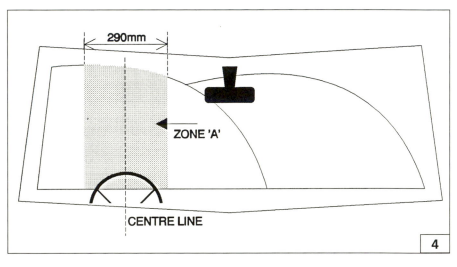

is 40 mm. (approx. 1.6 in.) and there is no ruling regarding cumulative damage. Specialist windscreen companies can often repair a cracked screen for a lot less than the cost of replacement. Moreover, the cost of repair is often covered by comprehensive insurance policies without excess but check first that your no-claims discount won't suffer!

☐ 5. The horn control should be present, secure and readily accessible to the driver, and the horn should be loud enough to be heard by other road users. Gongs, bells and sirens are not permitted (except as part of an anti-theft device) and multi- tone horns (which alternate between two or more notes) are not permitted at all. On cars first used after 1 August 1973, the horn should produce a constant, continuous or uniform note which is neither harsh nor grating.

☐ 6. After 1 August 1978 there must be one exterior mirror on the driver's side of the vehicle and either an exterior mirror fitted to the passenger's side or an interior mirror. The required mirrors should be secure and in good condition.

☐ 7. Check that the handbrake operates effectively without coming to the end of its working travel. The lever and its mechanism must be complete, securely mounted, unobstructed in its travel and in a sufficiently good condition to remain firmly in the "On" position even when knocked from side to side. The rule regarding bodywork corrosion applies in the vicinity of the handbrake lever mounting: there must be none within 30 cm (12 in.).

☐ 8. The foot brake pedal assembly should be complete, unobstructed, and in a good working condition, including the pedal rubber (which should not have been worn smooth). There should be no excessive movement of the pedal at right angles to its normal direction. When fully depressed, the pedal should not be at the end of its travel. The pedal should not feel spongy (indicating air in the hydraulic system), nor should it tend to creep downwards while held under pressure (which indicates an internal hydraulic leak).

☐ 9. Seats must be secure on their mountings and seat backs must be capable of being locked in the upright position. However, if your Beetle is of an age where it was not part of the original design for the seat back to be locked, it will not be an MoT failure point.

☐ 10. On Beetles first used on or after 1 January 1965, but before 1 April 1981, the driver's and front passenger's seats must be fitted with belts, though these can be simple diagonal belts rather than the three-point belts (lap and diagonal belts for adults with at least three anchorage points) required by later cars. For safety's sake, however, we do not recommend this type of belt. Rear seat belts are a requirement for cars first used after 31 March 1987. Examine seat belt webbing and fittings to make sure that all are in good condition and that anchorages are firmly attached to the car's structure. Locking mechanisms should be capable of remaining locked, and of being released if required, when under load. Flexible buckle stalks (if fitted) should be free of corrosion, broken cable strands or other weaknesses. Note that any belts fitted which are not part of a legal requirement may be examined by the tester but will not form part of the official test.

☐ 11. On inertia reel belts, check that on retracting the belts the webbing winds into the retracting unit automatically, albeit with some manual assistance to start with.

☐ 12. Note the point raised earlier regarding corrosion around seat belt anchorage points. The MoT tester will not carry out any dismantling here, but he will examine floor mounted anchorage points from underneath the car if that is possible.

☐ 13. Before getting out of the car, make sure that both doors can be opened from the inside.

OUTSIDE THE CAR

☐ 14. Before closing the driver's door check the condition of the inner sill. Usually the MoT tester will do this by applying finger or thumb pressure to various parts of the panel while the floor covering remains in place. For your own peace of mind, look beneath the sill covering, taking great care not to tear any rubber covers. Then close the driver's door and make sure that it latches securely and repeat these checks on the nearside inner sill and door.

Now check all of the lights, front and rear, (and the number plate lights) while your assistant operates the light switches.

☐ 15. As we said earlier, you can carry out a rough and ready check on head lamp alignment for yourself, although it will certainly not be as accurate as having it done for you at the MoT testing station. Drive your car near to a wall, as shown. Check that your tyres are correctly inflated and the car is on level ground.

Draw on the wall, with chalk:

a horizontal line about 2 metres long, and at same height as centre of head lamp lens.

two vertical lines about 1 metre long, each forming a cross with the horizontal line and the same distance apart as the head lamp centres.

another vertical line to form a cross on the horizontal line, midway between the others.

Now position your car so that:

it faces the wall squarely, and its centre line is in line with centre line marked on the wall.

the steering is straight.

head light lenses are 5.0 metres (16 ft) from the wall.

Switch on the headlamps' 'main' and 'dipped' beams in turn, and measure their centre points. You will be able to judge any major discrepancies in intensity and aim prior to having the beams properly set by a garage with beam measuring equipment.

Headlamps should be complete, clean, securely mounted, in good working order and not adversely affected by the operation of another lamp, and these basic requirements affect all the lamps listed below. Headlamps must dip as a pair from a single switch. Their aim must be correctly adjusted and they should not be affected (even to the extent of flickering) when lightly tapped by hand. Each head lamp should match its partner in terms of size, colour and intensity of light, and can be white or yellow.

☐ 16. Side lights should show white light to the front and red light to the rear. Lenses should not be broken, cracked or incomplete.

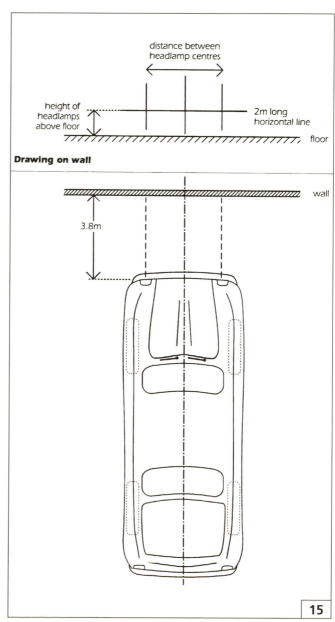

distance between headlamp centres

height of headlamps above floor

2m long horizontal line

floor

Drawing on wall

wall

3.8m

15

☐ 17. Vehicles first used before 1 April 1986 do not have to have a hazard warning device, but if one is fitted, it must be tested, and it must operate with the ignition switched either on or off. The lights should flash 60-120 times per minute, and indicators must operate independently of any other lights.

☐ 18. Check your stop lights. Pre-1971 cars need only one, but when two are fitted, both are tested, so you will not get away with one that works and one that doesn't! Stop lamps should produce a steady red light when the foot brake is applied.

☐ 19. There must be two red rear reflectors - always fitted by the manufacturers, of course! - which are clean, and securely and symmetrically fitted to the car.

☐ 20. Cars first used on or after 1 April 1980 must have at least one rear fog lamp, fitted to the centre or offside of the car and, as far as fog lamps are concerned, the MoT tester is interested in this lamp on these cars only. It must comply with the basic requirements (listed under headlamps) and emit a steady red light. Its tell-tale lamp, inside the car, must work to inform the driver that it is switched on.

☐ 21. There must be a registration number plate at the front and rear of the car and both must be clean, secure, complete and unobscured. Letters and figures must be correctly formed and correctly spaced and not likely to be misread due to an uncovered securing bolt or whatever. The year letter counts as a figure. The space between letters and figures must be at least twice that between adjacent letters or figures.

☐ 22. Number plate lamps must be present, working, and must not flicker when tapped by hand, just as for other lamps. Where more than one lamp or bulb was fitted as original equipment, all must be working.

The MoT tester will examine tyres and wheels while walking around the car and again when he is under the car.

☐ 23. Front tyres should match each other and rear tyres should match each other, both sets matching in terms of size, aspect ratio and type of structure. For example, you must never fit tyres of different sizes or types, such as cross-ply or radial, on the same 'axle' - both front or rear wheels counting as 'on the same axle' in this context. If cross-ply or bias belted tyres are fitted to the rear of the car, you must not fit radials to the front. If cross-ply tyres are fitted to the rear, bias belted tyres should not be fitted to the front. (We recommend that you do not mix tyre types anywhere on the car.)

☐ 24. Failure of the test can be caused by a cut, lump, tear or bulge in a tyre, exposed ply or cord, a badly seated tyre, a re-cut tyre, a tyre fouling part of the vehicle, or a seriously damaged or misaligned valve stem which could cause sudden deflation of the tyre. To pass the test, the grooves of the tread pattern must be at least 1.6 mm. deep throughout a continuous band comprising the central three-quarters of the breadth of tread, and round the entire outer circumference of the tyre.

The following six photographs and information in this section have been supplied, with grateful thanks, by Dunlop/SP Tyres.

☐ 24A. Modern tyres have tread wear indicators built into the tread groves (usually about eight of them spread equidistantly around the circumference). These appear as continuous bars running across the tread when the original pattern depth has worn down to 1.6 mm. There will be a distinct reduction in wet grip well before the tread wear indicators start to show, and you should replace tyres before they get to this stage, even though this is the legal minimum in the UK.

NEW TYRE — TWI — ILLEGAL TYRE 24A

☐ 24B. Lumps and bulges in the tyre wall usually arise from accidental damage or even because of faults in the tyre construction. You should run your hand all the way around the side wall of the tyre, with the car either jacked off the ground, or moving the car half a wheels revolution, so that you can check the part of the tyre that was previously resting on the ground. Since you can't easily check the insides of the tyres in day-to-day use, it is even more important that you spend time carefully checking the inside of each tyre - the MoT tester will certainly do so! Tyres with bulges in them must be scrapped and replaced with new, since they can fail suddenly, causing your car to lose control.

☐ 24C. Abrasion of the tyre side wall can take place either in conjunction with bulging, or by itself, and this invariably results from an impact, such as the tyre striking the edge of a kerb or a pothole in the road. Once again, the tyre may be at imminent risk or failure and you should take advice from a tyre specialist on whether the abrasion is just superficial, or whether the tyre will need replacement.

24B

24C

24D

☐ 24D. All tyres will suffer progressively from cracking, albeit in most cases superficially, due to the effects of sunlight. If old age has caused the tyres on your car to degrade to this extent, replace them.

☐ 24E. If the outer edges of the tread are worn noticeably more than at the centre, the tyres have been run under-inflated which not only ruins tyres, but causes worse fuel consumption, dangerous handling and is, of course, illegal.

Over-inflation causes the centre part of the tyre to wear more quickly than the outer edges. This is also illegal but in addition, it causes the steering and grip to suffer and the tyre becomes more susceptible to concussion damage.

24E

24F

☐ 24F. Incorrect wheel alignment causes one side of the tyre to wear more severely than the other. If your car should ever hit a kerb or large pothole, it is worthwhile having the wheel alignment checked since this costs considerably less than new front tyres!

☐ 25. Road wheels must be secure and must not be badly damaged, distorted or cracked, or have badly distorted bead rims (perhaps due to "kerbing"), or loose or missing wheel nuts, studs or bolts.

☐ 26. Check the bodywork for any sharp edges or projections, caused by corrosion or damage, which could prove dangerous to other road users, including pedestrians.

☐ 27. Check that the fuel cap fastens securely and that its sealing washer is neither torn nor deteriorated, or its mounting flange damaged sufficiently to allow fuel to escape (for example, while the car is cornering).

UNDER THE BONNET (LUGGAGE COMPARTMENT)

☐ 28. The car should have a Chassis Number or Vehicle Identification Number fitted to the bodywork. The modern VIN plate is required on all vehicles first used on or after 1 August 1980. This can be on a plate secured to the vehicle or, etched or stamped on the bodywork. In general, Beetles have an identification plate in the luggage compartment and the chassis number under the rear seat. See *Chapter 8, Facts and Figures* and *Chapter 2, Buying Spares* for more information.

☐ 29. While peering under the bonnet check that hydraulic reservoir is securely mounted and not damaged. Ensure that the cap is present, that the fluid levels are satisfactory and that there are no fluid leaks.

☐ 30. Still under the bonnet, make a thorough search for evidence of excessive corrosion, severe distortion or fracture in any load bearing panelling within 30 cm. (12 in.) of important mounting points such as the master cylinder/servo mounting, front suspension mountings etc.

UNDER THE CAR - FRONT END

SAFETY FIRST!
On some occasions there is no alternative but for your assistant to sit in the car whilst you go beneath. Therefore: 1) Place the car ramps as well as axle stands beneath the car's structure so that it cannot fall. 2) Don't allow your assistant to move vigorously or get in or out of the car while you are beneath it. If either of these are problematical, DON'T CARRY OUT THIS CHECK - leave it to your garage.

☐ 31. Have an assistant turn the steering wheel from side to side while you watch for movement in the steering mechanism. Make sure that the steering box is securely clamped to the axle tube (on relevant models), that the ball joints show no signs of wear and that the ball joint dust covers are in sound condition. Ensure that all split pins, locking nuts and so on are in place and correctly fastened, throughout the steering and suspension systems.

☐ 32. Check the steering column universal joint and clamp bolts (where applicable) for wear and looseness by asking your assistant to turn the steering wheel from side to side while you watch what happens to the wheels. More than 75 mm. (approx. 3 in.) of free play at the perimeter of the steering wheel, due to wear in the steering components, is sufficient grounds for a test failure. Note that the 75 mm. criterion is based on a steering wheel of 380 mm. (15 in.) diameter and will be less for smaller steering wheels. Also check for the presence and security of any locking device in the steering column assembly (i.e. it must work if fitted) (depending on year and model).

☐ 33. Examine the torsion bars (and their attachments) to ensure that they are free from cracks, fractures and excessive corrosion and pitting. In addition, check the end fixings for security and excessive free play.

☐ 34. With the front of the car raised, and securely supported on axle stands (with the wheels clear of the ground), grasp each front wheel/tyre in turn at top and bottom, and attempt to 'rock' the wheel in and out. If more than just perceptible movement is evident at the rim, this could be due to wear in the king (swivel) pins and bushes (on earlier models), or in the front wheel bearings. Repeat the test while an assistant applies the foot brake. This will effectively lock the hub to the stub axle assembly, so any movement remaining will be in the king pins and bushes.

☐ 35. Check the condition of the master cylinder, positioned immediately behind the brake pedal. It's awkward to get to, but you must make the effort. It should be securely mounted and show no signs of leaks. Make sure that the brake light connections are sound - the terminals often rust solid and break off.

☐ 36. Spin each front wheel in turn, listening for roughness in the bearings. There must be none!

☐ 37. Visually inspect the shock absorbers for signs of leaks. Don't confuse road spray with leaking hydraulic oil. Where fitted, coil springs must be sound and free from cracks or other visible damage.

☐ 38. With the wheels on the ground again, push down firmly a couple of times on each front wing of the car, then let go at the bottom of a stroke. The car should return to approximately its original level within two or three strokes. Continuing oscillations will earn your VW a 'failure' ticket for worn front 'shockers'!

UNDER THE CAR - REAR SUSPENSION

☐ 39. Check the condition of the rear shock absorbers in the same way as the front. A 'bounce' test can be carried out as for the front shock absorbers as an approximate check on how efficient or otherwise the damping effect is.

☐ 40. Check the axle tube oil seal gaiter for its condition. If it is split in any way, it must be replaced immediately.

☐ 41. With the back of the car raised on axle stands (both rear wheels off the ground), rotate the rear wheels and check, as well as you can, for roughness in the bearings, just as you did at the front. Don't be mislead by the 'drag' from the axle shafts.

BRAKES

☐ 42. The MoT brake test is carried out on a special 'rolling road' set-up, which measures the efficiency in terms of percentage. For the foot brake, the examiner is looking for 50 per cent; the handbrake must measure 25 per cent. Frankly, without a rolling road of your own, there is little that you can do to verify whether or not your car will come up to the required figures. What you can do, though, is carry out an entire check of the brake system, which will also cover all other aspects the examiner will be checking, and be as sure as you can that the system is working efficiently.

☐ 43. The MoT examiner will not dismantle any part of the system, but you can do so. So, take off each front wheel in turn, and examine as follows:

DISC BRAKES

Check the front brake discs themselves, looking for excessive grooving or crazing, the calliper pistons/dust seals (looking for signs of fluid leakage and deterioration of the seals), and the brake pads - ideally, replace them if less than approximately 3 mm. (1/8th in.) friction material remains on each pad.

DRUM BRAKES

Remove each brake drum and check the condition of the linings (renew if worn down to anywhere near the rivet heads), the brake drum (watch for cracking, ovality and serious scoring, etc.) and the wheel cylinders. Check the cylinder's dust covers to see if they contain brake fluid. If so, or if it is obvious that the cylinder(s) have been leaking, in which case they require replacement.

IMPORTANT! See *Chapter 3, Service Intervals, Step-by-Step* for important information, including SAFETY FIRST! information before working on your car's brakes.

☐ 44. Ensure that the drum brake adjusters (where fitted) are free to rotate (i.e. not seized!). If they are stuck fast, apply a little penetrating oil to the adjusters taking great care not to get any onto the brake shoes. Work them gently until they are free, at which point a little brake grease can be applied to the threads to keep them in this condition. With the rear brakes correctly adjusted, check handbrake action. The lever should rise three or four 'clicks' before the brake operates fully - if it goes further, the cable or rear brakes require adjustment. Ensure too that the handbrake lever remains locked in the 'on' position when fully applied, even if the lever is knocked sideways.

☐ 45. Closely check the state of ALL visible pipework - that's brakes and fuel lines. If any section of the steel tubing shows signs of corrosion, replace it, for safety as well as to gain an MoT pass. Note also that where the manufacturers fitted a clip to secure a piece of pipe, then it must be present and the pipe must be secured by it. Look too for leakage of fluid around pipe joints, and from the master cylinder. The fluid level in the master cylinder reservoir must also be at its correct level - if not, find out why and rectify the problem! At the front and rear of the car, bend the flexible hydraulic pipes through 180 degrees (by hand) near each end of each pipe, checking for signs of cracking. If any is evident, or if the pipes have been chafing on the tyres, wheels, steering or suspension components, replace them with new items, re-routing them to avoid future problems.

☐ 46. Have an assistant press down hard on the brake pedal while you check all flexible pipes for bulges. As an additional check, firmly apply the foot brake and hold the pedal down for a few minutes. It should not slowly sink to the floor (if it does, you have a hydraulic system problem). Press and release the pedal a few times - it should not feel 'spongy' (due to the presence of air in the system). If there is the risk of any problems with the braking system's hydraulics, have a qualified mechanic check it over before using the car.

☐ 47. A test drive should reveal obvious faults (such as pulling to one side, due to a seized calliper piston, for example), but otherwise all will be revealed on the rollers at the MoT station...

BODYWORK STRUCTURE

A structurally deficient car is a dangerous vehicle, and rust can affect many important areas, including the inner and outer sills, the floor pan, under the wheel arches behind the front wheels and in front of the rears and the rear chassis mounting points. Examine these areas, and also the spare wheel well, the jacking mounting points and the rear three quarter area under the rear seat. See *Chapter 3, Service Intervals Step-by-Step* for illustrations.

☐ 48. Essentially, fractures, cracks or serious corrosion in any load bearing panel or member (to the extent that the affected sections are weakened) need to be dealt with. In addition, failure will result from any deficiencies in the structural metalwork within 30 cm. (12 in.) of the seat belt mountings, and also the steering and suspension component attachment points. Repairs made to any structural areas must be carried out by 'continuous' seam welding, and the repair should restore the affected section to at least its original strength.

☐ 49. The MoT examiner will be looking for metal which gives way under squeezing pressure between finger and thumb, and will use his wicked little 'Corrosion Assessment Tool' (i.e. a plastic-headed tool, known as the 'toffee hammer'!), which in theory at least should be used for detecting rust by lightly tapping the surface. If scraping the surface of the metal shows weakness beneath, the car will fail.

☐ 50. Note that the security of doors and other openings must also be assessed, including the hinges, locks and catches. Corrosion damage or other weakness in the vicinity of these items can mean failure. It must be possible to open both doors from inside and outside the car.

EXTERIOR BODYWORK

☐ 51. Check for another area which can cause problems. Look out for surface rust, or accident damage, on the exterior bodywork, which leaves sharp or jagged edges and which may be liable to cause injury. Ideally, repairs should be carried out by welding in new metal, but for non-structural areas, riveting a plate over a hole, bridging the gap with glass fibre or body filler or even taping over the gap can be legally acceptable, at least as far as the MoT test is concerned.

FUEL SYSTEM

☐ 52. Another recent extension of the regulations brings the whole of the fuel system under scrutiny, from the tank to the engine. The system should be examined with and without the engine running, and there must be no leaks from any of the components. The tank must be securely mounted, and the filler cap must fit properly - 'temporary' caps are not permitted. Note that this applies even to early models of the Beetle where the fuel cap is actually under the bonnet.

EMISSIONS

Oh dear! - even the thought of this aspect can cause headaches. In almost every case, a proper 'engine tune' will help to ensure that your car is running at optimum efficiency, and there should be no difficulty in passing the test, unless your engine, the distributor or the carburettor really are well worn.

☐ 53. For Beetles first used before 1 August, 1975, the only test carried out is for 'visual smoke emission'. The engine must be fully warmed up, allowed to idle, then revved slightly. If smoke emitted is regarded by the examiner as being 'excessive', the car will fail. Often smoke emitted during this test is as a result of worn valve stem seals, allowing oil into the combustion chambers during tickover, to be blown out of the exhaust as 'blue smoke' when the engine is revved. In practice, attitudes vary widely between MoT stations on this aspect of the test.

☐ 54. For cars first used between 1 August, 1975 and 31 July, 1983, a 'smoke' test also applies. Again, the engine must be fully warmed up, and allowed to idle, before being revved to around 2,500 rpm for 20 seconds (to 'purge' the system). If dense blue or black smoke is emitted for more than five seconds, the car will fail. In addition, the exhaust gas is analysed. A maximum of 6 per cent carbon monoxide (CO), and 1,200 parts per million (ppm) hydrocarbons is allowable. The percentage of these gases are established using an exhaust gas analyser - home user versions are available for testing CO readings - see Chapter 3, Service Intervals Step-by-Step. Vehicles first used after 1st August 1983 have to follow the same stipulations, but with a reduced CO emissions target of 4.5%.

☐ 55. A CO reading which is slightly too high can usually be cured by carrying out simple servicing procedures as described in Chapter 3. It's important to ensure that the fuel is being burnt when and where it should be, which means getting the points, dwell angle, timing and carburation spot-on. However, if the reading is substantially adrift, it points to there being a serious problem and professional help should be sought.

CHAPTER 8 - FACTS & FIGURES

SECTION 1 - VEHICLE DETAILS

This Chapter serves two main purposes. First, we aim to help you find the identification numbers on your car and then we show which settings you will need to use in order to service your car. The "Data" sections of this chapter will also make essential reading when you come to carrying out the servicing on your car since you will then need to know things like valve clearance settings, spark plug gap, torque settings and a whole host of other adjustments and measurements that you will need to carry out in the course of maintaining your car. VAG always recommend that you quote the correct part number when ordering any spare parts. However, where this is not known, it's important to be able to quote the vehicle chassis and engine numbers instead. Bear in mind that, with engine interchangeability being as easy as it is with the Beetle, the engine in your car could well not be the original. Quite possibly, it could be a different engine capacity altogether. VW used several different numbering systems for the Beetle. For most owners, the system in use from the latter part of 1964 will be the most relevant, though the others are given for interest.

1949

Type	Description
IIA	Basic lhd saloon
IIB	Basic rhd saloon
11C	Export lhd saloon
11D	Export rhd saloon
14A	Hebmuller cabrio lhd
15A	Karmann cabrio lhd
15B	Karmann cabrio rhd

EARLY 1950

11E	Basic saloon lhd
11F	Basic saloon rhd
11G	Export saloon lhd
11H	Export saloon rhd

LATE 1950 ONWARD

101	Basic chassis lhd
102	Basic chassis rhd
103	Export chassis lhd
104	Export chassis rhd
111	Basic saloon lhd
112	Basic saloon rhd
113	Export saloon lhd
114	Export saloon rhd
115	Basic saloon with sunroof lhd
116	Basic saloon with sunroof rhd
117	Export saloon with sunroof (steel) lhd
118	Export saloon with sunroof (steel) rhd
151	Karmann cabrio lhd
152	Karmann cabrio rhd

In 1964 the numbering system was amended slightly. With effect from all models produced in the 1965 model year (ie from August 1964) the first two numbers are the Type No and the third one (odd numbers for lhd cars and even for rhd models) is the model year. The rest are chassis numbers. There are three places to look for reference numbers on your Beetle. The engine number is on the crankcase at the generator support flange. The chassis number is on the frame tunnel under the rear seat and it is also shown on the Type Identification plate on the front cross panel under the luggage compartment lid. The engine and chassis numbers should match up with the DVLC V5 form (the 'logbook') in the U.K. Photographs of the positioning of the numbers are shown in Chapter 2.

PART NUMBERS

The seemingly endless part numbers all have a meaning and a relevance. For example, let's take the part 113 867 011 K, which is actually for a left hand door trim panel. The first three show the type and model of car. The next number indicates which of the 10 main parts groups is required and the following two denote the subgroups. The final three numbers relate to the actual part itself and if there have been modifications to the part where it is not interchangeable, it is shown by placing a letter at the end. Thus, our example reads as follows:-

113	Type, model, version
8	Main parts group
67	Sub parts group
011	Part designation
K	Modification letter

BASIC ENGINE CONFIGURATION

All Beetles feature a 4-cylinder, horizontally opposed pushrod overhead valve engine. It is air cooled by the large fan at the front of the engine and by ducting, bringing air in from vents at the rear of the car. The thermostat opens at between 65° to 70°C (149° to 158°F). The wet sump lubrication system features a gauze strainer in the sump and has an initial capacity of 5.3 pints (3.0 litres) and an oil-change capacity of 4.4 pints (2.5 litres). The firing order is 1, 4, 3, 2. No. 1 cylinder is the right front, No. 2 cylinder is the right rear, No. 3 cylinder is the left front and No. 4 cylinder is the left rear.

COMPRESSION

You should have around 100 psi on all four cylinders. Whatever they read, they should be within 10 psi of each other. Drastic differences (more than absolute pressures unless they are very low, in which case the engine is probably worn out in lots of obvious ways) mean that something is amiss and demands your immediate attention. Note that number 3 cylinder will usually be a little down on the others because it runs hottest.

TIMING

It's possible to static time all engines except dual port motors equipped with a vacuum retard distributor. The latter is recognisable by the fact that there are two hoses running to the distributor rather than one. These engines must be timed using a strobe light, but it's as well to do this on all engines. The latest range of DIY test equipment is particularly accurate and it also allows you to check things like your points dwell angle and set your idle speed accurately. All timing relates to TDC - Top Dead Centre. It's either spot-on (0°) or it's before (BTDC) or after (ATDC). Check out the statistics in this chapter to see exactly what setting your particular engine requires.

INSIDE INFORMATION: You may find that your Beetle will give enhanced performance if you advance the ignition timing over the correct figure. However, you should NEVER do so since it can lead to the curse of the Beetle engine - engine overheating and damaged valves and pistons.

US MODELS FITTED WITH SMOG CONTROL EQUIPMENT

Cars fitted with stock distributor and carburettor

1968-72	0 degrees (top dead centre)
1971-74	(those vehicles fitted a vacuum retard distributor) 5 degrees after top dead centre (carburettor throttle valve must be closed)
1971-74	(cars not equipped with a vacuum retard distributor) 7.5 degrees before top dead centre (carburettor throttle valve must be closed)

NB: Remember that those cars fitted with the vacuum retard smog distributors will not give a smooth idle unless the distributor timing is fully retarded at idle and the carburettor valve is fully closed.

ELECTRICAL

All Beetles had 6v electrics until the 1967 model year. In 1968, when the Beetle changed to upright headlamps, the electrics were uprated to 12v on all UK models except for the basic 1200 Beetle, which remained 6v for another year in order to use up the remaining 6v parts in Volkswagen's stores. All standard 6v batteries produced 66 amp hours and all standard 12v batteries, 36 amp hours.

STARTER MOTOR

Incorporated in the pinion is a freewheel device which prevents damage should the key not be released immediately the engine fires. All post '62 cars have a non-repeat switch which prevents the starter motor being operated once the engine is running.

ALTERNATOR/DYNAMO

There were two types of 6v dynamo; up to 1966, a 90 mm bore unit was used with the voltage regulator bolted on top of it. 6v Beetles produced from 1967 used a 105 mm dynamo (the same size as the 12v dynamo) and had the regulator fitted under the rear seat. From 1974/5, the Beetle was fitted with a 12v Bosch alternator.

LIGHT BULBS

	6v Watts	12v Watts
Headlamp (main/dip beam)	45/40	45/40
Halogen	N/A	60/55
Sidelamp	4	4
Stop/tail lamp	21/5	21/5
Indicator lamp	21	21
Rear number plate lamp	10	10
Warning lamps	1.2	1.2
Speedometer lamp	1.2	2
Interior lamp	10	10

FUSES AND FUSEBOXES

All models of German Beetle used the ceramic type of fuse. Prior to 1954, two fuseboxes were fitted under the bonnet, one containing 6 fuses on the left-hand side next to the fuel tank and one containing four fuses on the back of the instrument panel.

A. Fusebox fitted next to the fuel tank:	Amps
1. Headlamp main beam (right).	(8)
2. Headlamp main beam (left), main beam warning lamp.	(8)
3. Headlamp dip beam (right).	(8)
4. Headlamp dip beam (left).	(8)
5. Front sidelamps (right and left).	(8)
6. Windscreen wipers, horn.	(8)

B. Fusebox fitted on the back of the instrument panel:	Amps
1. Interior lamp.	(8)
2. Fusebox (6 fuses), stop lamp.	(8)
3. Rear sidelamp (left).	(8)
4. Rear sidelamp (right), number plate lamp.	(8)

From January 1954, there remained two fuseboxes, again sited under the bonnet but with only 6 fuses fitted - two in a block alongside the fuel tank and four in a block at the back of the instrument panel.

A. Fusebox situated to the left of the fuel tank:	Amps
1. Headlamp main beam (right)	(8)
2. Headlamp main beam (left)	(8)

B. Fusebox situated on the back of the instrument panel:	Amps
1. Interior lamp, horn.	(8)
2. Windscreen wipers, stop lamps, indicators.	(8)
3. Front sidelamps (left and right), rear sidelamp (left).	(8)
4. Rear sidelamp (right), number plate lamp.	(8)

It wasn't long before the specification was changed and two extra fuses were added to protect the headlamp dip beam circuits, as follows:

Fusebox situated on the back of the instrument panel:	Amps
1. Interior lamp, horn.	(8)
2. Windscreen wipers, stop lamps, indicators.	(8)
3. Front sidelamps (left and right), rear sidelamp (left).	(8)
4. Rear sidelamp (right), number plate lamp.	(8)

Fusebox situated to the left of the fuel tank: **Amps**
1. Headlamp main beam (right. (8)
2. Headlamp main beam (left), main beam warning lamp. (8)
3. Headlamp dip beam (right). (8)
4. Headlamp dip beam (left). (8)

With effect from the 1960 model year, the fusebox was relocated to a position under the dashboard inside the car. The fuses were accessed from inside the car and the wiring from under the bonnet. (The exception was the 1303/1303S, where the fusebox could be dropped down as a unit inside the car.) The fusebox was under the right-hand side of the dash on all models except the 1303 and 1303S, where it was positioned under the centre of the dash. Over the years, the number of fuses increased from 8 to 12, as shown in the following table:

1200, 1300 models from August 1960 to July 1966 **Amps**
1. Indicators, stop lamps, horn, windscreen wipers. (16)
2. Headlamp main beam (left), main beam warning lamp. (8)
3. Headlamp main beam (right). (8)
4. Headlamp dip beam (left). (8)
5. Headlamp dip beam (right). (8)
6. Front and rear sidelamps (left) (8)
7. Front and rear sidelamps (right), number-plate lamp. (8)
8. Radio, interior lamp (8)

1200, 1300, 1500 models from August 1966 to July 1970 **Amps**
1. Indicators, stop lamps, horn. (16)
2. Windscreen wipers. (8)
3. Headlamp main beam (left), main beam warning lamp. (8)
4. Headlamp main beam (right). (8)
5. Headlamp dip beam (left). (8)
6. Headlamp dip beam (right). (8)
7. Front and rear sidelamps (right), number plate lamp. (8)
8. Front and rear sidelamps (left). (8)
9. Radio. (8)
10. Headlamp flasher, interior lamp. (16)

1200, 1300 models from August 1970 **Amps**
1. Front & rear sidelamps, rear sidelamp (right), number plate lamp. (8)
2. Rear sidelamp (left). (8)
3. Headlamp dip beam (left). (8)
4. Headlamp dip beam (right). (8)
5. Headlamp main beam (left), main beam warning lamp. (8)
6. Headlamp main beam (right). (8)
7. Not connected (8)
8. Hazard flashers. (8)
9. Interior lamp, headlamp flasher. (16)
10. Windscreen wipers, heated rear window. (16)
11. Horn, brake lamps. (8)
12. Indicators, fuel gauge, warning lamp for dual circuit brakes. (8)

On some models, there is an 8 amp fuse situated under the rear seat near the voltage regulator for the heated rear window main current.

1302S **Amps**
1. Front and rear tail lamps (left), number plate lamp. (8)
2. Front and rear tail lamps (right). (8)
3. Headlamp dip beam (right). (8)
4. Headlamp dip beam (left). (8)
5. Headlamp main beam (right). (8)
6. Headlamp main beam (left), main beam warning lamp. (8)
7. Headlamp flasher, interior lamp. (8)
8. Hazard flashers. (8)
9. NOT CONNECTED (16)
10. Stop lamps, horn. (8)
11. Windscreen wipers (16)
12. Indicators, warning lamps, fuel gauge. (8)

1303/1303S models **Amps**
1. Front sidelamps (left and right), rear tail lamp (right), number plate lamp. (8)
2. Rear tail lamp (left). (8)
3. Headlamp main beam (left). (8)
4. Headlamp main beam (right). (8)
5. Headlamp dip beam (left), main beam warning light. (8)
6. Headlamp dip beam (right). (8)
7. NOT CONNECTED. (16)
8. Hazard flashers. (8)
9. Headlamp flasher, interior lamp. (8)
10. Stop lamps, horn. (8)
11. Windscreen wipers. (16)
12. Warning lamps, gauges. (8)

Note that all fuses are numbered from the left. The figures in brackets relate to the amperage rating of the fuses. In NO circumstances should a fuse of a different rating be substituted, either greater or lower. The fuse locations for different world markets differed on occasion. The locations shown here are for the UK market.

WHEELS AND TYRES
Wheels

Wheel type	Steel disc with 5 bolt (early) or 4 bolt (late) fixing.
Size	4J x 15 (early), 41/2J x 15 (late), 51/2J x 15 (late, optional)

Tyres

Almost all Beetles nowadays are fitted with radial ply tyres and we very strongly recommend their use for reasons of safety and longevity.

Tyre size

All cars from 1955 to 1965	5.60 x 15 - 4PR cross-ply
All cars from 1965 onwards	5.60 x 15 - 4PR or 6.00 x 15 - 4PR cross-ply; 155 SR 15, 165 SR 15 or 175/70 SR 15radial-ply

Tyre pressures

A number of authorities show different pressures but a good starting point are the pressures shown here. Always check with your tyre supplier if in any doubt.

	Pressure lb/in sq.	(kg/cm sq.)
	Front	Rear
5.60 x 15 - 4PR cross-ply, (1954 to 1965):		
1 to 2 occupants	16 (1.1)	20 (1.4)
3 to 5 occupants	17 (1.2)	23 (1.6)
5.60 x 15 - 4PR, 6.00 x 15 - 4PR cross-ply (August 1965 onward):		
1 to 2 occupants	16 (1.1)	24 (1.7)
3 to 5 occupants	17 (1.2)	26 (1.8)

155 SR 15, 165 SR 15 and
175/70 SR 15 radial-ply

1 to 2 occupants	18 (1.3)	27 (1.9)
3 to 5 occupants	18 (1.3	27 (1.9)

Spare tyre pressure (the pressure from the tyre operates the windscreen washer): Max 42 lb/in sq. (2.9 kg/cm sq.) Note that the pressure to the washer cuts out at about 28 lb/in sq. (1.9 kg/cm sq.)

NB Always carry a tyre pressure gauge so that you can reduce the spare tyre pressure to the appropriate level if you need to use it on the car.

SUSPENSION

Front suspension

Independent twin transverse laminated leaf torsion bars, each having a trailing arm to the steering knuckles or link.

Exceptions: 1302S, 1303, 1303S

Independent MacPherson struts with built-in shock absorbers and coil springs. Anti-roll bars were standard.

Rear suspension

Independent single divided transverse solid torsion bar with trailing spring plate to outer end of swing axle tube which pivots at the transmission. Separate shock absorbers.

Exceptions: 1500 and 1300 Automatic Stick shift, 1302S, 1303, 1303S

Independent single divided transverse solid torsion bar with trailing link to outer end of diagonal semi-trailing arm. Double jointed driveshafts and separate shock absorbers.

STEERING

All Beetle models up to approximately 1980 utilised a worm and sector steering gear arrangement. Later models, with the exception of the 1303 and 1303S, were fitted with worm and roller type steering gear. 1303 and 1303S models from approximately 1975 onward have rack and pinion steering gear. The steering geometry for all models is as follows:-

	Trailing arm suspension	MacPherson strut suspension
Front wheel alignment (tracking)	30' ± 15' toe-in	30' ± 15' toe-in
Camber angle	+30' ± 20'	+1° +20' -40'
Castor angle	3° 20' ± 1°	2° ± 35'

BRAKES

All standard Beetles (ie not deluxe versions) were fitted with a mechanical cable braking system, operating on all four wheels, until 1961. Early hydraulic systems had only a single circuit master cylinder, but all models were equipped with a dual circuit system in 1968 except the 1200, which followed suit a year later. The handbrake operates the rear brake shoes via a cable. All models featured drum brakes all round, apart from the 1500, 1302S and 1303S models, which had front disc brakes with the same specification, as follows:-

Diameter	10.9 in (277 mm)
Disc thickness	0.374 in (9.5 mm)
Minimum disc thickness	0.335 in (8.5 mm)

PERFORMANCE

Outright performance has never been a Beetle strong point, as these typical owner figures show. The fact that there are some 21 million satisfied customers shows that they know something that can't be quantified by a stop-watch. The bullet-proof nature of the engine (when cared for properly) and the ability to cruise all day at the top speed are just two of those intangible qualities that other manufacturers dream of.

	1200	1300	1500	1303S
Max speed - overall (mph)	72	75	78	81
Automatic Stick Shift	—	72	75	—
1st gear	15	15	15	15
2nd gear	41	45	45	45
3rd gear	65	60	60	60
4th gear	72	75	78	81
0 to 30 mph (secs)	6.5	5.6	4.8	4.7
Automatic Stick Shift	—	7.8	5.6	—
0 to 50 mph (secs)	16.2	13.9	12.6	12.5
Automatic Stick Shift	—	20.7	16.1	—
Fuel consumption (mpg)	29/36	26/34	25/34	28/32

SECTION 2 - MAINTENANCE INFORMATION AND SETTINGS

1200 (1954 ONWARD)

Capacity	1192 cc
Bore	77 mm
Stroke	64 mm
Compression ratio	6.6:1 to August 1960
Power and torque	30 bhp / 56 lbs ft @ 2000 RPM
Valve clearances	0.004 in (0.1 mm) inlet and exhaust
Compression ratio	7.0:1 from August 1960
Power and torque	34 bhp / 61 lbs ft @ 2000 RPM
Valve clearances	0.008 in (0.2 mm) inlet
	0.012 in (0.3 mm) exhaust
Compression ratio	7.3:1 code D
Power and torque	34 bhp / 55 lbs ft @ 1700 RPM
Valve clearances	0.004 in (0.1 mm) inlet and exhaust
Ignition timing	
1955 to 1966	10° BTDC
Except above	7.5° BTDC
Points gap	0.016 in (0.4 mm)
Dwell angle	
Normal	44 to 50°
Wear limits	42 to 58°
Sparking plugs	
Standard	NGK B5-HS (or other manufacturer's equivalent)
Electrode gap	0.024 in (0.6 mm)
Thread size	14 mm
Carburettor	
Early models	Solex 28PCI, 28 PCIT, 28 PCIT-1
Later models	Solex 30 PICT-3
Fuel pump	Pierburg mechanical

Overall length	160.2 in (4070 mm)
Overall width	61 in (1550 mm)
Kerb weight	1675 lbs (760 kgs)
Overall height	59 in (1500 mm)

1300

Capacity	1285 cc
Bore	77 mm
Stroke	69 mm
Compression ratio	7.3:1 code F from August 1970
Power and torque	40 bhp / 69 lbs ft @ 2600 RPM
Compression ratio	7.5:1 code AB and AR from August 1970
Power and torque	44 bhp / 63 lbs ft @ 3000 RPM
Compression ratio	6.6:1 low compression code AC
Power and torque	40 bhp / 58 lbs ft @ 3000 RPM
Valve clearances (all models)	0.006 in (0.15 mm) inlet and exhaust
Ignition timing	
Engine numbers: F0,000,001-F2,140,820 with vacuum advance	7.5° BTDC vacuum hose off
Engine numbers: AB0,000,001 -AB0,313,345 with double vacuum and centrifugaladvance	5° ATDC vacuum hoses off
Engine numbers: AB0,313,346 onward with vacuum advance	7.5° BTDC vacuum hose off
Points gap	0.016 in (0.4 mm)
Dwell angle	
Normal	44° to 50°
Wear limits	42° to 58°
Sparking plugs	
Standard	NGK B5-HS (or other manufacturer's equivalent)
Electrode gap	0.024 in (0.6 mm)
Thread size	14 mm
Carburettor	Solex 30 PICT-1, 30 PICT-2, 31 PICT-3, 31 PICT-4
Fuel pump	Pierburg mechanical
Overall length	158.6 in (4030 mm)
Overall width	61 in (1550 mm)
Kerb weight	1808 lbs (820 kgs)
Overall height	59 in (1500 mm)

1500

Capacity	1493 cc
Bore	83 mm
Stroke	69 mm
Compression ratio	7.5:1 code H
Power and torque	44 bhp / 78 ft lbs @ 2600 RPM
Valve clearances	0.006 in (0.15 mm) inlet and exhaust

Ignition timing	
Engine numbers: H0,204,001 - H0,879,926	7.5° BTDC
Engine numbers: H0,879,927 - H1,124,669 auto transmission	0°
Engine numbers: H1,124,670 - H1,259,314	7.5° BTDC
Other engine numbers in 'H' range	0°
Points gap	0.016 in (0.4 mm)
Dwell angle	
Normal	44° to 50°
Wear limits	42° to 58°
Sparking plugs	
Standard	NGK B5-HS (or other manufacturer's equivalent)
Electrode gap	0.028 in (0.7 mm)
Thread size	14 mm
Carburettor	
Early models	Solex 30 PICT-1, 30 PICT-2
Later models	Solex 31 PICT-3
Fuel pump	Pierburg mechanical
Overall length	160.6 in (4080 mm)
Overall width	62.4 in (1585 mm)
Kerb weight	1918 lbs (870 kgs)
Overall height	59 in (1500 mm)

1600

Capacity	1584 cc
Bore	85.5 mm
Stroke	69 mm
Compression ratio	7.5:1 code AD,AE,AH,AR,AS
Power and torque	50 bhp / 77 lbs ft @ 2800 RPM
Compression ratio	6.6:1 low compression code AF
Power and torque	46 bhp / 72 lbs ft @ 2600 RPM
Valve clearances (all models)	0.006 in (0.15 mm) inlet and exhaust
Ignition timing	
Engine numbers: B6,000,001 - B6,440,900	0° (manual - vacuum hose off auto - vacuum hose on)
Engine codes: AD, AE, AF, AK, AH, with double vacuum	5° BTDC vacuum hoses on
Engine codes: AD, AK, AH, AR, AS with single vacuum	7.5° BTDC vacuum hoses off
Points gap	0.016 in (0.4 mm)
Dwell angle	
Normal	44° to 50°
Wear limits	42° to 58°
Sparking plugs	
Standard	NGK B5-HS (or other manufacturer's equivalent)
Electrode gap	0.024 in (0.6 mm)
Thread size	14 mm
Carburettor	Solex 34 PICT-3, 34 PICT-4

FACTS & FIGURES

Fuel pump	Pierburg mechanical
Overall length	160.6 in (4080 mm)
Overall width	62.4 in (1585 mm)
Kerb weight	1918 lbs (870 kgs)
Overall height	59 in (1500 mm)

TRANSMISSION

Manual transmission

All manual transmission Beetles feature a single, dry plate disc with a diaphragm spring or, on early models, a toggle release. The clutch is cable operated and the free play at the pedal should be 0.4 to 1.0 in (10 to 25 mm).

Transmission capacity (all models)

Initial fill	5.3 pints (3 litres)
Change	4.4 pints (2.5 litres)

Automatic (stick shift) transmission

The stick shift Beetle was something of a hybrid, featuring a conventional gearbox with a clutch, operated pneumatically by an electronic switch, and a torque converter but with no clutch pedal.

Transmission capacity (all models)

Initial fill	5.3 pints (3 litres)
Change	4.4 pints (2.5 litres)
Torque converter capacity	7.5 pints (3.6 litres)

TORQUE SETTINGS

Maximum torque settings, shown in imperial (lb/ft) and metric (kg/m) together with the socket size required.

Engine - general

In general nuts and bolts in and around the engine bay should be tightened as follows, unless otherwise specified:

Socket size (mm)	lb/ft	kg/m
10	5	0.7
11	7	1.0
12	10	1.5
13	14	2.0
14	18	2.5
17	22	3.0

Engine - specific

	lb/ft	kg/m	Socket size (mm)
Crankcase nuts:			
36 bhp engines	14	2.0	13/14
40 bhp engines	22	3.0	17
1500 cc engines (with plastic insert)	25	3.5	17
All other engines	18	2.5	17
Cylinder head nuts:			
36 bhp engines	26	3.7	17
All other engines	23	3.2	15/16/17

Rocker shaft nuts:			
36 and 40 bhp engines	14	2.0	13/14
1500 cc engines	18	2.5	13
1600 cc engines	14	2.0	13
Flywheel gland nut	220	30.0	36
Connecting rod bolts:			
36 bhp engines	36	5.0	14
All other engines	23	3.2	14
Oil drain plug (where applicable)	25	3.5	21
Oil screen nuts	6	0.7	10
Oil screen bolt	9	0.85	19
Oil pump nuts	7	1.0	10
Generator pulley nut	44	6.0	21
Generator pulley bolt	32 to 36	4.5 to 5.0	30
Engine mounting bolts	22	3.0	17
Engine to frame	18	2.5	14
Transaxle to frame	18	2.5	14
Spark plugs	22 to 29	3.0 to 4.0	21

Clutch and transmission

Clutch pressure plate bolts	18	2.5	14
Transmission filler/drain plugs	14	2.0	17 (Allen key)

Steering and suspension

Tie rod nuts	18	2.5	14
Rear axle nut	220	30.0	36
Road wheel bolts	72	10	19
Shock absorber nut	14 to 22	2.0 to 3.0	13
Shock absorber bolt	22 to 25	3.0 to 3.5	17
Steering damper nut	18	2.5	14
Steering damper bolt	29 to 32	4.0 to 4.5	17
Shock absorber to front strut bolt(where applicable)	50 to 60	7.0 to 8.5	—
Rear shock absorber bolt	44	6.0	17

Brakes

Brake plate bolts (drums)	36	5.0	16
Bleeder bolt	4.6	0.5	—
Master cylinder mounting bolts	18	2.5	14
Wheel cylinder mounting bolts (drum brakes)	18	2.5	13/14
Bearing retainer bolts (rear brake plates)	43	6.0	16
Disc calliper bolts	43	6.0	—
Brake hose/pipe unions	11 to 15	1.5 to 2.0	—

CHAPTER 9 - TOOLS & EQUIPMENT

Basic maintenance on any Beetle can be carried out using a fairly simple, relatively inexpensive tool kit. There is no need to spend a fortune all at once - most owners who do their own servicing acquire their implements over a long period of time. However, there are some items you simply cannot do without in order properly to carry out the work necessary to keep your VW on the road. Therefore, in the following lists, we have concentrated on those items which are likely to be valuable aids to maintaining your car in a good state of tune, and to keep it running sweetly and safely and in addition we have featured some of the tools that are 'nice-to-have' rather than 'must have' because as your tool chest grows, there are some tools that help to make servicing just that bit easier and more thorough to carry out.

Two vital points - firstly always buy the best quality tools you can afford. 'Cheap and cheerful' items may look similar to more expensive implements, but experience shows that they often fail when the going gets tough, and some can even be dangerous. With proper care, good quality tools will last a lifetime, and can be regarded as an investment. The extra outlay is well worth it, in the long run.

Secondly, the Beetle is an unusual car - the engine is air, rather than water cooled and it's at the opposite end of the car to most. As such, tools and equipment suitable for 'normal' cars may not be usable on your Vee-Dub. Ask the pointed question 'Can this tool be used on a VW Beetle' before you buy!

The following lists are shown under headings indicating the type of use applicable to each group of tools and equipment.

LIFTING: It is inevitable that you will need to raise the car from the ground in order to gain access to the underside of it.

We strongly recommend that you invest in a good quality

> *SAFETY FIRST!*
> *There are, of course, important safety implications when working underneath any vehicle. Sadly, many DIY enthusiasts have been killed or seriously injured when maintaining their automotive pride and joy, usually for the want of a few moments' thought. So - THINK SAFETY! In particular, NEVER venture beneath any vehicle supported only by a jack - of ANY type. A jack is ONLY intended to be a means of lifting a vehicle, NOT for holding it 'airborne' while being worked on.*

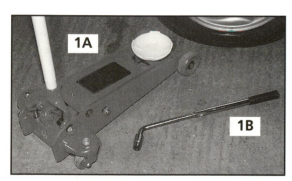

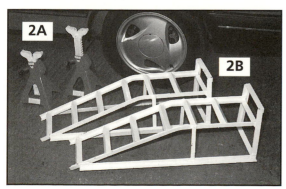

trolley jack, such as the Kamasa 2 1/4 ton unit shown here (1.A) while an excellent 'nice-to-have' is this extendible wheel nut spanner from the same company (1.B). This is also ideal for carrying in the car in case of punctures. If you've ever tried removing a wheel nut tightened by a garage gorilla, you know why this tool is so good!

Having raised the vehicle from the floor, always support it under a sound section of the 'chassis', or, if working at the rear of the car, beneath the rear axle. Use only proper axle stands (2.A), intended for the purpose, with solid wooden blocks on top, if necessary, to spread the load. These Kamasa stands are exceptionally strong and are very rapidly adjusted, using the built-in ratchet stops. Screw-type stands have an infinite amount of adjustments but are fiddly and time-consuming to use. *NEVER, NEVER* use bricks to support a car - they can crumble without warning, with horrifying results. Always chock all wheels not in the air, to prevent the car from rolling.

Frankly, if you don't need to remove the road wheels for a particular job, the use of car ramps (2.B), which are generally more stable than axle stands - is preferable, in order to gain the necessary working height. However, even then there are dangers. Ensure that the car is 'square' to the ramps before attempting to drive up onto

Thanks are due to Kamasa Tools for their kind assistance with this chapter. Almost all of the tools shown here and in Chapter 3 were kindly supplied by them.

TOOLS & EQUIPMENT

them, and preferably place the ramps on two long lengths of old carpet, extending towards the vehicle. The carpet should help prevent the ramps from sliding as the wheels mount them. If you have an assistant guiding you onto the ramps, be absolutely sure that he/she is well out of the way as you drive forwards. NEVER allow anyone to stand in front of the car, or immediately beside it - the ramps could tip. Be very careful, too, not to 'overshoot' the ramps. When the car is safely positioned on the ramps, fully apply the handbrake, and firmly chock the pair of wheels still on the ground.

Whenever you are working underneath your VW, preferably work with someone else, so that there are always two people around in case of an emergency. If this is not possible, and especially if you are working on the car at a location away from your house, make sure that someone knows exactly where you are and how long you intend to work on the vehicle, so that checks can be made if you are not home when expected.

In conclusion, here's a few more words on using and choosing jacks and supports.

JACKS: Manufacturer's jack - for emergency wheel changing ONLY - NOT to be used when working on the vehicle

'Bottle' jack - screw or hydraulic types - can be used as a means of lifting the car, in conjunction with axle stands to hold it clear of the ground. Ensure that the jack you buy is low enough to pass beneath the floorpan of your VW.

Trolley jack - extremely useful as it is so easily manoeuvrable. Again, use only for lifting the vehicle, in conjunction with axle stands to support it clear of the ground. Ensure that the lifting head of the jack will pass beneath the lowest points on the floorpan of your VW. Aim for the highest quality jack you can afford. Cheap types seldom last long, and can be VERY dangerous (suddenly allowing a car to drop to ground level, without warning, for example).

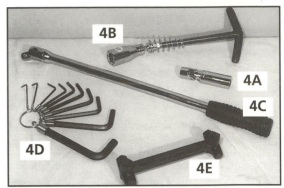

AXLE STANDS: Available in a range of sizes. Ensure that those you buy are sturdy, with the three legs reasonably widely spaced, and with a useful range of height adjustment.

CAR RAMPS: Available in several heights - high ones are easier for working beneath the car, but too steep a ramp angle can cause problems if you have low front spoilers, a sports exhaust or lowered suspension.

The ultimate ramps are the 'wind-up' variety - easy to drive onto at their lowest height setting, then raised by means of screw threads to a convenient working height.

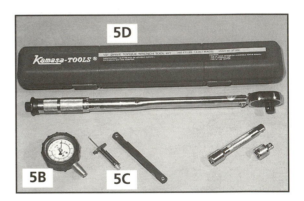

SPANNERS:

Being of German origin, your Beetle features metric fasteners - nuts, bolts, studs and screws. Though there are some direct imperial equivalents (13/16 in. equals 21 mm, for example) don't ever be tempted to use a non-metric spanner that is 'almost the right size'. Apart from the obvious danger of damaging the fastener beyond repair, there's also the very real possibility that you'll do the same to your hands!

This Kamasa spanner set (3.A) is very useful in that it includes the more unusual types of spanner size in the same set. There are also 'stubby' ratchet handles available (3.B) for that cramped engine bay!

Note - in every case, ring spanners provide a more positive grip on a nut/bolt head than open-ended types, which can spread and/or slip when used on tight fasteners. Similarly, 'impact' type socket spanners with hexagonal apertures give better grip on a tight fastener than the normal 12 point 'bi-hex' variety.

Open-ended spanners - set(s) covering the range 3/8 to 15/16 in. AF.

Ring spanners - set(s) covering the range 3/8 to 15/16 in. AF (alternatively, combination spanner set(s) (with one ring end, and one 'open' end of the same AF size, for each spanner) covering the same range.

Socket spanners - 3/8 in. and 1/2 in. square drive, covering the same range.

A long extension bar is a typical 'nice-to-have' tool. (4.C)

Adjustable spanner - nine inch, to start off with. (8.F)

Allen key set. (4.D)

Spark plug spanner, with rubber 'plug grip' insert either for use with the ratchet set (3.A) or the harder to use T-bar type. (4.B)

Rear axle drain plug spanner. (4.E)

Brake adjuster spanner.

Torque wrench. This is very nearly a 'must-have' item and for any serious mechanic, it becomes a 'must-have' once you have one. Prevents overtightening and stud shearing. (5.D)

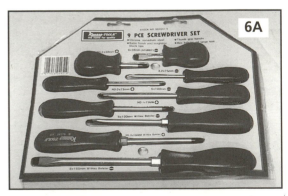

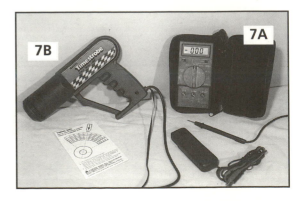

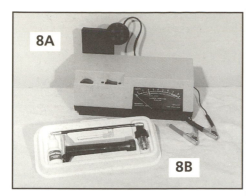

SCREWDRIVERS:

General-purpose set of cross-head variety and a general purpose set of flat-bladed screw-drivers. (All available in various-sized sets.) (6.A)

Impact driver, useful for releasing seized screws. (12.A)

Stud removing tools. A 'nice-to-have' when studs shear and all else fails. (12.B)

'TUNING' AIDS:

Depending on how much of the servicing you want to carry out yourself, you'll need all of these - see Chapter 3, Service Intervals Step-by-Step for information on how to use them. The more expensive can be purchased gradually, as you save more and more money by doing your own servicing!

Compression gauge, preferably screw-in, rather than 'push-in' variety.

Set of feeler gauges. (5.C)

'Automatic' valve clearance adjuster (can help to correctly set valve clearances when rockers have worn pads).

Spark plug adjuster tool. (Although many people lever the spark-plug electrode with a screwdriver, it's best gripped and bent with pliers if you don't have an adjuster.)

Dwell meter/multi-meter (preferably with built-in tachometer). (7.A)

Xenon stroboscopic timing light (neon types can be used, but the orange light produced is less bright than the white light produced by the xenon lamps, so that the timing marks are correspondingly less easy to see). This is one of several from the highly regarded Gunson range. (7.B)

Carburettor balancing/adjusting tool.

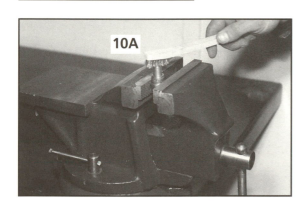

Simple CO meter. Gunson have now introduced an accurate exhaust gas analyser that is expensive but affordable. (8.A)

Colourtune (8.B) enables you to adjust the carb. by watching the changing colour of the spark. Trouble is, with the position of the Beetle's plugs, you can't possibly see the Colourtune!

SUNDRY ITEMS:

Tool box - steel types are sturdiest.

Extension lead.

Small/medium size ball pein hammer this one part of the huge Kamasa range. (9.A)

Soft-faced hammer (available here, from Kamasa Tools, as a set). (9.B)

Special, brass bristle wire brush for cleaning spark plugs. (10.A)

12 volt test lamp (can be made using 12 volt bulb, bulb holder, two short lengths of cable and two small crocodile clips).

Copper-based anti-seize compound - useful during assembly of threaded components, including spark plugs, to make future dismantling easier!

Grease gun.

Oil can (with 15W/50 multigrade oil, for general purpose lubrication).

Water dispellant 'electrical' aerosol spray.

Pair of pliers ('standard' jaw). (11.A)

Pair of 'long-nosed' pliers. (11.B)

Pair of 'side cutters'. (11.C)

Kamasa also sell pliers in sets, as this shoal indicates. (11.D)

Self-grip wrench or -preferably - set of three. (11.E)

Junior hacksaw. (9.C)

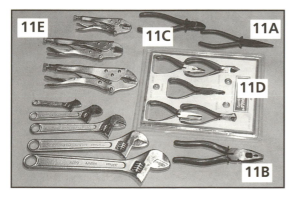

Tyre pump.

Tyre pressure gauge. (5.B)

Tyre tread depth gauge. (5.C)

Drifts - a set is an extremely useful 'nice-to-have'. (9.D)

Hub pullers, useful when you go beyond the straightfor-ward servicing stage. (12.C)

Electric drill. Not a servicing tool as such but a 'must-have' nevertheless. The Kamasa rechargeable drill (13.A) is superb, enabling you to reach tight spots without trailing leads - and much safer out of doors. Recommended!

Appendix 1 - Lubrication Chart

1. Engine
See Jobs 1 and 49
Castrol GTX
Overseas For territories with regular air temperatures below 5 degrees C, there are various grades of Castrol lubricants available. Consult your local supplier.

2. Oil bath air cleaner (where applicable)
See Job 24
Castrol GTX engine oil

3. Transmission
See Jobs 16 and 87
Castrol Hypoy light, EP 80W gear oil or Castrol TQD automatic transmission fluid for Automatic Stick Shift semi-automatic cars.

4. CV Joints (where applicable)
See Job 86
Castrol MS3 Grease

5. Handbrake cables (where applicable)
See Job 47
Castrol LM Grease

6. Front wheel bearings
See Job 43
Castrol LM Grease

7. King pins and ball joints
See Job 18
King pins (2 nipples per side) and ball joints (4 nipples per side)
Castrol LM Grease

8. Steering gear (where applicable)
See Jobs 40 and 41
Castrol EPX 80W/90

9. Front axle tubes
See Job 18
Front axle tubes (2 nipples per side)
Castrol LM Grease

10. Brake fluid reservoir
See Jobs 2, 45 and 46
Castrol Girling Universal Brake and Clutch Fluid.

11. Brake mechanism - areas of metal-to-metal contact
Proprietary brand of high melting point brake grease - such as Castrol PH Grease - not conventional high melting point grease.
General
Castrol Easing Fluid (aerosol)
Castrol Everyman Oil (in a can)

NB Not every model will have all the grease points shown here. In general, the later the model, the fewer the grease nipples.

(Illustration, courtesy Volkswagen)

APPENDIX 2
AMERICAN AND BRITISH TERMS

It was Mark Twain who described the British and the Americans as, "two nations divided by a common language". such cynicism has no place here but we do acknowledge that our common language evolves in different directions. We hope that this glossary of terms, commonly encountered when servicing your car, will be of assistance to American owners and, in some cases, English speaking owners in other parts of the world, too.

American	British
Antenna	Antenna
Axleshaft	Halfshaft
Back-up	Reverse
Carburetor	Carburettor
Cotter pin	Split pin
Damper	Shock absorber
DC Generator	Dynamo
Defog	Demist
Drive line	Transmission
Driveshaft	Propeller shaft
Fender	Wing or mudguard
Firewall	Bulkhead
First gear	Bottom gear
Float bowl	Float chamber
Freeway, turnpike	Motorway
Frozen	Seized
Gas tank	Petrol tank
Gas pedal	Accelerator or throttle pedal
Gasoline, Gas or Fuel	Petrol or fuel
Ground (electricity)	Earth
Hard top	Fast back
Header	Exhaust manifold
Headlight dimmer	Headlamp dipswitch
High gear	Top gear
Hood	Bonnet
Industrial Alcohol or Denatured Alcohol	Methylated spirit
Kerosene	Paraffin
Lash	Free-play
License plate	Number plate
Lug nut	Wheel nut
Mineral spirit	White spirit
Muffler	Silencer
Oil pan	Sump
Panel wagon/van	Van
Parking light	Side light
Parking brake	Hand brake
'Pinging'	'Pinking'
Quarter window	Quarterlight
Recap (tire)	Remould or retread
Rocker panel	Sill panel

American	British
Rotor or disk (brake)	Disc
Sedan	Saloon
Sheet metal	Bodywork
Shift lever	Gear lever
Side marker lights, side turn signal or position indicator	Side indicator lights
Soft-top	Hood
Spindle arm	Steering arm
Stabiliser or sway bar	Anti-roll bar
Throw-out bearing	Release or thrust bearing
Tie-rod (or connecting rod)	Track rod (or steering)
Tire	Tyre
Transmission	Drive line
Trouble shooting	Fault finding/diagnosis
Trunk	Boot
Turn signal	Indicator
Valve lifter	Tappet
Valve cover	Rocker cover
Valve lifter or tappet	Cam follower or tappet
Vise	Vice
Windshield	Windscreen
Wrench	Spanner

Useful conversions:

	Multiply by
US gallons to Litres	3.785
Litres to US gallons	0.2642
UK gallons to US gallons	1.20095
US gallons to UK gallons	0.832674

Fahrenheit to Celsius (Centigrade) -
Subtract 32, multiply by 0.5555

Celsius to Fahrenheit -
Multiply by 1.8, add 32

SPECIALISTS & SUPPLIERS

APPENDIX 3
SPECIALISTS AND SUPPLIERS

All of the products and specialists listed below have contributed in various ways to this book. All of the consumer products used are available through regular high street outlets or by mail order from specialist suppliers.

Autobarn, Manor Farm House, Kersoe, Pershore, Worcs. WR10 3JD
Tel: 0386 710780 or 710710
Specialising in the supply of original V.A.G. parts.

Autoline (Dinitrol), Eagle House, Redstone Industrial Estate, Boston, Lincs, PE21 8EA.
Tel: 0205 354500
Dinitrol Rust prevention treatment of various grades.

Automotive Chemicals Ltd, Bevis Green Works, Wallmersley, Bury, Lancs, BL9 8RE.
Tel: 061 797 5899
Aerosol spray paint

Automotive Products, Tachbrook Road, Leamington Spa, Warwicks, CV31 3ER.
Tel: 0926 472251
Manufacturers of AP Lockheed 'original equipment' brakes.

Beetle Specialist Workshop, Ballards Place, Eardiston, Tenbury Wells, Worcs. WR15 8JR.
Tel: 058 470 348
Beetle restoration specialist.

Castrol (UK) Ltd, Burmah House, Pipers Way, Swindon, Wiltshire, SN3 1RE.
Tel: 0793 512712
One of the best quality and best known lubricant ranges.

Gunson Ltd, Pudding Mill Lane, Stratford, London, E15 2PJ.
Tel: 081 555 7421
Electrical and electronic engine tuning equipment.

Kamasa Tools, Saxon Industries, Lower Everland Road, Hungerford, Berkshire, RG17 0DX.
Huge range of hand and power tools, used throughout this book.

Macvolks, Lane Farm, Kingswood, Nr Aylesbury, HP18 0RB.
Tel: 0296 770707.
Beetle/Volkswagen service and repair specialist who assisted greatly in the production of this book.

Motorworld Bodyshop, Langford Lane, Kidlington, Oxford, OX5 1JA.
Tel: 0865 373811
Top quality body repairs to all makes of vehicle.

NGK Spark Plugs (UK) Ltd, 7-8-9 Garrick Industrial Centre, Hendon, London, NW9 6AQ.
Tel: 081 202 2151
Top quality spark plugs.

Partco. See Yellow Pages for your local Partco centre (look under 'Motor Factors').
Just about all regular service items. Suppliers of almost every type of consumable and component used in automotive repair.

SP Tyres UK Ltd, Fort Dunlop, Birmingham, B24 9QT.
Tel: 021 384 4444
Manufacturers of Dunlop tyres in both modern and 'period' patterns.

VAG (UK) Ltd., Yeoman's Drive, Blakelands, Milton Keynes, Bucks. MK15 5AN.
Tel: 0908 679121
Importers of all VW vehicles and suppliers of Beetle O/E service parts.

W David & Sons Ltd (Isopon), Ridgemount House, 1 Totteridge Lane, Whetstone, London, N20 0EY.
Tel: 081 445 0372
Manufacturers of Isopon filler and Fastglas fiberglass kits - top quality products.

APPENDIX 4
SERVICE HISTORY

This Chapter helps you keep track of all the servicing carried out on your car and can even save you money! A car with a 'service history' is always worth more than one without. Although this book's main purpose is to give invaluable advice to anyone carrying out his or her own servicing, you could make full use of this section, even if you have a garage or mechanic carry out the work for you. It enables you to specify the jobs you want to have carried out to your car and, once again, it enables you to keep that all-important service history. And even if your car doesn't have a 'history' going back to when it was new, keeping this Chapter complete will add to your car's value when you come to sell it. Mind you, it obviously won't be enough to just to tick the boxes: keep all your receipts when you buy oil, filters and other consumables or parts. That way, you'll also be able to return any faulty parts if needs be.

IMPORTANT NOTE! The Service Jobs listed here are intended as a check list and a means of keeping a record of your car's service history. It is most important that you refer to *Chapter 3, Service Intervals, step-by-step* for full details of how to carry out each Job listed here and for essential SAFETY information, all of which will be essential when you come to carry out the work.

Before carrying out a service on your car, you will need to purchase the right parts. Please refer to *Chapter 2, Buying Spares* for information on how to buy the right parts at the right prices and *Chapter 8, Facts and Figures* for information on how to find your car's model type, 'identity numbers', and so on; information that you will need in order to buy the right parts, first time!

Wherever possible, the Jobs listed in this section have been placed in a logical order or placed into groups that will help you make progress on the car. We have tried to save you too much in the way of unnecessary movement by grouping Jobs around areas of the car and also - most important, this! - into groups of jobs that apply when the car is on the ground, when one front wheel is removed, when the front or rear of the car is off the ground, and so on. Therefore, at each Service Interval, you will see the work grouped into Jobs that need carrying out in the engine bay, around the car or under the car and another division into Bodywork and Interior Jobs, and Mechanical and Electrical Jobs.

You'll also see space at each Service Interval for you to write down the date, price and seller's name every time you buy consumables or accessories. And once again, do remember to keep your receipts! There's also space for you to date and sign the Service Record or for a garage's stamp to be applied.

As you move through the Service Intervals, you will notice that the work carried out at, say, *1,500 Miles or Every Month*, whichever comes first, is repeated at each one of the following Service Intervals. The same applies to the *6,000 Miles or Six Months* Interval: much of it is repeated at *12,000 Miles or Twelve Months*. Every time a Job or set of Jobs is 'repeated' from an earlier Interval, we show it in a tinted area on the page. You can then see more clearly which jobs are unique to the level of Service Interval that you are on. And you may be surprised to find that all the major Intervals, right up to *36,000 Miles or Thirty Six Months* contain Jobs that are unique to that Service Interval. That's why we have continued this Service History right up to the 3 Year Interval. There are sufficient Service History sheets for you to keep a record of your car's servicing for three years, and when that is full, you can purchase a set of continuation sheets from Porter Publishing at the address and telephone number shown at the end of this Chapter. If you keep your car and wish to continue your service record, you will be able to start the 3 year sequence all over again, in the knowledge that your car has been serviced as well as anyone could wish for!

500 MILES, WEEKLY, OR BEFORE A LONG JOURNEY

This list is shown, complete, only once. It would have been a bit much to have provided the list 52 times over for use once a week throughout the year! They are, however, included with every longer Service list from 3,000 miles/Three Months-on so that each of the 'weekly' Jobs is carried out as part of every Service.

500 Mile Mechanical and Electrical - The Engine Bay

Job 1. Check engine oil level.

500 Mile Mechanical and Electrical - Around the Car

Job 2. Check brake fluid level.

Job 3. Check windscreen washer reservoir level.

Job 4. Check windscreen washers.

Job 5. Check windscreen wipers.

Job 6. Check headlamps/sidelamps.

Job 7. Check front indicators.

Job 8. Check horn.

Job 9. Rear sidelamps/indicators.

Job 10. Check number plate lamp.

Job 11. General condition of tyres.

Job 12. Check tyre pressures.

Job 13. Security of wheel bolts.

Job 14. Battery electrolyte level.

500 Mile Bodywork and Interior - Around the Car

Job 15. Clean bodywork.

1,500 MILES - OR EVERY MONTH, whichever comes first

These Jobs are similar to the 500 Mile Jobs but don't need carrying out quite so regularly. Once again, these Jobs are not shown with a separate listing for each 1,500 miles/1 Month interval but they are included as part of every 3,000 miles/Three Month Service list and for every longer Service interval.

1,500 Mile Mechanical and Electrical - The Engine Bay

Job 16. AUTOMATIC STICK SHIFT MODELS ONLY. Check torque converter fluid level.

1,500 Mile Mechanical and Electrical - Around the Car

Job 17. Lubricate door hinges.

1,500 Mile Mechanical and Electrical - Under the Car

Job 18. Grease front suspension.

1,500 Mile Bodywork and Interior - Around the Car

Job 19. Touch-up paintwork.

Job 20. Aerial/antenna.

Job 21. Clean interior.

Job 22. Improve visibility!

1,500 Mile Bodywork - Under the Car

Job 23. Clean mud traps.

Date serviced: ....

Carried out by: ....
Garage Stamp or signature:

Parts/Accessories purchased (date, parts, source) ....
....
....
....
....

3,000 MILES - OR EVERY THREE MONTHS, whichever comes first

All the Service Jobs in the tinted area have been carried forward from earlier service intervals and are to be repeated at this Service.

3,000 Mile Mechanical and Electrical - The Engine Bay

First carry out those Jobs listed under earlier Service Intervals.

☐ Job 1. Check engine oil level.

☐ Job 16. AUTOMATIC STICK SHIFT MODELS ONLY. Check torque converter fluid level.

☐ Job 24. Clean out air cleaner & refill.

☐ Job 25. Lubricate carburettor control linkage.

☐ Job 26. Clean fuel pump filter (where applicable).

☐ Job 27. FUEL INJECTION CARS ONLY Adjust idle speed.

☐ Job 28. Check pipes and hoses.

☐ Job 29. Fan belt for wear & tension.

☐ Job 30. Check HT circuit.

☐ Job 31. Adjust spark plugs.

☐ Job 32. Clean contact breaker points.

☐ Job 33. Check ignition timing.

☐ Job 34. Distributor vacuum advance.

☐ Job 35. Lubricate distributor cam shaft bearing & breaker arm fibre block.

☐ Job 36. AUTOMATIC STICK SHIFT CARS ONLY. Clean auto transmission control valve filter.

3,000 Mile Mechanical and Electrical - Around the Car

First carry out all the Jobs listed under earlier Service Intervals.

☐ Job 2. Check brake fluid level.

☐ Job 3. Check windscreen washer reservoir level.

☐ Job 4. Check windscreen washers.

☐ Job 5. Check windscreen wipers.

☐ Job 6. Headlamps/sidelamps.

☐ Job 7. Check front indicators.

☐ Job 8. Check horn.

☐ Job 9. Rear sidelamps/indicators.

☐ Job 10. Number plate lamp.

☐ Job 11. General condition of tyres.

☐ Job 12. Check tyre pressures.

☐ Job 13. Security of wheel bolts.

☐ Job 14. Battery electrolyte level.

☐ Job 17. Lubricate door hinges.

☐ Job 37. **EARLY MODELS ONLY** Adjust/lubricate pedals.

☐ Job 38. Lubricate petrol reserve tap.

☐ Job 39. **AUTOMATIC STICK SHIFT CARS ONLY** Check starter inhibit switch.

☐ Job 40. **MODELS UP TO 1965 ONLY** Check steering box oil level.

☐ Job 41. Check steering mechanism.

3,000 Mile Mechanical and Electrical - Under the Car

First carry out the Job listed under an earlier Service Interval.

☐ Job 18. Grease front suspension.

☐ Job 42. **CABLE BRAKE MODELS ONLY** Check cable brakes.

☐ Job 43. Check front wheel bearings.

☐ Job 44. **DISC BRAKE MODELS ONLY** Check brake pads.

☐ Job 45. **HYDRAULIC BRAKE MODELS ONLY**. Hydraulic front drum brakes.

☐ Job 46. Check hydraulic rear brakes.

☐ Job 47. Lubricate handbrake cables.

☐ Job 48. Check handbrake travel.

☐ Job 49. Change engine oil.

☐ Job 50. Valve to rocker clearance.

☐ Job 51. Check for oil leaks.

☐ Job 52. **AUTOMATIC STICK SHIFT & 1302, 1302S, 1303 & 1303S MODELS ONLY**. Check CV joints for tightness.

☐ Job 53. **MANUAL SHIFT MODELS ONLY** Check clutch adjustment.

☐ Job 54. Exhaust/heat exchangers.

3,000 Mile Mechanical and Electrical - Road Test

☐ Job 55. Clean controls.

☐ Job 56. Check instruments.

☐ Job 57. Accelerator pedal.

☐ Job 58. Handbrake function.

☐ Job 59. Brakes and steering.

3,000 Mile Bodywork and Interior - Around the Car

First carry out all the Jobs listed under earlier Service Intervals.

☐ Job 15. Clean bodywork.

☐ Job 19. Touch-up paintwork.

☐ Job 20. Aerial/antenna.

☐ Job 21. Clean interior.

☐ Job 22. Improve visibility!

☐ Job 60. Check windscreen.

☐ Job 61. Wiper blades and arms.

☐ Job 62. Check rear view mirrors.

☐ Job 63. Chrome trim and badges.

3,000 Mile Bodywork - Under the Car

First carry out the Job listed under an earlier Service Intervals.

☐ Job 23. Clean mud traps.

☐ Job 64. Inspect underside.

Date serviced:..

Cazrried out by:..

Garage Stamp or signature:

Parts/Accessories purchased (date, parts, source) ....

....

....

....

6,000 MILES - OR EVERY SIX MONTHS, whichever comes first

All the Service Jobs in the tinted area have been carried forward from earlier service intervals are to be repeated at this Service.

6,000 Mile Mechanical and Electrical - The Engine Bay

First carry out all the Jobs listed under earlier Service Intervals as applicable.

☐ Job 1. Check engine oil level.

☐ Job 16. **AUTOMATIC STICK SHIFT MODELS ONLY**. Check torque converter fluid level.

☐ Job 24. Clean out air cleaner & refill.

☐ Job 25. Lubricate carburettor control linkage.

☐ Job 26. Clean fuel pump filter (where applicable).

☐ Job 27. **FUEL INJECTION CARS ONLY** Adjust idle speed.

☐ Job 28. Check pipes and hoses.

☐ Job 29. Check fan belt for wear & tension.

☐ Job 30. Check HT circuit.

☐ Job 31. Adjust spark plugs.

☐ Job 32. Clean contact breaker points.

☐ Job 33. Check ignition timing.

☐ Job 34. Check distributor vacuum advance.

☐ Job 35. Lubricate distributor cam shaft bearing & breaker arm fibre block.

☐ Job 36. **AUTOMATIC STICK SHIFT CARS ONLY**. Clean auto transmission control valve filter.

☐ Job 65. Replace spark plugs.

☐ Job 66. Renew contact breaker points.

☐ Job 67. Cylinder compressions.

☐ Job 68. Check exhaust emissions.

☐ Job 69. Adjust carburettor idle speed.

☐ Job 70. Check automatic choke.

☐ Job 71. **AFC FUEL INJECTION CARS ONLY** Replace fuel filter.

☐ Job 72. Check all fuel connections.

☐ Job 73. Check warm air control flap.

6,000 Mile Mechanical and Electrical - Around the Car

First carry out all the Jobs listed under earlier Service Intervals.

☐ Job 2. Check brake fluid level.

☐ Job 3. Check windscreen washer reservoir level.

☐ Job 4. Check windscreen washers.

☐ Job 5. Check windscreen wipers.

☐ Job 6. Headlamps/sidelamps.

☐ Job 7. Check front indicators.

☐ Job 8. Check horn.

☐ Job 9. Rear sidelamps/indicators.

☐ Job 10. Check number plate lamp.

☐ Job 11. General condition of tyres.

☐ Job 12. Check tyre pressures.

☐ Job 13. Security of wheel bolts.

☐ Job 14. Battery electrolyte level.

☐ Job 17. Lubricate door hinges.

☐ Job 37. **EARLY MODELS ONLY** Adjust/lubricate pedals.

☐ Job 38. Lubricate petrol reserve tap.

☐ Job 39. **AUTOMATIC STICK SHIFT CARS ONLY**. Check starter inhibit switch.

☐ Job 40. **MODELS UP TO 1965 ONLY** Check steering box oil level.

☐ Job 41. Steering mechanism.

☐ Job 74. Check battery/terminals.

☐ Job 75. Check headlamp alignment.

☐ Job 76. **AUTOMATIC STICK SHIFT CARS ONLY**. Check automatic stick shift switch contacts.

6,000 Mile Mechanical and Electrical - Under the Car

First carry out all the Jobs listed under earlier Service Intervals.

☐ Job 18. Grease front suspension.

☐ Job 42. **CABLE BRAKE MODELS ONLY** Check cable brakes.

☐ Job 43. Front wheel bearings.

☐ Job 44. **DISC BRAKE MODELS ONLY**. Check brake pads.

☐ Job 45. **HYDRAULIC BRAKE MODELS ONLY**. Hydraulic front drum brakes.

☐ Job 46. **HYDRAULIC BRAKE MODELS ONLY**. Check hydraulic rear brakes.

☐ Job 47. Lubricate handbrake cables.

☐ Job 48. Check handbrake travel.

☐ Job 49. Change engine oil.

☐ Job 50. Valve to rocker clearance.

☐ Job 51. Check for oil leaks.

☐ Job 52. **AUTOMATIC STICK SHIFT & 1302, 1302S, 1303, & 1303S MODELS ONLY** Check CV joints for tightness.

☐ Job 53. **MANUAL SHIFT MODELS ONLY** Check clutch adjustment.

☐ Job 54. Exhaust/heat exchangers.

☐ Job 77. Brake pipes and fuel lines.

☐ Job 78. Check front dampers.

☐ Job 79. **1302 & 1303 SERIES CARS ONLY** Check front springs.

☐ Job 80. Check steering components.

☐ Job 81. Front wheel alignment.

☐ Job 82. Check rear dampers.

☐ Job 83. **1302 & 1303 SERIES CARS ONLY** Check rear springs.

☐ Job 84. Heater control cables & levers.

☐ Job 85. Power unit mountings.

☐ Job 86. Drive shaft/CV joint gaiters.

☐ Job 87. Check transmission oil level.

☐ Job 88. **AUTOMATIC STICK SHIFT CARS ONLY**. Check clutch adjustment.

6,000 Mile Mechanical and Electrical - Road Test

First carry out all the Jobs listed under earlier Service Intervals.

☐ Job 55. Clean controls.

☐ Job 56. Check instruments.

☐ Job 57. Accelerator pedal.

☐ Job 58. Handbrake function.

☐ Job 59. Brakes and steering.

6,000 Mile Bodywork and Interior - Around the Car

First carry out all the Jobs listed under earlier Service Intervals.

☐ Job 15. Clean bodywork.

☐ Job 19. Touch-up paintwork.

☐ Job 20. Aerial/antenna.

☐ Job 21. Clean interior.

☐ Job 22. Improve visibility!

☐ Job 60. Check windscreen.

☐ Job 61. Wiper blades and arms.

☐ Job 62. Check rear view mirrors.

☐ Job 63. Chrome trim and badges.

☐ Job 89. Lubricate luggage lid release and hinges.

☐ Job 90. Lubricate door locks and striker plates.

☐ Job 91. Lubricate engine lid lock.

☐ Job 92. Check seats and seat belts.

☐ Job 93. Check floors including spare wheel well.

6,000 Mile Bodywork - Under the Car

First carry out those Jobs listed under earlier Service Intervals.

☐ Job 23. Clean mud traps.

☐ Job 64. Inspect underside.

☐ Job 94. Rustproof underbody.

☐ Job 95. Clear all drain holes.

Date serviced: ....

Carried out by: ....
Garage Stamp or signature:

Parts/Accessories purchased (date, parts, source) ....
....
....
....
....
....
....
....
....

9,000 MILES - OR EVERY NINE MONTHS, whichever comes first

All the Service Jobs at this Service Interval have been carried forward from earlier service intervals and are to be repeated at this Service.

9,000 Mile Mechanical and Electrical - The Engine Bay

First carry out all the Jobs listed under earlier Service Intervals as applicable.

☐ Job 1. Check engine oil level.

☐ Job 16. **AUTOMATIC STICK SHIFT MODELS ONLY**. Check torque converter fluid level.

☐ Job 24. Clean out air cleaner & refill.

☐ Job 25. Lubricate carburettor control linkage.

☐ Job 26. Clean fuel pump filter (where applicable).

☐ Job 27. **FUEL INJECTION CARS ONLY** Adjust idle speed.

☐ Job 28. Check pipes and hoses.

☐ Job 29. Check fan belt for wear & tension.

☐ Job 30. Check HT circuit.

☐ Job 31. Adjust spark plugs.

☐ Job 32. Clean contact breaker points.

☐ Job 33. Check ignition timing.

☐ Job 34. Check distributor vacuum advance.

☐ Job 35. Lubricate distributor cam shaft bearing & breaker arm fibre block.

☐ Job 36. **AUTOMATIC STICK SHIFT CARS ONLY**. Clean auto transmission control valve filter.

9,000 Mile Mechanical and Electrical - Around the Car

☐ Job 2. Check brake fluid level.

☐ Job 3. Check windscreen washer reservoir level.

☐ Job 4. Check windscreen washers.

☐ Job 5. Check windscreen wipers.

☐ Job 6. Headlamps/sidelamps.

☐ Job 7. Check front indicators.

☐ Job 8. Check horn.

☐ Job 9. Rear sidelamps/indicators.

☐ Job 10. Check number plate lamp.

☐ Job 11. General condition of tyres.

☐ Job 12. Check tyre pressures.

☐ Job 13. Security of wheel bolts.

☐ Job 14. Battery electrolyte level.

☐ Job 17. Lubricate door hinges.

☐ Job 37. **EARLY MODELS ONLY** Adjust/lubricate pedals.

☐ Job 38. Lubricate petrol reserve tap.

☐ Job 39. **AUTOMATIC STICK SHIFT CARS ONLY**. Check starter inhibit switch.

☐ Job 40. **MODELS UP TO 1965 ONLY** Check steering box oil level.

☐ Job 41. Steering mechanism.

9,000 Mile Mechanical and Electrical - Under the Car

First carry out all the Jobs listed under earlier Service Intervals.

☐ Job 18. Grease front suspension.

☐ Job 42. **CABLE BRAKE MODELS ONLY** Check cable brakes.

☐ Job 43. Front wheel bearings.

☐ Job 44. **DISC BRAKE MODELS ONLY**. Check brake pads.

☐ Job 45. **HYDRAULIC BRAKE MODELS ONLY**. Hydraulic front drum brakes.

☐ Job 46. **HYDRAULIC BRAKE MODELS ONLY**. Check hydraulic rear brakes.

☐ Job 47. Lubricate handbrake cables.

☐ Job 48. Check handbrake travel.

☐ Job 49. Change engine oil.

☐ Job 50. Valve to rocker clearance.

☐ Job 51. Check for oil leaks.

☐ Job 52. **AUTOMATIC STICK SHIFT & 1302, 1302S, 1303, & 1303S MODELS ONLY** Check CV joints for tightness.

☐ Job 53. **MANUAL SHIFT MODELS ONLY** Check clutch adjustment.

☐ Job 54. Exhaust/heat exchangers.

SERVICE HISTORY

9,000 Mile Mechanical and Electrical - Road Test

- ☐ Job 55. Clean controls.
- ☐ Job 56. Check instruments.
- ☐ Job 57. Accelerator pedal.
- ☐ Job 58. Handbrake function.
- ☐ Job 59. Brakes and steering.

9,000 Mile Bodywork and Interior - Around the Car

- ☐ Job 15. Clean bodywork.
- ☐ Job 19. Touch-up paintwork.
- ☐ Job 20. Aerial/antenna.
- ☐ Job 21. Clean interior.
- ☐ Job 22. Improve visibility!
- ☐ Job 60. Check windscreen.
- ☐ Job 61. Wiper blades and arms.
- ☐ Job 62. Check rear view mirrors.
- ☐ Job 63. Chrome trim and badges.

9,000 Mile Bodywork - Under the Car

- ☐ Job 23. Clean mud traps.
- ☐ Job 64. Inspect underside.

Date serviced:..

Carried out by: ....
Garage Stamp or signature:

Parts/Accessories purchased (date, parts, source) ....

....

....

....

....

12,000 MILES - OR EVERY TWELVE MONTHS, whichever comes first

All the Service Jobs in the tinted area have been carried forward from earlier service intervals and are to be repeated at this Service.

12,000 Mile Mechanical and Electrical - The Engine Bay

- ☐ Job 1. Check engine oil level.
- ☐ Job 16. **AUTOMATIC STICK SHIFT MODELS ONLY**. Check torque converter fluid level.
- ☐ Job 24. Clean out air cleaner & refill.
- ☐ Job 25. Lubricate carburettor control linkage.
- ☐ Job 26. Clean fuel pump filter (where applicable).
- ☐ Job 27. **FUEL INJECTION CARS ONLY** Adjust idle speed.
- ☐ Job 28. Check pipes and hoses.
- ☐ Job 29. Check fan belt for wear and tension.
- ☐ Job 30. Check HT circuit.
- ☐ Job 31. Adjust spark plugs.
- ☐ Job 32. Clean contact breaker points.
- ☐ Job 33. Check ignition timing.
- ☐ Job 34. Distributor vacuum advance.
- ☐ Job 35. Lubricate distributor cam shaft bearing & breaker arm fibre block.
- ☐ Job 36. **AUTOMATIC STICK SHIFT CARS ONLY**. Clean auto transmission control valve filter.
- ☐ Job 65. Replace spark plugs.
- ☐ Job 66. Renew contact breaker points.
- ☐ Job 67. Cylinder compressions.
- ☐ Job 68. Check exhaust emissions.
- ☐ Job 69. Adjust carburettor idle speed.
- ☐ Job 70. Check automatic choke.
- ☐ Job 71. **AFC FUEL INJECTION CARS ONLY**. Replace fuel filter.
- ☐ Job 72. All fuel connections.
- ☐ Job 73. Warm air control flap.

- ☐ Job 96. Change in-line fuel filter.

12,000 Mile Mechanical and Electrical - Around the Car

First carry out all the Jobs listed under earlier Service Intervals.

- ☐ Job 2. Check brake fluid level.
- ☐ Job 3. Check windscreen washer reservoir level.
- ☐ Job 4. Check windscreen washers.
- ☐ Job 5. Check windscreen wipers.
- ☐ Job 6. Headlamps/sidelamps.
- ☐ Job 7. Check front indicators.
- ☐ Job 8. Check horn.
- ☐ Job 9. Rear sidelamps/indicators.
- ☐ Job 10. Check number plate lamp.
- ☐ Job 11. General condition of tyres.
- ☐ Job 12. Check tyre pressures.
- ☐ Job 13. Security of wheel bolts.
- ☐ Job 14. Battery electrolyte level.
- ☐ Job 17. Lubricate door hinges.
- ☐ Job 37. **EARLY MODELS ONLY** Adjust/lubricate pedals.
- ☐ Job 38. Lubricate petrol reserve tap.
- ☐ Job 39. **AUTOMATIC STICK SHIFT CARS ONLY**. Check starter inhibit switch.
- ☐ Job 40. **MODELS UP TO 1965 ONLY** Check steering box oil level.
- ☐ Job 41. Steering mechanism.
- ☐ Job 74. Check battery/terminals.
- ☐ Job 75. Headlamp alignment.
- ☐ Job 76. **AUTOMATIC STICK SHIFT CARS ONLY**. Check automatic stick shift switch contacts.

- ☐ Job 97. Test dampers.
- ☐ Job 98. Alarm remote control transmitters.

12,000 Mile Mechanical and Electrical - Under the Car

First carry out all the Jobs listed under earlier Service Intervals.

☐ Job 18. Grease front suspension.

☐ Job 42. **CABLE BRAKE MODELS ONLY** Check cable brakes.

☐ Job 43. Front wheel bearings.

☐ Job 44. **DISC BRAKE MODELS ONLY.** Check brake pads.

☐ Job 45. **HYDRAULIC BRAKE MODELS ONLY.** Hydraulic front drum brakes.

☐ Job 46. **HYDRAULIC BRAKE MODELS ONLY.** Check hydraulic rear brakes.

☐ Job 47. Lubricate handbrake cables.

☐ Job 48. Check handbrake travel.

☐ Job 49. Change engine oil.

☐ Job 50. Valve to rocker clearance.

☐ Job 51. Check for oil leaks.

☐ Job 52. **AUTOMATIC STICK SHIFT & 1302, 1302S, 1303, & 1303S MODELS ONLY** Check CV joints for tightness.

☐ Job 53. **MANUAL SHIFT MODELS ONLY** Check clutch adjustment.

☐ Job 54. Exhaust/heat exchangers.

☐ Job 77. Brake pipes and fuel lines.

☐ Job 78. Check front dampers.

☐ Job 79. **1302 & 1303 SERIES CARS ONLY.** Check front springs.

☐ Job 80. Steering components.

☐ Job 81. Front wheel alignment.

☐ Job 82. Check rear dampers.

☐ Job 83. **1302 & 1303 SERIES CARS ONLY.** Check rear springs.

☐ Job 84. Heater control cables & levers.

☐ Job 85. Power unit mountings.

☐ Job 86. Drive shaft/CV joint gaiters.

☐ Job 87. Transmission oil level.

☐ Job 88. **AUTOMATIC STICK SHIFT CARS ONLY**. Check clutch adjustment.

☐ Job 99. Check suspension rubbers.

☐ Job 100. **AUTOMATIC STICK SHIFT CARS ONLY**. Change automatic transmission oil.

☐ Job 101. **EARLY CARS ONLY** Check kingpins.

☐ Job 102. **DISC BRAKE CARS ONLY** Front brake callipers.

☐ Job 103. Check steering free play.

☐ Job 104. Check track rod ends.

☐ Job 105. Steering box mountings.

12,000 Mile Mechanical and Electrical - Road Test

☐ Job 55. Clean controls.

☐ Job 56. Check instruments.

☐ Job 57. Accelerator pedal.

☐ Job 58. Handbrake function.

☐ Job 59. Brakes and steering.

12,000 Mile Bodywork and Interior - Around the Car

First carry out all the Jobs listed under earlier Service Intervals.

☐ Job 15. Clean bodywork.

☐ Job 19. Touch-up paintwork.

☐ Job 20. Aerial/antenna.

☐ Job 21. Clean interior.

☐ Job 22. Improve visibility!

☐ Job 60. Check windscreen.

☐ Job 61. Wiper blades and arms.

☐ Job 62. Check rear view mirrors.

☐ Job 63. Chrome trim and badges.

☐ Job 89. Lubricate luggage lid release and hinges.

☐ Job 90. Lubricate door locks and striker plates.

☐ Job 91. Lubricate engine lid lock.

☐ Job 92. Seats and seat belts.

☐ Job 93. Check floors including spare wheel well.

☐ Job 106. Seat runners.

☐ Job 107. Toolkit and jack.

12,000 Mile Bodywork - Under the Car

First carry out all the Jobs listed under earlier Service Intervals.

☐ Job 23. Clean mud traps.

☐ Job 64. Inspect underside.

Job 108. Steam clean underside.
SPECIALIST SERVICE

☐ Job 94. Rustproof underbody.

☐ Job 95. Clear all drain holes.

Date serviced:...

Carried out by: ....
Garage Stamp or signature:

Parts/Accessories purchased (date, parts, source) ....
....
....
....
....
....
....
....
....
....

15,000 MILES - OR EVERY FIFTEEN MONTHS, whichever comes first

All the Service Jobs at this Service Interval have been carried forward from earlier service intervals and are to be repeated at this Service.

15,000 Mile Mechanical and Electrical - The Engine Bay

First carry out all the Jobs listed under earlier Service Intervals as applicable.

- [ ] Job 1. Check engine oil level.
- [ ] Job 16. **AUTOMATIC STICK SHIFT MODELS ONLY.** Check torque converter fluid level.
- [ ] Job 24. Clean out air cleaner & refill.
- [ ] Job 25. Lubricate carburettor control linkage.
- [ ] Job 26. Clean fuel pump filter (where applicable).
- [ ] Job 27. **FUEL INJECTION CARS ONLY** Adjust idle speed.
- [ ] Job 28. Check pipes and hoses.
- [ ] Job 29. Check fan belt for wear & tension.
- [ ] Job 30. Check HT circuit.
- [ ] Job 31. Adjust spark plugs.
- [ ] Job 32. Clean contact breaker points.
- [ ] Job 33. Check ignition timing.
- [ ] Job 34. Check distributor vacuum advance.
- [ ] Job 35. Lubricate distributor cam shaft bearing & breaker arm fibre block.
- [ ] Job 36. **AUTOMATIC STICK SHIFT CARS ONLY.** Clean auto transmission control valve filter.

15,000 Mile Mechanical and Electrical - Around the Car

First carry out all the Jobs listed under earlier Service Intervals.

- [ ] Job 2. Check brake fluid level.
- [ ] Job 3. Check windscreen washer reservoir level.
- [ ] Job 4. Check windscreen washers.
- [ ] Job 5. Check windscreen wipers.
- [ ] Job 6. Headlamps/sidelamps.
- [ ] Job 7. Check front indicators.
- [ ] Job 8. Check horn.
- [ ] Job 9. Rear sidelamps/indicators.
- [ ] Job 10. Check number plate lamp.
- [ ] Job 11. General condition of tyres.
- [ ] Job 12. Check tyre pressures.
- [ ] Job 13. Security of wheel bolts.
- [ ] Job 14. Battery electrolyte level.
- [ ] Job 17. Lubricate door hinges.
- [ ] Job 37. **EARLY MODELS ONLY** Adjust/lubricate pedals.
- [ ] Job 38. Lubricate petrol reserve tap.
- [ ] Job 39. **AUTOMATIC STICK SHIFT CARS ONLY.** Check starter inhibit switch.
- [ ] Job 40. **MODELS UP TO 1965 ONLY** Check steering box oil level.
- [ ] Job 41. Steering mechanism.

15,000 Mile Mechanical and Electrical - Under the Car

First carry out all the Jobs listed under earlier Service Intervals.

- [ ] Job 18. Grease front suspension.
- [ ] Job 42. **CABLE BRAKE MODELS ONLY** Check cable brakes.
- [ ] Job 43. Front wheel bearings.
- [ ] Job 44. **DISC BRAKE MODELS ONLY.** Check brake pads.
- [ ] Job 45. **HYDRAULIC BRAKE MODELS ONLY.** Hydraulic front drum brakes.
- [ ] Job 46. **HYDRAULIC BRAKE MODELS ONLY.** Check hydraulic rear brakes.
- [ ] Job 47. Lubricate handbrake cables.
- [ ] Job 48. Check handbrake travel.
- [ ] Job 49. Change engine oil.
- [ ] Job 50. Valve to rocker clearance.
- [ ] Job 51. Check for oil leaks.
- [ ] Job 52. **AUTOMATIC STICK SHIFT & 1302, 1302S, 1303, & 1303S MODELS ONLY** Check CV joints for tightness.
- [ ] Job 53. **MANUAL SHIFT MODELS ONLY** Check clutch adjustment.
- [ ] Job 54. Exhaust/heat exchangers.

15,000 Mile Mechanical and Electrical - Road Test

- [ ] Job 55. Clean controls.
- [ ] Job 56. Check instruments.
- [ ] Job 57. Accelerator pedal.
- [ ] Job 58. Handbrake function.
- [ ] Job 59. Brakes and steering.

15,000 Mile Bodywork and Interior - Around the Car

- [ ] Job 15. Clean bodywork.
- [ ] Job 19. Touch-up paintwork.
- [ ] Job 20. Aerial/antenna.
- [ ] Job 21. Clean interior.
- [ ] Job 22. Improve visibility!
- [ ] Job 60. Check windscreen.
- [ ] Job 61. Wiper blades and arms.
- [ ] Job 62. Check rear view mirrors.
- [ ] Job 63. Chrome trim and badges.

15,000 Mile Bodywork - Under the Car

- [ ] Job 23. Clean mud traps.
- [ ] Job 64. Inspect underside.

Date serviced: ....

Carried out by: ....
Garage Stamp or signature:

Parts/Accessories purchased (date, parts,
source) ....
....
....
....
....
....
....
....
....
....

18,000 MILES - OR EVERY EIGHTEEN MONTHS, whichever comes first

All the Service Jobs in the tinted area
have been carried forward from earlier
service intervals and are to be repeated
at this Service.

18,000 Mile Mechanical and Electrical - The Engine Bay

- [ ] Job 1. Check engine oil level.
- [ ] Job 16. **AUTOMATIC STICK SHIFT MODELS ONLY**. Check torque converter fluid level.
- [ ] Job 24. Clean out air cleaner & refill.
- [ ] Job 25. Lubricate carburettor control linkage.
- [ ] Job 26. Clean fuel pump filter (where applicable).
- [ ] Job 27. **FUEL INJECTION CARS ONLY** Adjust idle speed.
- [ ] Job 28. Check pipes and hoses.
- [ ] Job 29. Check fan belt for wear and tension.
- [ ] Job 30. Check HT circuit.
- [ ] Job 31. Adjust spark plugs.
- [ ] Job 32. Clean contact breaker points.
- [ ] Job 33. Check ignition timing.
- [ ] Job 34. Distributor vacuum advance.
- [ ] Job 35. Lubricate distributor cam shaft bearing & breaker arm fibre block.
- [ ] Job 36. **AUTOMATIC STICK SHIFT CARS ONLY**. Clean auto transmission control valve filter.
- [ ] Job 65. Replace spark plugs.
- [ ] Job 66. Renew contact breaker points.
- [ ] Job 67. Cylinder compressions.
- [ ] Job 68. Check exhaust emissions.
- [ ] Job 69. Adjust carburettor idle speed.
- [ ] Job 70. Check automatic choke.
- [ ] Job 71. **AFC FUEL INJECTION CARS ONLY**. Replace fuel filter.
- [ ] Job 72. All fuel connections.
- [ ] Job 73. Warm air control flap.

- [ ] Job 109. LATE MODEL CARS ONLY WITH PAPER AIR FILTER. Change air filter.

18,000 Mile Mechanical and Electrical - Around the Car

First carry out all the Jobs listed under
earlier Service Intervals.

- [ ] Job 2. Check brake fluid level.
- [ ] Job 3. Check windscreen washer reservoir level.
- [ ] Job 4. Check windscreen washers.
- [ ] Job 5. Check windscreen wipers.
- [ ] Job 6. Headlamps/sidelamps.
- [ ] Job 7. Check front indicators.
- [ ] Job 8. Check horn.
- [ ] Job 9. Rear sidelamps/indicators.
- [ ] Job 10. Check number plate lamp.
- [ ] Job 11. General condition of tyres.
- [ ] Job 12. Check tyre pressures.
- [ ] Job 13. Security of wheel bolts.
- [ ] Job 14. Battery electrolyte level.
- [ ] Job 17. Lubricate door hinges.
- [ ] Job 37. **EARLY MODELS ONLY** Adjust/lubricate pedals.
- [ ] Job 38. Lubricate petrol reserve tap.
- [ ] Job 39. **AUTOMATIC STICK SHIFT CARS ONLY**. Check starter inhibit switch.
- [ ] Job 40. **MODELS UP TO 1965 ONLY** Check steering box oil level.
- [ ] Job 41. Steering mechanism.
- [ ] Job 74. Check battery/terminals.
- [ ] Job 75. Headlamp alignment.
- [ ] Job 76. **AUTOMATIC STICK SHIFT CARS ONLY**. Check automatic stick shift switch contacts.

18,000 Mile Mechanical and Electrical - Under the Car

First carry out all the Jobs listed under earlier Service Intervals.

- [ ] Job 18. Grease front suspension.
- [ ] Job 42. CABLE BRAKE MODELS ONLY Check cable brakes.
- [ ] Job 43. Front wheel bearings.
- [ ] Job 44. DISC BRAKE MODELS ONLY. Check brake pads.
- [ ] Job 45. HYDRAULIC BRAKE MODELS ONLY. Hydraulic front drum brakes.
- [ ] Job 46. HYDRAULIC BRAKE MODELS ONLY. Check hydraulic rear brakes.
- [ ] Job 47. Lubricate handbrake cables.
- [ ] Job 48. Check handbrake travel.
- [ ] Job 49. Change engine oil.
- [ ] Job 50. Valve to rocker clearance.
- [ ] Job 51. Check for oil leaks.
- [ ] Job 52. AUTOMATIC STICK SHIFT & 1302, 1302S, 1303, & 1303S MODELS ONLY Check CV joints for tightness.
- [ ] Job 53. MANUAL SHIFT MODELS ONLY Check clutch adjustment.
- [ ] Job 54. Exhaust/heat exchangers.
- [ ] Job 77. Brake pipes and fuel lines.
- [ ] Job 78. Check front dampers.
- [ ] Job 79. 1302 & 1303 SERIES CARS ONLY. Check front springs.
- [ ] Job 80. Steering components.
- [ ] Job 81. Front wheel alignment.
- [ ] Job 82. Check rear dampers.
- [ ] Job 83. 1302 & 1303 SERIES CARS ONLY. Check rear springs.
- [ ] Job 84. Heater control cables & levers.
- [ ] Job 85. Power unit mountings.
- [ ] Job 86. Drive shaft/CV joint gaiters.
- [ ] Job 87. Transmission oil level.
- [ ] Job 88. AUTOMATIC STICK SHIFT CARS ONLY. Check clutch adjustment.

18,000 Mile Mechanical and Electrical - Road Test

Carry out all the Jobs listed under earlier Service Intervals.

- [ ] Job 55. Clean controls.
- [ ] Job 56. Check instruments.
- [ ] Job 57. Accelerator pedal.
- [ ] Job 58. Handbrake function.
- [ ] Job 59. Brakes and steering.

18,000 Mile Bodywork and Interior - Around the Car

Carry out all the Jobs listed under earlier Service Intervals.

- [ ] Job 15. Clean bodywork.
- [ ] Job 19. Touch-up paintwork.
- [ ] Job 20. Aerial/antenna.
- [ ] Job 21. Clean interior.
- [ ] Job 22. Improve visibility!
- [ ] Job 60. Check windscreen.
- [ ] Job 61. Wiper blades and arms.
- [ ] Job 62. Check rear view mirrors.
- [ ] Job 63. Chrome trim and badges.
- [ ] Job 89. Lubricate luggage lid release and hinges.
- [ ] Job 90. Lubricate door locks and striker plates.
- [ ] Job 91. Lubricate engine lid lock.
- [ ] Job 92. Seats and seat belts.
- [ ] Job 93. Check floors including spare wheel well.

18,000 Mile Bodywork - Under the Car

Carry out all the Jobs listed under earlier Service Intervals.

- [ ] Job 23. Clean mud traps.
- [ ] Job 64. Inspect underside.
- [ ] Job 94. Rustproof underbody.
- [ ] Job 95. Clear all drain holes.

Date serviced:..

Carried out by: ....
Garage Stamp or signature:

Parts/Accessories purchased (date, parts, source) ....
....
....
....
....
....
....
....
....
....

21,000 MILES - OR EVERY TWENTY ONE MONTHS, whichever comes first

All the Service Jobs at this Service Interval have been carried forward from earlier service intervals and are to be repeated at this Service.

21,000 Mile Mechanical and Electrical - The Engine Bay

First carry out all the Jobs listed under earlier Service Intervals as applicable.

☐ Job 1. Check engine oil level.

☐ Job 16. **AUTOMATIC STICK SHIFT MODELS ONLY.** Check torque converter fluid level.

☐ Job 24. Clean out air cleaner & refill.

☐ Job 25. Lubricate carburettor control linkage.

☐ Job 26. Clean fuel pump filter (where applicable).

☐ Job 27. **FUEL INJECTION CARS ONLY** Adjust idle speed.

☐ Job 28. Check pipes and hoses.

☐ Job 29. Check fan belt for wear & tension.

☐ Job 30. Check HT circuit.

☐ Job 31. Adjust spark plugs.

☐ Job 32. Clean contact breaker points.

☐ Job 33. Check ignition timing.

☐ Job 34. Check distributor vacuum advance.

☐ Job 35. Lubricate distributor cam shaft bearing & breaker arm fibre block.

☐ Job 36. **AUTOMATIC STICK SHIFT CARS ONLY.** Clean auto transmission control valve filter.

21,000 Mile Mechanical and Electrical - Around the Car

First carry out all the Jobs listed under earlier Service Intervals.

☐ Job 2. Check brake fluid level.

☐ Job 3. Check windscreen washer reservoir level.

☐ Job 4. Check windscreen washers.

☐ Job 5. Check windscreen wipers.

☐ Job 6. Headlamps/sidelamps.

☐ Job 7. Check front indicators.

☐ Job 8. Check horn.

☐ Job 9. Rear sidelamps/indicators.

☐ Job 10. Check number plate lamp.

☐ Job 11. General condition of tyres.

☐ Job 12. Check tyre pressures.

☐ Job 13. Security of wheel bolts.

☐ Job 14. Battery electrolyte level.

☐ Job 17. Lubricate door hinges.

☐ Job 37. **EARLY MODELS ONLY** Adjust/lubricate pedals.

☐ Job 38. Lubricate petrol reserve tap.

☐ Job 39. **AUTOMATIC STICK SHIFT CARS ONLY.** Check starter inhibit switch.

☐ Job 40. **MODELS UP TO 1965 ONLY** Check steering box oil level.

☐ Job 41. Steering mechanism.

21,000 Mile Mechanical and Electrical - Under the Car

First carry out all the Jobs listed under earlier Service Intervals.

☐ Job 18. Grease front suspension.

☐ Job 42. **CABLE BRAKE MODELS ONLY** Check cable brakes.

☐ Job 43. Front wheel bearings.

☐ Job 44. **DISC BRAKE MODELS ONLY.** Check brake pads.

☐ Job 45. **HYDRAULIC BRAKE MODELS ONLY.** Hydraulic front drum brakes.

☐ Job 46. **HYDRAULIC BRAKE MODELS ONLY.** Check hydraulic rear brakes.

☐ Job 47. Lubricate handbrake cables.

☐ Job 48. Check handbrake travel.

☐ Job 49. Change engine oil.

☐ Job 50. Valve to rocker clearance.

☐ Job 51. Check for oil leaks.

☐ Job 52. **AUTOMATIC STICK SHIFT & 1302, 1302S, 1303, & 1303S MODELS ONLY** Check CV joints for tightness.

☐ Job 53. **MANUAL SHIFT MODELS ONLY** Check clutch adjustment.

☐ Job 54. Exhaust/heat exchangers.

21,000 Mile Mechanical and Electrical - Road Test

☐ Job 55. Clean controls.

☐ Job 56. Check instruments.

☐ Job 57. Accelerator pedal.

☐ Job 58. Handbrake function.

☐ Job 59. Brakes and steering.

21,000 Mile Bodywork and Interior - Around the Car

- [ ] Job 15. Clean bodywork.
- [ ] Job 19. Touch-up paintwork.
- [ ] Job 20. Aerial/antenna.
- [ ] Job 21. Clean interior.
- [ ] Job 22. Improve visibility!
- [ ] Job 60. Check windscreen.
- [ ] Job 61. Wiper blades and arms.
- [ ] Job 62. Check rear view mirrors.
- [ ] Job 63. Chrome trim and badges.

21,000 Mile Bodywork - Under the Car

- [ ] Job 23. Clean mud traps.
- [ ] Job 64. Inspect underside.

Date serviced: ....

Carried out by: ....
Garage Stamp or signature:

Parts/Accessories purchased (date, parts, source) ....
....
....
....
....
....
....
....
....

24,000 MILES - OR EVERY TWENTY FOUR MONTHS, whichever comes first

All the Service Jobs in the tinted area have been carried forward from earlier service intervals and are to be repeated at this Service.

24,000 Mile Mechanical and Electrical - The Engine Bay

- [ ] Job 1. Check engine oil level.
- [ ] Job 16. **AUTOMATIC STICK SHIFT MODELS ONLY**. Check torque converter fluid level.
- [ ] Job 24. Clean out air cleaner & refill.
- [ ] Job 25. Lubricate carburettor control linkage.
- [ ] Job 26. Clean fuel pump filter (where applicable).
- [ ] Job 27. **FUEL INJECTION CARS ONLY** Adjust idle speed.
- [ ] Job 28. Check pipes and hoses.
- [ ] Job 29. Check fan belt for wear and tension.
- [ ] Job 30. Check HT circuit.
- [ ] Job 31. Adjust spark plugs.
- [ ] Job 32. Clean contact breaker points.
- [ ] Job 33. Check ignition timing.
- [ ] Job 34. Distributor vacuum advance.
- [ ] Job 35. Lubricate distributor cam shaft bearing & breaker arm fibre block.
- [ ] Job 36. **AUTOMATIC STICK SHIFT CARS ONLY**. Clean auto transmission control valve filter.
- [ ] Job 65. Replace spark plugs.
- [ ] Job 66. Renew contact breaker points.
- [ ] Job 67. Cylinder compressions.
- [ ] Job 68. Check exhaust emissions.
- [ ] Job 69. Adjust carburettor idle speed.
- [ ] Job 70. Check automatic choke.
- [ ] Job 71. **AFC FUEL INJECTION CARS ONLY**. Replace fuel filter.
- [ ] Job 72. All fuel connections.
- [ ] Job 73. Warm air control flap.

- [ ] Job 96. Change in-line fuel filter.
- [ ] Job 110. Replace fan belt.

24,000 Mile Mechanical and Electrical - Around the Car

First carry out all the Jobs listed under earlier Service Intervals.

- [ ] Job 2. Check brake fluid level.
- [ ] Job 3. Check windscreen washer reservoir level.
- [ ] Job 4. Check windscreen washers.
- [ ] Job 5. Check windscreen wipers.
- [ ] Job 6. Headlamps/sidelamps.
- [ ] Job 7. Check front indicators.
- [ ] Job 8. Check horn.
- [ ] Job 9. Rear sidelamps/indicators.
- [ ] Job 10. Check number plate lamp.
- [ ] Job 11. General condition of tyres.
- [ ] Job 12. Check tyre pressures.
- [ ] Job 13. Security of wheel bolts.
- [ ] Job 14. Battery electrolyte level.
- [ ] Job 17. Lubricate door hinges.
- [ ] Job 37. **EARLY MODELS ONLY** Adjust/lubricate pedals.
- [ ] Job 38. Lubricate petrol reserve tap.
- [ ] Job 39. **AUTOMATIC STICK SHIFT CARS ONLY**. Check starter inhibit switch.
- [ ] Job 40. **MODELS UP TO 1965 ONLY** Check steering box oil level.
- [ ] Job 41. Steering mechanism.
- [ ] Job 74. Check battery/terminals.
- [ ] Job 75. Headlamp alignment.
- [ ] Job 76. **AUTOMATIC STICK SHIFT CARS ONLY**. Check automatic stick shift switch contacts.
- [ ] Job 97. Test dampers.
- [ ] Job 98. Alarm remote control transmitters.

24,000 Mile Mechanical and Electrical - Under the Car

First carry out all the Jobs listed under earlier Service Intervals.

- [ ] Job 18. Grease front suspension.
- [ ] Job 42. **CABLE BRAKE MODELS ONLY** Check cable brakes.
- [ ] Job 43. Front wheel bearings.
- [ ] Job 44. **DISC BRAKE MODELS ONLY.** Check brake pads.
- [ ] Job 45. **HYDRAULIC BRAKE MODELS ONLY.** Hydraulic front drum brakes.
- [ ] Job 46. **HYDRAULIC BRAKE MODELS ONLY.** Check hydraulic rear brakes.
- [ ] Job 47. Lubricate handbrake cables.
- [ ] Job 48. Check handbrake travel.
- [ ] Job 49. Change engine oil.
- [ ] Job 50. Valve to rocker clearance.
- [ ] Job 51. Check for oil leaks.
- [ ] Job 52. **AUTOMATIC STICK SHIFT & 1302, 1302S, 1303, & 1303S MODELS ONLY** Check CV joints for tightness.
- [ ] Job 53. **MANUAL SHIFT MODELS ONLY** Check clutch adjustment.
- [ ] Job 54. Exhaust/heat exchangers.
- [ ] Job 77. Brake pipes and fuel lines.
- [ ] Job 78. Check front dampers.
- [ ] Job 79. **1302 & 1303 SERIES CARS ONLY.** Check front springs.
- [ ] Job 80. Steering components.
- [ ] Job 81. Front wheel alignment.
- [ ] Job 82. Check rear dampers.
- [ ] Job 83. **1302 & 1303 SERIES CARS ONLY.** Check rear springs.
- [ ] Job 84. Heater control cables & levers.
- [ ] Job 85. Power unit mountings.
- [ ] Job 86. Drive shaft/CV joint gaiters.
- [ ] Job 87. Transmission oil level.
- [ ] Job 88. **AUTOMATIC STICK SHIFT CARS ONLY.** Check clutch adjustment.
- [ ] Job 99. Check suspension rubbers.
- [ ] Job 100. **AUTOMATIC STICK SHIFT CARS ONLY.** Change automatic transmission oil.

- [ ] Job 101. **EARLY CARS ONLY** Check kingpins.
- [ ] Job 102. **DISC BRAKE CARS ONLY** Front brake callipers.
- [ ] Job 103. Check steering free play.
- [ ] Job 104. Check track rod ends.
- [ ] Job 105. Steering box mountings.
- [ ] Job 111. **MANUAL TRANSMISSION CARS ONLY.** Change transmission oil.
- [ ] Job 112. **HYDRAULIC BRAKE CARS ONLY.** Renew brake fluid.
- [ ] Job 113. **DISC BRAKE CARS ONLY** Check brake discs.
- [ ] Job 114. Check brake drums.
- [ ] Job 115. Brake back plates.

24,000 Mile Mechanical and Electrical - Road Test

Carry out all the Jobs listed under earlier Service Intervals.

- [ ] Job 55. Clean controls.
- [ ] Job 56. Check instruments.
- [ ] Job 57. Accelerator pedal.
- [ ] Job 58. Handbrake function.
- [ ] Job 59. Brakes and steering.

24,000 Mile Bodywork and Interior - Around the Car

Carry out all the Jobs listed under earlier Service Intervals.

- [ ] Job 15. Clean bodywork.
- [ ] Job 19. Touch-up paintwork.
- [ ] Job 20. Aerial/antenna.
- [ ] Job 21. Clean interior.
- [ ] Job 22. Improve visibility!
- [ ] Job 60. Check windscreen.
- [ ] Job 61. Wiper blades and arms.
- [ ] Job 62. Check rear view mirrors.
- [ ] Job 63. Chrome trim and badges.
- [ ] Job 89. Lubricate luggage lid release and hinges.
- [ ] Job 90. Lubricate door locks and striker plates.

- [ ] Job 91. Lubricate engine lid lock.
- [ ] Job 92. Seats and seat belts.
- [ ] Job 93. Check floors including spare wheel well.
- [ ] Job 106. Seat runners.
- [ ] Job 107. Toolkit and jack.

- [ ] Job 116. Check lamp seals.
- [ ] Job 117. Maintain window mechanism.

24,000 Mile Bodywork - Under the Car

Carry out all the Jobs listed under earlier Service Intervals.

- [ ] Job 23. Clean mud traps.
- [ ] Job 64. Inspect underside.
- [ ] Job 108. Steam clean underside.

SPECIALIST SERVICE

- [ ] Job 94. Rustproof underbody.
- [ ] Job 95. Clear all drain holes.

Date serviced: ....

Carried out by: ....
Garage Stamp or signature:

Parts/Accessories purchased (date, parts, source) ....

SERVICE HISTORY

27,000 MILES - OR EVERY TWENTY SEVEN MONTHS, whichever comes first

All the Service Jobs at this Service Interval have been carried forward from earlier service intervals and are to be repeated at this Service.

27,000 Mile Mechanical and Electrical - The Engine Bay

- [ ] Job 1. Check engine oil level.
- [ ] Job 16. AUTOMATIC STICK SHIFT MODELS ONLY. Check torque converter fluid level.
- [ ] Job 24. Clean out air cleaner & refill.
- [ ] Job 25. Lubricate carburettor control linkage.
- [ ] Job 26. Clean fuel pump filter (where applicable).
- [ ] Job 27. FUEL INJECTION CARS ONLY Adjust idle speed.
- [ ] Job 28. Check pipes and hoses.
- [ ] Job 29. Check fan belt for wear and tension.
- [ ] Job 30. Check HT circuit.
- [ ] Job 31. Adjust spark plugs.
- [ ] Job 32. Clean contact breaker points.
- [ ] Job 33. Check ignition timing.
- [ ] Job 34. Distributor vacuum advance.
- [ ] Job 35. Lubricate distributor cam shaft bearing & breaker arm fibre block.
- [ ] Job 36. AUTOMATIC STICK SHIFT CARS ONLY. Clean auto transmission control valve filter.

27,000 Mile Mechanical and Electrical - Around the Car

- [ ] Job 2. Check brake fluid level.
- [ ] Job 3. Check windscreen washer reservoir level.
- [ ] Job 4. Check windscreen washers.
- [ ] Job 5. Check windscreen wipers.
- [ ] Job 6. Headlamps/sidelamps.

- [ ] Job 7. Check front indicators.
- [ ] Job 8. Check horn.
- [ ] Job 9. Rear sidelamps/indicators.
- [ ] Job 10. Check number plate lamp.
- [ ] Job 11. General condition of tyres.
- [ ] Job 12. Check tyre pressures.
- [ ] Job 13. Security of wheel bolts.
- [ ] Job 14. Battery electrolyte level.
- [ ] Job 17. Lubricate door hinges.
- [ ] Job 37. EARLY MODELS ONLY Adjust/lubricate pedals.
- [ ] Job 38. Lubricate petrol reserve tap.
- [ ] Job 39. AUTOMATIC STICK SHIFT CARS ONLY. Check starter inhibit switch.
- [ ] Job 40. MODELS UP TO 1965 ONLY Check steering box oil level.
- [ ] Job 41. Steering mechanism.

27,000 Mile Mechanical and Electrical - Under the Car

- [ ] Job 18. Grease front suspension.
- [ ] Job 42. CABLE BRAKE MODELS ONLY Check cable brakes.
- [ ] Job 43. Front wheel bearings.
- [ ] Job 44. DISC BRAKE MODELS ONLY. Check brake pads.
- [ ] Job 45. HYDRAULIC BRAKE MODELS ONLY. Hydraulic front drum brakes.
- [ ] Job 46. HYDRAULIC BRAKE MODELS ONLY. Check hydraulic rear brakes.
- [ ] Job 47. Lubricate handbrake cables.
- [ ] Job 48. Check handbrake travel.
- [ ] Job 49. Change engine oil.
- [ ] Job 50. Valve to rocker clearance.
- [ ] Job 51. Check for oil leaks.
- [ ] Job 52. AUTOMATIC STICK SHIFT & 1302, 1302S, 1303, & 1303S MODELS ONLY Check CV joints for tightness.
- [ ] Job 53. MANUAL SHIFT MODELS ONLY Check clutch adjustment.
- [ ] Job 54. Exhaust/heat exchangers.

27,000 Mile Mechanical and Electrical - Road Test

- [ ] Job 55. Clean controls.
- [ ] Job 56. Check instruments.
- [ ] Job 57. Accelerator pedal.
- [ ] Job 58. Handbrake function.
- [ ] Job 59. Brakes and steering.

27,000 Mile Bodywork and Interior - Around the Car

- [ ] Job 15. Clean bodywork.
- [ ] Job 19. Touch-up paintwork.
- [ ] Job 20. Aerial/antenna.
- [ ] Job 21. Clean interior.
- [ ] Job 22. Improve visibility!
- [ ] Job 60. Check windscreen.
- [ ] Job 61. Wiper blades and arms.
- [ ] Job 62. Check rear view mirrors.
- [ ] Job 63. Chrome trim and badges.

27,000 Mile Bodywork - Under the Car

- [ ] Job 23. Clean mud traps.
- [ ] Job 64. Inspect underside.

Date serviced: ....

Carried out by: ....
Garage Stamp or signature:

Parts/Accessories purchased (date, parts, source) ....
....
....
....
....
....

30,000 MILES - OR EVERY THIRTY MONTHS, whichever comes first

All the Service Jobs at this Service Interval have been carried forward from earlier service intervals and are to be repeated at this Service.

30,000 Mile Mechanical and Electrical - The Engine Bay

☐ Job 1. Check engine oil level.

☐ Job 16. **AUTOMATIC STICK SHIFT MODELS ONLY**. Check torque converter fluid level.

☐ Job 24. Clean out air cleaner & refill.

☐ Job 25. Lubricate carburettor control linkage.

☐ Job 26. Clean fuel pump filter (where applicable).

☐ Job 27. **FUEL INJECTION CARS ONLY** Adjust idle speed.

☐ Job 28. Check pipes and hoses.

☐ Job 29. Check fan belt for wear and tension.

☐ Job 30. Check HT circuit.

☐ Job 31. Adjust spark plugs.

☐ Job 32. Clean contact breaker points.

☐ Job 33. Check ignition timing.

☐ Job 34. Distributor vacuum advance.

☐ Job 35. Lubricate distributor cam shaft bearing & breaker arm fibre block.

☐ Job 36. **AUTOMATIC STICK SHIFT CARS ONLY**. Clean auto transmission control valve filter.

30,000 Mile Mechanical and Electrical - Around the Car

☐ Job 2. Check brake fluid level.

☐ Job 3. Check windscreen washer reservoir level.

☐ Job 4. Check windscreen washers.

☐ Job 5. Check windscreen wipers.

☐ Job 6. Headlamps/sidelamps.

☐ Job 7. Check front indicators.

☐ Job 8. Check horn.

☐ Job 9. Rear sidelamps/indicators.

☐ Job 10. Check number plate lamp.

☐ Job 11. General condition of tyres.

☐ Job 12. Check tyre pressures.

☐ Job 13. Security of wheel bolts.

☐ Job 14. Battery electrolyte level.

☐ Job 17. Lubricate door hinges.

☐ Job 37. **EARLY MODELS ONLY** Adjust/lubricate pedals.

☐ Job 38. Lubricate petrol reserve tap.

☐ Job 39. **AUTOMATIC STICK SHIFT CARS ONLY**. Check starter inhibit switch.

☐ Job 40. **MODELS UP TO 1965 ONLY** Check steering box oil level.

☐ Job 41. Steering mechanism.

30,000 Mile Mechanical and Electrical - Under the Car

☐ Job 18. Grease front suspension.

☐ Job 42. **CABLE BRAKE MODELS ONLY** Check cable brakes.

☐ Job 43. Front wheel bearings.

☐ Job 44. **DISC BRAKE MODELS ONLY.** Check brake pads.

☐ Job 45. **HYDRAULIC BRAKE MODELS ONLY**. Hydraulic front drum brakes.

☐ Job 46. **HYDRAULIC BRAKE MODELS ONLY.** Check hydraulic rear brakes.

☐ Job 47. Lubricate handbrake cables.

☐ Job 48. Check handbrake travel.

☐ Job 49. Change engine oil.

☐ Job 50. Valve to rocker clearance.

☐ Job 51. Check for oil leaks.

☐ Job 52. **AUTOMATIC STICK SHIFT & 1302, 1302S, 1303, & 1303S MODELS ONLY** Check CV joints for tightness.

☐ Job 53. **MANUAL SHIFT MODELS ONLY** Check clutch adjustment.

☐ Job 54. Exhaust/heat exchangers.

30,000 Mile Mechanical and Electrical - Road Test

☐ Job 55. Clean controls.

☐ Job 56. Check instruments.

☐ Job 57. Accelerator pedal.

☐ Job 58. Handbrake function.

☐ Job 59. Brakes and steering.

30,000 Mile Bodywork and Interior - Around the Car

☐ Job 15. Clean bodywork.

☐ Job 19. Touch-up paintwork.

☐ Job 20. Aerial/antenna.

☐ Job 21. Clean interior.

☐ Job 22. Improve visibility!

☐ Job 60. Check windscreen.

☐ Job 61. Wiper blades and arms.

☐ Job 62. Check rear view mirrors.

☐ Job 63. Chrome trim and badges.

30,000 Mile Bodywork - Under the Car

☐ Job 23. Clean mud traps.

☐ Job 64. Inspect underside.

Date serviced: ....

Carried out by: ....
Garage Stamp or signature:

Parts/Accessories purchased (date, parts, source) ....

....

....

....

....

....

....

SERVICE HISTORY

33,000 MILES - OR EVERY THIRTY THREE MONTHS, whichever comes first

All the Service Jobs at this Service Interval have been carried forward from earlier service intervals and are to be repeated at this Service.

33,000 Mile Mechanical and Electrical - The Engine Bay

- [ ] Job 1. Check engine oil level.
- [ ] Job 16. **AUTOMATIC STICK SHIFT MODELS ONLY**. Check torque converter fluid level.
- [ ] Job 24. Clean out air cleaner & refill.
- [ ] Job 25. Lubricate carburettor control linkage.
- [ ] Job 26. Clean fuel pump filter (where applicable).
- [ ] Job 27. **FUEL INJECTION CARS ONLY** Adjust idle speed.
- [ ] Job 28. Check pipes and hoses.
- [ ] Job 29. Check fan belt for wear and tension.
- [ ] Job 30. Check HT circuit.
- [ ] Job 31. Adjust spark plugs.
- [ ] Job 32. Clean contact breaker points.
- [ ] Job 33. Check ignition timing.
- [ ] Job 34. Distributor vacuum advance.
- [ ] Job 35. Lubricate distributor cam shaft bearing & breaker arm fibre block.
- [ ] Job 36. **AUTOMATIC STICK SHIFT CARS ONLY**. Clean auto transmission control valve filter.

33,000 Mile Mechanical and Electrical - Around the Car

- [ ] Job 2. Check brake fluid level.
- [ ] Job 3. Check windscreen washer reservoir level.
- [ ] Job 4. Check windscreen washers.
- [ ] Job 5. Check windscreen wipers.
- [ ] Job 6. Headlamps/sidelamps.

- [ ] Job 7. Check front indicators.
- [ ] Job 8. Check horn.
- [ ] Job 9. Rear sidelamps/indicators.
- [ ] Job 10. Check number plate lamp.
- [ ] Job 11. General condition of tyres.
- [ ] Job 12. Check tyre pressures.
- [ ] Job 13. Security of wheel bolts.
- [ ] Job 14. Battery electrolyte level.
- [ ] Job 17. Lubricate door hinges.
- [ ] Job 37. **EARLY MODELS ONLY** Adjust/lubricate pedals.
- [ ] Job 38. Lubricate petrol reserve tap.
- [ ] Job 39. **AUTOMATIC STICK SHIFT CARS ONLY**. Check starter inhibit switch.
- [ ] Job 40. **MODELS UP TO 1965 ONLY** Check steering box oil level.
- [ ] Job 41. Steering mechanism.

33,000 Mile Mechanical and Electrical - Under the Car

- [ ] Job 18. Grease front suspension.
- [ ] Job 42. **CABLE BRAKE MODELS ONLY** Check cable brakes.
- [ ] Job 43. Front wheel bearings.
- [ ] Job 44. **DISC BRAKE MODELS ONLY.** Check brake pads.
- [ ] Job 45. **HYDRAULIC BRAKE MODELS ONLY.** Hydraulic front drum brakes.
- [ ] Job 46. **HYDRAULIC BRAKE MODELS ONLY.** Check hydraulic rear brakes.
- [ ] Job 47. Lubricate handbrake cables.
- [ ] Job 48. Check handbrake travel.
- [ ] Job 49. Change engine oil.
- [ ] Job 50. Valve to rocker clearance.
- [ ] Job 51. Check for oil leaks.
- [ ] Job 52. **AUTOMATIC STICK SHIFT & 1302, 1302S, 1303, & 1303S MODELS ONLY** Check CV joints for tightness.
- [ ] Job 53. **MANUAL SHIFT MODELS ONLY** Check clutch adjustment.
- [ ] Job 54. Exhaust/heat exchangers.

33,000 Mile Mechanical and Electrical - Road Test

- [ ] Job 55. Clean controls.
- [ ] Job 56. Check instruments.
- [ ] Job 57. Accelerator pedal.
- [ ] Job 58. Handbrake function.
- [ ] Job 59. Brakes and steering.

33,000 Mile Bodywork and Interior - Around the Car

- [ ] Job 15. Clean bodywork.
- [ ] Job 19. Touch-up paintwork.
- [ ] Job 20. Aerial/antenna.
- [ ] Job 21. Clean interior.
- [ ] Job 22. Improve visibility!
- [ ] Job 60. Check windscreen.
- [ ] Job 61. Wiper blades and arms.
- [ ] Job 62. Check rear view mirrors.
- [ ] Job 63. Chrome trim and badges.

33,000 Mile Bodywork - Under the Car

- [ ] Job 23. Clean mud traps.
- [ ] Job 64. Inspect underside.

Date serviced:...

Carried out by: ....
Garage Stamp or signature:

Parts/Accessories purchased (date, parts, source) ....
....
....
....
....
....
....

36,000 MILES - OR EVERY THIRTY SIX MONTHS, whichever comes first.

All the Service Jobs in the tinted area have been carried forward from earlier service intervals and are to be repeated at this Service.

36,000 Mile Mechanical and Electrical - The Engine Bay

- [ ] Job 1. Check engine oil level.
- [ ] Job 16. **AUTOMATIC STICK SHIFT MODELS ONLY.** Check torque converter fluid level.
- [ ] Job 24. Clean out air cleaner & refill.
- [ ] Job 25. Lubricate carburettor control linkage.
- [ ] Job 26. Clean fuel pump filter (where applicable).
- [ ] Job 27. **FUEL INJECTION CARS ONLY** Adjust idle speed.
- [ ] Job 28. Check pipes and hoses.
- [ ] Job 29. Check fan belt for wear and tension.
- [ ] Job 30. Check HT circuit.
- [ ] Job 31. Adjust spark plugs.
- [ ] Job 32. Clean contact breaker points.
- [ ] Job 33. Check ignition timing.
- [ ] Job 34. Distributor vacuum advance.
- [ ] Job 35. Lubricate distributor cam shaft bearing & breaker arm fibre block.
- [ ] Job 36. **AUTOMATIC STICK SHIFT CARS ONLY.** Clean auto transmission control valve filter.
- [ ] Job 65. Replace spark plugs.
- [ ] Job 66. Renew contact breaker points.
- [ ] Job 67. Cylinder compressions.
- [ ] Job 68. Check exhaust emissions.
- [ ] Job 69. Adjust carburettor idle speed.
- [ ] Job 70. Check automatic choke.
- [ ] Job 71. **AFC FUEL INJECTION CARS ONLY.** Replace fuel filter.

- [ ] Job 72. All fuel connections.
- [ ] Job 73. Warm air control flap.
- [ ] Job 96. Change in-line fuel filter.
- [ ] Job 109. **LATE MODEL CARS ONLY WITH PAPER AIR FILTER.** Change air filter.

36,000 Mile Mechanical and Electrical - Around the Car

First carry out all the Jobs listed under earlier Service Intervals.

- [ ] Job 2. Check brake fluid level.
- [ ] Job 3. Check windscreen washer reservoir level.
- [ ] Job 4. Check windscreen washers.
- [ ] Job 5. Check windscreen wipers.
- [ ] Job 6. Headlamps/sidelamps.
- [ ] Job 7. Check front indicators.
- [ ] Job 8. Check horn.
- [ ] Job 9. Rear sidelamps/indicators.
- [ ] Job 10. Check number plate lamp.
- [ ] Job 11. General condition of tyres.
- [ ] Job 12. Check tyre pressures.
- [ ] Job 13. Security of wheel bolts.
- [ ] Job 14. Battery electrolyte level.
- [ ] Job 17. Lubricate door hinges.
- [ ] Job 37. **EARLY MODELS ONLY** Adjust/lubricate pedals.
- [ ] Job 38. Lubricate petrol reserve tap.
- [ ] Job 39. **AUTOMATIC STICK SHIFT CARS ONLY.** Check starter inhibit switch.
- [ ] Job 40. **MODELS UP TO 1965 ONLY** Check steering box oil level.
- [ ] Job 41. Steering mechanism.
- [ ] Job 74. Check battery/terminals.
- [ ] Job 75. Headlamp alignment.
- [ ] Job 76. **AUTOMATIC STICK SHIFT CARS ONLY.** Check automatic stick shift switch contacts.
- [ ] Job 97. Test dampers.
- [ ] Job 98. Alarm remote control transmitters.

36,000 Mile Mechanical and Electrical - Under the Car

First carry out all the Jobs listed under earlier Service Intervals.

- [ ] Job 18. Grease front suspension.
- [ ] Job 42. **CABLE BRAKE MODELS ONLY** Check cable brakes.
- [ ] Job 43. Front wheel bearings.
- [ ] Job 44. **DISC BRAKE MODELS ONLY.** Check brake pads.
- [ ] Job 45. **HYDRAULIC BRAKE MODELS ONLY.** Hydraulic front drum brakes.
- [ ] Job 46. **HYDRAULIC BRAKE MODELS ONLY.** Check hydraulic rear brakes.
- [ ] Job 47. Lubricate handbrake cables.
- [ ] Job 48. Check handbrake travel.
- [ ] Job 49. Change engine oil.
- [ ] Job 50. Valve to rocker clearance.
- [ ] Job 51. Check for oil leaks.
- [ ] Job 52. **AUTOMATIC STICK SHIFT & 1302, 1302S, 1303, & 1303S MODELS ONLY** Check CV joints for tightness.
- [ ] Job 53. **MANUAL SHIFT MODELS ONLY** Check clutch adjustment.
- [ ] Job 54. Exhaust/heat exchangers.
- [ ] Job 77. Brake pipes and fuel lines.
- [ ] Job 78. Check front dampers.
- [ ] Job 79. **1302 & 1303 SERIES CARS ONLY.** Check front springs.
- [ ] Job 80. Steering components.
- [ ] Job 81. Front wheel alignment.
- [ ] Job 82. Check rear dampers.
- [ ] Job 83. **1302 & 1303 SERIES CARS ONLY.** Check rear springs.
- [ ] Job 84. Heater control cables & levers.
- [ ] Job 85. Power unit mountings.
- [ ] Job 86. Drive shaft/CV joint gaiters.
- [ ] Job 87. Transmission oil level.
- [ ] Job 88. **AUTOMATIC STICK SHIFT CARS ONLY.** Check clutch adjustment.

☐ Job 99. Check suspension rubbers.

☐ Job 100. **AUTOMATIC STICK SHIFT CARS ONLY.** Change automatic transmission oil.

☐ Job 101. **EARLY CARS ONLY** Check kingpins.

☐ Job 102. **DISC BRAKE CARS ONLY** Front brake callipers.

☐ Job 103. Check steering free play.

☐ Job 104. Check track rod ends.

☐ Job 105. Steering box mountings.

☐ Job 118. Renew brake pipes, seals & hoses.

☐ Job 119. Lubricate gear change.

36,000 Mile Mechanical and Electrical - Road Test

Carry out all the Jobs listed under earlier Service Intervals.

☐ Job 55. Clean controls.

☐ Job 56. Check instruments.

☐ Job 57. Accelerator pedal.

☐ Job 58. Handbrake function.

☐ Job 59. Brakes and steering.

36,000 Mile Bodywork and Interior - Around the Car

Carry out all the Jobs listed under earlier Service Intervals.

☐ Job 15. Clean bodywork.

☐ Job 19. Touch-up paintwork.

☐ Job 20. Aerial/antenna.

☐ Job 21. Clean interior.

☐ Job 22. Improve visibility!

☐ Job 60. Check windscreen.

☐ Job 61. Wiper blades and arms.

☐ Job 62. Check rear view mirrors.

☐ Job 63. Chrome trim and badges.

☐ Job 89. Lubricate luggage lid release and hinges.

☐ Job 90. Lubricate door locks and striker plates.

☐ Job 91. Lubricate engine lid lock.

☐ Job 92. Seats and seat belts.

☐ Job 93. Check floors including spare wheel well.

☐ Job 106. Seat runners.

☐ Job 107. Toolkit and jack.

36,000 Mile Bodywork - Under the Car

Carry out all the Jobs listed under earlier Service Intervals.

☐ Job 23. Clean mud traps.

☐ Job 64. Inspect underside.

☐ Job 108. Steam clean underside.

SPECIALIST SERVICE

☐ Job 94. Rustproof underbody.

☐ Job 95. Clear all drain holes.

Date serviced: ....

Carried out by: ....
Garage Stamp or signature:

Parts/Accessories purchased (date, parts, source) ....
....
....
....
....
....
....

YOU HAVE NOW COMPLETED ALL OF THE SERVICE JOBS LISTED IN THIS SERVICE GUIDE, 'THE LONGEST' INTERVAL BETWEEN ANY JOBS BEING 36,000 MILES OR THREE YEARS. WHEN YOU HAVE FILLED IN EACH OF THE SERVICE INTERVALS SHOWN HERE, YOU MAY PURCHASE CONTINUATION SHEETS TO ENABLE YOU TO CONTINUE AND COMPLETE YOUR SERVICE HISTORY FOR AS LONG AS YOU OWN THE CAR.

PLEASE CONTACT

PORTER PUBLISHING
AT:

**The Storehouse
Little Hereford Street
Bromyard
Hereford
HR7 4DE
England.
Tel: 0885 488800**